the man
jesus loved

the man jesus loved

homoerotic narratives from the new testament

THEODORE W. JENNINGS, JR.

THE
PILGRIM
PRESS
Cleveland

For Gerardo

The Pilgrim Press
700 Prospect Avenue East
Cleveland, Ohio 44115-1100
pilgrimpress.com

© 2003 by Theodore W. Jennings, Jr.

All rights reserved. Published 2003

Printed in the United States of America on acid-free paper

08   07   06   05   04   03   5   4   3   2   1

Contents

Part Three
MARRIAGE AND FAMILY VALUES ———————————— 171

Preface

If one surfs the Internet, one may find a number of sites through key words like "gay Jesus." But does that suggestion have any solid biblical support? This book is an attempt to carefully and patiently explore texts from the Gospels that suggest something about Jesus' own erotic attachments and the attitude toward same-sex relationships that may be fairly extrapolated from the traditions about Jesus. What emerges is evidence for the "dangerous memory" of Jesus as the lover of another man and as one whose attitudes toward such relationships, as well as toward gender and what are today called "marriage and family values," are incompatible with modern heterosexism and homophobia. I hope that this study will provide support for continuing attempts to produce significant and enduring change in church and society toward the affirmation of gay, lesbian, transgendered, and bisexual people.

I began work on this project many years ago and had in fact written much of the material in part 1 when it was interrupted by other projects and responsibilities. Many people — especially James Creech, who read that early draft, and Ronna Case — encouraged me to return to this project to complete it. How good to recall that both were there to encourage me when I undertook to write my first book more than two decades and several books ago. Friendship is truly life's greatest blessing.

I am grateful to the Chicago Theological Seminary, which not only invited me back to teach more than ten years ago but also has been strongly supportive of my attempt to develop a program of gay and lesbian studies as an integral part of the seminary curriculum. Within that program I have had the opportunity to teach several seminars, but the one that has most affected this study is one on "Homosexuality and Hermeneutics." The students in that seminar have made invaluable contributions to the work that I have undertaken — listening to my ideas, challenging them, and offering ideas and suggestions of their own. I am deeply grateful to them. The manuscript has also benefited from the careful reading and

ix

thoughtful suggestions of several of my colleagues on the faculty, including now President Susan Thistlethwaite, Dow Edgerton, and Ken Stone.

An earlier version of chapter 2, "The Lover and His Beloved," appeared in the *Chicago Theological Seminary Register* (vol. 91, no. 3, 2001), and the discussion of Markan texts on marriage and family in chapters 10 and 11 is based on earlier work on the Gospel of Mark to be published as *The Insurrection of the Crucified: "The Gospel of Mark" as Theological Manifesto*. I am grateful to Scott Haldeman of CTS, the editor of the *Register* and of Exploration Press, for permission to adapt these materials. I am grateful to Timothy Staveteig of Pilgrim Press for his willingness to take on this project and to Bob Land and John Eagleson for their diligence and alacrity in copyediting the manuscript. I am also grateful to Mark Charon for the depiction of Jesus and the disciple he loved that he created for the cover of this book.

For years Ronna Case, to whom I have had the good fortune of being married for nearly thirty years, has exclaimed upon discovering some or another writing project upon which I was engaged, "Oh dear, we'll have to pack!" Of late she has been keeping an especially close eye on the luggage. Although I don't plan on going anywhere, it has been my joy to play Ruth to her Naomi.

Chapter 1

Homosexuality and Biblical Interpretation

In the course of the last quarter century, the churches have been engaged in a protracted debate concerning homosexuality. At the heart of this debate has been a set of questions concerning the interpretation of the Bible. Issues of interpretation are hotly contested because some biblical passages appear to condemn at least some same-sex relationships or erotic practices.

An initial phase of the debate was couched in the context of the "sexual revolution" at the end of the 1960s. To a certain extent, the question of "homosexuality" was the leading wedge of an attempt to enable the church to confront in a new context the issues of sexual ethics.

The debate as originally posed had to do with the presupposition that certain persons were congenitally or at least irreversibly oriented toward finding sexual satisfaction among persons of their own gender. This "discovery," based on the Kinsey report, warranted for some a revision of the proscription of same-sex erotic practices.

An early attempt to argue this case came in the context of the revision of civil statutes criminalizing same-sex erotic practices in England, a revision in which the official Church of England was engaged (through the Wolfenden Commission). Derrick Sherwin Bailey's landmark study titled *Homosexuality in the Western Christian Tradition* was primarily concerned with the emergence of the legal criminalization of same-sex practices, but the work paid significant attention to the biblical texts that were supposed to be the foundation of such laws.[1]

---

1. Derrick Sherwin Bailey, *Homosexuality in the Western Christian Tradition* (London: Longmans, Green, 1955). Although Bailey's work exploded the alleged biblical basis for sodomy statutes, the U.S. Supreme Court appears not to have noticed (*Bowers v. Hardwick*). Then as now, the reading of the Bible has important consequences for civil society as a whole.

1

Bailey's work demonstrated that a great many biblical passages that nineteenth-century legalists had assumed entailed a proscription of homosexuality were in fact not pertinent. That is, Bailey succeeded in greatly limiting the number of texts that were deemed relevant to the discussion.

We were then left with two verses from Leviticus and three from the New Testament that seemed to require additional work, for these texts appear to proscribe same-sex genital practice among males (and, in one case, among females). What, if anything, should be made of these texts?

One hermeneutical strategy has been to disqualify these texts on the grounds that in no way do they deal with homosexual orientation, which is indeed true; neither the term nor the category was known much more than a century ago. Persons were not classified according to sexual orientation prior to the late nineteenth century. Before that time, only behavior was noted: who has sex with whom. The much vexed question about whether some persons actually had exclusive orientation to, or preference for, same-sex erotic satisfaction was not the issue. The hermeneutical strategy employed by some people today is to say that some persons are exclusively homosexual in orientation. For these persons, same-sex practice cannot be understood as unnatural and thus should be accepted, whatever the Bible says about those others of us for whom it is presumably unnatural.

This hermeneutical strategy of disqualifying of the pertinence of biblical texts for legislating a phenomenon not yet understood in the first century has certain limitations. In the first place, this latter approach accepts without question the modern category of homosexuality without dealing at all with the no-less-established category of bisexuality. But we are in a period when the very idea of homosexuality is itself questioned within the gay academy of theoreticians. The debate between constructivists and essentialists has rendered moot the whole category of homosexuality.

The attempt to finesse the question of practice by way of appeal to a category of persons who are innately homosexual must be regarded as resting upon shaky conceptual/theoretical foundations and, in any case, as having too limited a scope to deal with the issues of sexual practice that are at stake.

A further difficulty is involved in the kind of discussion that has predominated over the last quarter century. The focus has been on the question of accepting persons who either engage in or are attracted to the practice of same-sex erotic practices. "Homosexuals" have been petitioners who seek admittance to the ecclesial or social sphere. The question then has to do with toleration of difference and with widening the sphere of this tolerance to include "homosexuals." The move to toleration has proceeded in such a way as to leave in place the presumption that the sexual values, and especially the marriage and family values, of "straight culture" are basically correct. The argument then is that people who are in some way congenitally incapable of realizing these values should receive a kind of exemption.

This sort of discussion is inherently demeaning to the people it seeks to benefit, pleading for understanding and tolerance while leaving untouched the prevailing values and arrangements. Persons who identify themselves as gay, lesbian, bisexual, or "queer" increasingly find it no longer worthwhile to engage in this inherently degrading discussion.

Rereading the Bible

The current study departs from what has been the norm of discussion. This book takes the position that the homophobic and heterocentric position of the church (and of Western society generally) is a distortion of the Bible. I propose, as a corollary, that a gay affirmative reading of the Bible will actually respect the integrity of these texts and make their message both more clear and more persuasive.

This study is not a plea for acceptance or toleration of gay people, but it does suggest that the exclusion of persons on the basis of sexual orientation or same-sex practices brings with it a fundamental distortion of the Bible generally and of the traditions concerning Jesus in particular.

Now this case can be made only by rereading the biblical materials. The issue is not just a matter of the five isolated verses that presumably disqualify persons who engage in same-sex erotic behavior. It is a question of rereading the biblical witness much more broadly and appropriating the Bible for a gay-positive perspective.

This kind of a rereading of the Bible is related to the sort of rereading that has gone on in a variety of liberationist contexts. In the modern period, such a rereading has been necessary for a number of reasons. At the end of the eighteenth and the beginning of the nineteenth centuries, for example, a rereading was initiated to undermine the self-evidence of institutions of slavery. The Bible does not seem to abolish slavery. Indeed the apologists for chattel slavery could and did appeal both to "Mosaic" legislation and to the New Testament's apparent acceptance of institutions of slavery in order to legitimate the renewed practice of slavery in Protestant North America. The struggle, then, against slavery also was a struggle for the appropriate way of reading the Bible. That is, the question was one of hermeneutics.

This same hermeneutical issue or set of issues came into play in the struggle concerning segregation in the United States and apartheid in South Africa. In each case the issue had to do with the presence of biblical texts in both Testaments that were (mis)appropriated to legitimate white racism. But the issue was also in this case broader since it was a question of applying biblical principles (as opposed to proof texts) to questions of theological and ethical debate.

This struggle is by no means over. The work of Cain Hope Felder in developing an Afrocentric reading of the Bible is of considerable importance, as is the work of Itumeleng Mosala, and others in South Africa, for recapturing the Bible from white supremacist ideology.

A second illustration of the way in which a particular issue opens the way to a broader hermeneutical discussion has to do with a feminist reading of the Bible. Interestingly rereading the Bible from a feminist perspective began in the same context as the abolitionist and antiracist rereading of the Bible. The production of the "Woman's Bible" was the first rereading of the Bible from a liberationist (and revisionist) perspective.

The feminist rereading of the Bible continues today, and has growing relevance to a reappropriation of biblical texts, particularly in the work of Elisabeth Schüssler Fiorenza. Here we have moved beyond the question of accepting women in leadership positions in society and the church to an interrogation of the biblical worldview and to the meaning of the gospel as a whole. To be sure, many people (like Mary Daly) conclude that the biblical materials are hopelessly sexist and so should be abandoned. Others (like Rosemary Ruether), without discounting the patriarchal bias of the biblical authors, nevertheless find support in important aspects of this tradition for a rigorous critique of sexism and patriarchy in the world and in society.

One of the most urgent rereadings of the Bible in the twentieth century was in response to the horrors of the Holocaust prompted by the belated realization among Christian exegetes that traditional readings of the Bible have fostered anti-Semitism and actually contributed to and prepared the ground for the genocidal policies of Hitler. Here it has been a matter of reconsidering the apparently self-evident ways the New Testament was read and the way in which cherished doctrinal formulations were developed and interpreted. Even the name given by Christians to the sacred writings of Israel — the Old Testament — betrays a bias that is conducive to the emergence of anti-Judaism. The reconsideration of Jesus as a Jew (and of Paul as well) together with critical reflection on the ways texts seem to make the Jewish people generally responsible for the execution of Jesus (actually carried out, of course, by the Roman empire and thus by the Gentiles) has been immensely fruitful for producing fresh insight into the emergence of the Jesus movement as well as into the dangers of a traditional and ideologically distorted (mis)reading of the New Testament.

A further rereading of the Bible that has become widely influential is that undertaken from the standpoint of the struggle of the poor and oppressed to attain liberation and life. This hermeneutical strategy is most often associated with Latin American liberation theology, although it in fact embraces black liberation in the United States and Africa and has influenced the quite different context of Asian theology.

Now this liberationist rereading has shown itself to be of enduring importance, for it has not simply argued that we should be nice to poor people but that the welfare of the poor and marginalized is the test of our relationship to the God of both Testaments.

Indeed, in all the cases we have referred to, the proposed rereading of the Bible claims to provide decisive clarification of the meaning of the witness to the action, will, and goal of the divine in the world.

In all of these cases, a reading of the Bible is at stake that contests traditional readings. These traditional readings have so succeeded in substituting themselves for the text that they purport to "interpret" that new readings have often been regarded as "unbiblical." But in all cases, the rereading has resulted in greater clarity about the meaning of faithfulness to the God who is attested by Scripture.

I maintain that similar gains can be hoped for from a "gay-affirmative" or counterhomophobic rereading of the Bible. The gains I have in mind are not simply an acceptance of previously proscribed behavior but a greater clarity about the meaning of biblical texts and hence a greater clarity about the meaningfulness of biblical traditions for contemporary attitudes toward same-sex desire and practice.

Now I must add a caveat. I do not suppose that the hermeneutical enterprise that I am suggesting should displace the other hermeneutical strategies I have just listed. Rather I regard this approach as a collaborative enterprise. As Latin American theologians say, the search is for "integral liberation." A liberation of some at the expense of others cannot be liberation within the horizon of the new creation promised and already begun in Jesus.

At the "end of the rainbow" of the hermeneutical work that we begin here is an appropriation of the Bible that is not afraid of the body or of the erotic. Thus, the aim of a gay-positive reading of the Bible is as well to offer a liberating word to all persons, including "straights," concerning the place of the erotic in our lives. The consideration of the question of homosexuality in the churches a quarter century ago began in the context of the sexual revolution that asked whether traditional antierotic views associated with Christianity were to be regarded as binding upon us in the present. That question has been sidetracked by the focus on the question of homosexuality. A reexamination of homoeroticism in biblical narratives may also make possible a reconsideration of the place of the erotic in the life and thought of those who understand themselves as in some way indebted to these traditions and even answerable to them.

Strategies of "Gay Reading"

In the work that lies ahead, we must distinguish distinct strategies of reading that together make up a gay-affirmative rereading of biblical texts.

The first level of a gay-affirmative reading is one that has been pursued with considerable force over the last half century: contesting the presumed basis in Scripture for cultural and social denigration of and even legislation against persons who engage in same-gender sexual activity. The current result of this strategy is that several of the texts formerly read as referring to this behavior may no longer be so employed; they are the result of mistranslation. Another result is that any counterhomosexual texts can be applied, if at all, to behavior rather than to orientation.

These results may be regarded as important but insufficient. Therefore alternative strategies must be employed.

In the first place, a strategy may be employed that exposes homophobic readings as engaged in an obfuscation of the text — that is, as entailing a fundamental distortion of the biblical message. Here one must assert that a reading of these texts (for example, the narrative concerning Sodom) which uses them to license opposition to persons who engage in same-sex sexual relations actually blatantly distorts the texts. The distortion entailed is a measure of homophobia — that is, of a fear of homosexuality that brings the institutionally approved reading into irrationality.

While it is a positive animus against homosexuality, homophobia is also complemented by what may be called a heterosexist reading. This reading is so preoccupied with the model of heterosexual marriage and family values that it reads into the text its own presuppositions. This strategy does not necessarily entail a hatred or fear of homosexuality but rather a bias toward finding confirmation of the marriage and family values of heterosexual culture in the biblical texts. A reading that counters heterosexism then moves to a wider arena: not just delegitimating homophobic readings but contesting the reading that suggests the privileging of hetero-sexual institutions. Contesting heterosexism entails contesting the view that heterosexual institutions in fact are supported in the biblical texts. Note that while homophobic readings also appeal to heterosexist readings the reverse is not necessarily the case.[2]

A third level of reading is one that is "pro-gay." This kind of reading is anticipated by those who read the story of Jonathan and David or of Ruth and Naomi as gay-positive. This approach is analogous to, for example, feminist readings that demonstrate the presence of strong female charac-ters or of feminine attributes of the divine, or of readings like those of Cain Hope Felder that demonstrate the hidden presence of African people in the biblical texts. We are concerned then with the hidden presence of relationships that may be construed as gay in some sense.

To these strategies of reading we may add a fourth: reading the texts from the perspective of a contemporary gay or queer sensibility. Here the aim is to discover how the text appears when it is read from a stand-point affirmative of gay or queer reality — that is, what the text means now, when viewed from this perspective. While dependent upon the other strategies I have suggested, this reading goes beyond them by taking seri-ously the point of view of contemporary readers, as when the Bible is read from the standpoint of the impoverished of Latin America or women in North America.

The task of a gay reading thus entails a multiple strategy of inter-connected readings of texts. By attending to the distinction between and relations among these strategies, we become better acquainted with the biblical text itself as well as with the varied aspects of liberationist readings generally. In the material that follows, we cannot hope to accomplish more than to provide examples of the kinds of readings that may be employed. But the results of these readings may be useful not only to people who are concerned with the question of homosexuality, but also people who seek to understand the Bible in a fresh way and to liberate the tradition not only from homophobia and heterosexism but also to open the way to a non-erotophobic understanding of faith.

This Project

In this book, my intention is to break with the defensive strategy of dealing primarily with passages that are alleged to support homophobia and gay

---

2. See the discussion of relevant texts in chapters 10 and 11 below.

bashing. This strategy gives greater plausibility than is deserved to the traditional (mis)reading of the Bible. Instead I focus on examining what is, in fact, the preponderance of the evidence: that which includes and affirms homoerotic desire and relationships.

Most scholars today accept the drastic reduction of biblical texts that have been used to justify the condemnation of same-sex relationships and practice to a couple of verses of Leviticus together with a couple of verses of Paul. Even so, this approach has not generally led to the abandonment of the homophobic expropriation of the Bible. Instead the fallback position has been something like, "No matter how often or seldom the Bible speaks of same-sex activity (or homosexuality), it always condemns this practice." Thus the slenderness of the evidence supportive of homophobia is compensated for by an alleged unanimity. No one seems to be embarrassed that one could make the same case (with a far greater number of texts) for, say, the institution of slavery.

But I will seek to show that this alleged unanimity is a product of willful blindness to the Bible itself. In fact, the preponderance of biblical texts relevant to the discussion affirm and even celebrate same-sex relationships and practice.

In order to make this case as clearly as possible, I focus this study on an investigation of the traditions about Jesus that are passed down through the Gospels. Legend holds that a book was published entitled *Everything Jesus Said about Homosexuality.* When opened, the book consisted of nothing but blank pages. The point is well made but is also misleading. I contend that the Jesus tradition contains a good deal that is relevant to the discussion of same-sex erotic relationships, and that all of it is positive.

In order that this conclusion be seen as sharply as possible, I have taken the risk of beginning with the question: "Was Jesus gay?" I admit at the outset that the question, as thus posed, does not lend itself to a simple yes or no answer. First, the contemporary idea of gayness, like the modern idea of homosexuality, does not fit well with first-century ideas and perspectives. Ideas associated with talk of homosexuality or gayness today — ideas like the classification of persons according to supposed sexual orientation, the alleged dissimilarity between homosexual and heterosexual (or between gay and straight), the supposition that relations between persons of the same sex are also relationships between persons of the same age and status, the notion of a particular lifestyle or culture associated with sexual practice, and so on — would have been puzzling, even absurd, to people of antiquity (as they are to people of many cultures in the world today) and perhaps especially to those who engaged in and celebrated erotic relationships among persons of the same sex.

Not only do modern categories not fit well on ancient evidence, but any evidence we may have about the "personal" lives of historical persons from so long ago is generally suggestive and inferential rather than explicit and definitive, whether we think of Socrates or Plato, Alexander or Julius Caesar, Athanasius or Augustine. But such uncertainly is all the more true of Jesus, whose life, teachings, and deeds are filtered through a process of reflection and reconstruction that eventuates in the production of the primary documents, the Gospels, upon which we must rely for evidence.

Despite these difficulties the question, "was Jesus gay?" has important benefits as a way of directing and organizing our investigation of biblical texts.

First, as I indicated, this question provides a way of definitively breaking with the defensive hermeneutical strategy that has accomplished much, but which has the unfortunate appearance of pleading for some special exemption for or toleration of persons who identify themselves as gay or lesbian or bisexual.

Second, the question as thus posed allows us to focus attention on texts that have been largely ignored in the discussion, above all the material with which this study begins: the relationship between Jesus and the man identified as the disciple Jesus loved in the Fourth Gospel. As we shall see, the least forced reading of the texts that concern the "beloved disciple" is one which supposes that they refer to a relationship of love expressed by physical and personal intimacy — what we might today suppose to be a homoerotic or a "gay" relationship. Because this reading has been so marginal in the history of interpretation, and has in fact been virtually silenced by homophobia and indeed by erotophobia, some care is needed in developing the interpretation. This is the task of part 1.

In part 2, we turn to additional evidence from the traditions about Jesus from other Gospels. Thus we will look at material in the Gospel of Mark that seems to confirm what we have seen in the Gospel of John: that Jesus was remembered as having an erotic relationship with another man. While other Gospels do not reflect this strand of the material, we see that Matthew and Luke do suggest that Jesus was accepting, even approving of, a person whose chief characteristic is his love for his "boyfriend." Finally we see that the Gospels agree in suggesting that Jesus was not troubled by the gender role issues that are sometimes used to discredit same-sex relationships. Thus, in various ways, the Gospels present us with considerable evidence of the "dangerous memory" of Jesus as one who both accepted and modeled the intimate love of persons of the same sex.

In part 3, we turn to an issue that in the modern period has often been used to discredit same-sex relationships. In contemporary homophobic Christian rhetoric, homosexuality is regularly opposed to "marriage and family values." Same-sex relationships are said to undermine these key values of civilization, and allegedly of Christianity. While this claim would have been absurd to most people of antiquity, it nevertheless merits particular attention today because of the way it is used to assert that biblical values are destroyed by the acceptance, let alone celebration, of same-sex relationships. In this section, I simply demonstrate what is obvious to any reader of the Gospels: that Jesus, far from defending marriage and family values, was adamantly opposed to the institution of the family. The contemporary arguments about the importance of marriage and family values or the older notion that sex is proper only for procreation cannot be used to obfuscate the evidence concerning the Jesus tradition.

Such then is the outline of our study as it has been directed and organized by the leading question, "was Jesus gay?" This question helps to demonstrate that homophobic appropriations of the Bible depend upon blindness to the homoerotic elements of biblical narratives, especially the narratives concerning Jesus. On the other hand, reading the biblical narrative as "gay friendly" not only does no violence to the text, but actually illumines it in the sense of making good sense both of the episodes in question and also of the general point of view of the narratives as a whole. Indeed this approach may permit the Bible to be read as it was intended to be read by at least many of its authors: as good news for all, but especially for all those violated by the prestigious and the powerful.

Terminology

A brief word about terminology is in order. I have tended to use "gay" as a generic term to include gay men, lesbians, and bisexual and transgendered persons. The term "queer," which has been used in more recent discussion, is actually much better in the sense of inclusivity but it still has the tendency to block rather than facilitate understanding among readers, both "gay" and "straight," of my own generation.

I tend to use "same-sex" rather than "homosexual," and to use "cross-sex" rather than "heterosexual," in order to break with some of the intellectual baggage that attends the more familiar terms.

The manner of designating a relationship that may very well be mediated sexually but about which mediation we can, in the nature of things, have no direct knowledge can present a bit of a puzzle. Of course such assessment is true for virtually all relationships that we imagine may be sexual. My friends tend not to be guests on talk shows and thus do not generally say whether or how they have sex, for example, with their spouses or life partners. And since I'm not an avid watcher of such shows, I am as generally incurious about my friends' sex lives as they are about mine. The point isn't to bash talk shows but to say that in general we don't know much about who has sex with whom or how, even in relationships that we presume to be, in some way, sexually mediated or expressed. In general I have identified as "erotic" relationships in which sexual mediation may be supposed to be a feature of the relationship. I am not presuming knowledge of whether or how the people involved "had sex," but rather that the relationship is the sort in which we may suppose, in analogous circumstances, that some or another sexual practice would be involved. We suppose that sex is or would be a "natural" or likely extension (in private presumably) of what offers itself to be seen in public. In this sense I call the relationships between Jesus and the man he loved (and that between the centurion and his "lad") "homoerotic."

Part One

THE MAN JESUS LOVED

AT THE VERY LEAST, THE QUESTION, "was Jesus gay?" means that we are concerned with Jesus' personal relationships with other people. This question is seldom raised, in part because of a Christian erotophobia that implicitly regards erotic relationships as incompatible in some way with the image of Jesus as "without sin" or even as "divine." Even when the possibility of an erotic relationship does arise, this question is usually confined to imagining that Jesus' partner would have been female. The popular *Jesus Christ Superstar* supplied Mary of Magdala as a potential partner for Jesus as did Nikos Kazantzakis's *The Last Temptation of Christ*. Some early Mormon speculation has even proposed a different Mary (of Bethany) and her sister Martha as spouses for Jesus. The response on the part of mainline Christianity to these suggestions has generally been negative and even vehement.

However, if Christianity were to suppose that sexuality is not incompatible with sinlessness, then no reason in principle can be supplied for rejecting erotic attachments for Jesus. Then the question simply becomes whether the traditions concerning Jesus as they come to us in early Christian literature and especially in the four Gospels of the New Testament contain evidence of intimate relationships between Jesus and other people.

One way of approaching this question would be to ask whether Jesus is ever said to actually "love" another person in these documents. Terms for love occur surprisingly rarely in the traditions about Jesus. Indeed the only text in which they occur with any frequency is the Gospel of John. This fact by itself may be astonishing to people who have been inculcated with the belief that love is at the heart of the New Testament witness, a view that I do not dispute. Perhaps even more surprising is that, with a single exception, the only Gospel in which Jesus is said to love someone — even God, let alone another human being — is the Gospel of John.

To be sure, the "love" of Jesus for other people is expressed in a number of concrete ways in the other Gospels: in his attention to the poor, the hungry, the crowds, the sick, the demon possessed, and so on. But, for the most part, this expression is compassion for strangers and is never called "love" by the other narrators. Only in the Gospel of John do we have much material that bears on Jesus' relationship with those people who are close to him, with what we may term "interpersonal" relationships.

In this context, Jesus is said to love other persons. In two cases (13:1; 14:21), Jesus is said to love all his followers. In one case, Jesus is said to love a group of three people: Mary of Bethany, her sister (Martha), and their brother Lazarus (11:5). In two other cases, the reader is told that, in the view of other people, Jesus loved Lazarus (11:3, 36). However, no fewer than five times (13:23; 19:26; 20:2; 21:7, 20) the reader is told of a (male) disciple who is called simply the one whom Jesus loved.

Clearly then, a consideration of Jesus' strong personal relationships with other people must begin with an investigation of this relationship, even if we were not using the question, "was Jesus gay?" as a starting point. We should begin here even if we were concerned quite generally with Jesus' personal relationships or with the issue of Jesus' erotic attachments to anyone. Of course most people do not begin here, for homophobia and heterosexism conspire to direct attention away from the one person who is explicitly described as Jesus' beloved.

Because tradition and prejudice have conspired to hide from the reader's gaze the most obvious candidate for an erotic connection between Jesus and another human being, we have to develop the gay-affirmative reading of this relationship with some care.

In chapter 2, I attempt to show that the texts from the Gospel of John that deal with the disciple Jesus loved may be read quite "naturally" as indicating a homoerotic relationship between Jesus and another man. I seek to show that this reading is the least forced approach to these texts and that such a reading makes the best sense of the text as it stands. Subsequent chapters of part 1 deal with a number of issues that arise from such an interpretation of the text.

In chapter 3, I deal with a question that tradition and scholarship have addressed in this connection, the question of the identity or role of the "disciple Jesus loved." The chapter reviews a number of possible candidates for this identity and role and enables us to get a sense of the remarkable number of interpersonal relationships that are present in this narrative.

No other Gospel provides us with such a wealth of interpersonal detail in the depiction of the life and mission of Jesus. But this multiplicity of interpersonal relationships also makes it difficult to decide the question of the beloved disciple's identity.

While, in the nature of the case, we often cannot know for sure whether or how a specific erotic relationship is mediated or expressed sexually, we can at least discover whether the context within which such a relationship is reported is one that makes sexual mediation unthinkable or unlikely. In chapter 4, then, I turn to a consideration of the thought world of the Gospel of John to see whether good reasons exist for rejecting the possibility of sexual mediation for this relationship. I argue that they do not.

Because this interpretation of the relationship between Jesus and the man he loved may seem so unprecedented, in chapter 5 I survey some of the ways in which other readers have recognized the erotic character of this relationship.

Finally, in chapter 6, I turn to the question of the theological and ethical significance of the gay-affirmative interpretation of this relationship. I maintain that such an interpretation is helpful not only for gay readers of the Bible but also helps to clarify the nature, and relationship between, human and divine love.

The Texts

Prior to an attempt to interpret the material concerning Jesus and the disciple he loved, a review of the textual materials on which such an interpretation is based is necessary. We begin with a survey of the relevant sections of the Gospel of John.

The first reference to this figure comes in the account of Jesus' last meal with his disciples. John's account (John 13–17) is quite extraordinary.[1] Unlike the other three "Gospels," or the brief account we find in Paul (1 Cor. 11:3–26), nothing whatever occurs relating to an institution of the "Last Supper" as a meal to be celebrated by the community following Jesus' death. Instead, we find Jesus stripping naked and washing the feet of his friends — something that Peter at least regards as quite unseemly.[2]

The only feature that this account has in common with other accounts of Jesus' last meal with his disciples is the reference to the imminent

---

1. We will refer to the author by the traditional name of John, since some name must be used and any other would be both conjectural and confusing.

2. We attend a bit more to this text when we discuss the issue of gender role nonconformity in the Jesus tradition (chapter 9).

betrayal of Jesus by one of the disciples. Precisely in connection with this detail, we encounter for the first time the singling out of one of the disciples as in some special way loved by Jesus.

> Saying these things Jesus was troubled in spirit and testified and said: "Amen, Amen, I tell you that one of you will betray me." The disciples looked at one another being perplexed about whom he speaks. One of his disciples was lying in Jesus' lap, the one Jesus loved; so Simon Peter nods to this one and says: "Tell, who is he talking about." That one, falling back on Jesus' chest says to him: "Lord, who is it?" Jesus answers: "It is the one to whom I will give this morsel when I dip it." So when he had dipped the morsel he gave it to Judas, the son of Simon Iscariot. (John 13:21–26)[3]

This text is preceded and followed by the assertion that Jesus loved all the disciples (13:1, 34). Jesus' farewell discourse to the disciples continues to the end of chapter 17.

Following the long discourse and the account of his arrest, we come to Jesus' trial. Here we find a passage that, although it does not explicitly refer to the disciple Jesus loved, is sometimes considered as part of the relevant data:

> Simon Peter and another disciple followed Jesus. Since that disciple was known to the high priest, he went with Jesus into the courtyard of the high priest, but Peter was standing outside at the gate. So the other disciple, who was known to the high priest, went out, spoke to the woman who guarded the gate, and brought Peter in. (18:15–16)

Then follows the account of the trial, presumably overheard by both Peter and "another disciple." After the trial and execution of Jesus we come to the scene at the foot of the cross.

> But there stood by the cross of Jesus, his mother, the sister of his mother, Mary [the wife] of Clopas, and Mary the Magdalene. Jesus, seeing his mother and the disciple standing by whom he loved, he said to his mother "Woman, see your son." Then he says to the disciple, "See your mother!" And from that hour the disciple took her to his own. (19:25–27).

---

3. Throughout I have used the NRSV but with modifications where necessary to give a more literal sense of the Greek text.

The account of Jesus' death in this text is remarkably unlike that which we encounter in other narratives. After Jesus' side is pierced, the account concludes with the observation: "And the one who saw has testified and his testimony is true and that one knows that he speaks truly — that you also may believe" (19:35).

A reasonable conjecture, though not explicitly stated, is that "the one who saw" is the one previously identified as the disciple that Jesus loved. But at this point the conjecture rests on the use of the masculine possessive pronoun (his testimony), since the only male witness to the cross identified in the text is the disciple loved by Jesus.

Following the burial of Jesus, we have the account of the discovery of the empty tomb, which again is markedly different from what we find in the other Gospels:

> Now on the first [day] of the week Mary the Magdalene comes early, while it is yet dark, to the tomb, and sees that the stone had been taken from the tomb. So she runs and comes to Simon Peter and to the other disciple, the one Jesus loved, and says to them, "They took the Lord from the tomb and we don't know where they put him. Peter and the other disciple went out therefore and came to the tomb. And the two ran together; and the other disciple ran ahead more quickly than Peter and came first to the tomb, and stooping sees lying the sheets, but he didn't go in. So Simon Peter comes following him, and entered the tomb, and he sees the sheets lying, and the kerchief, which had been on his head, not with the sheets but separate, having been wrapped up in one place. Then the other disciple, who had come to the tomb first, also entered and he saw and believed; for as yet they did not know the writing, that he must rise from the dead. Then the disciples went back to their own homes. (20:1–10)

A number of resurrection appearance stories follow: first to Mary the Magdalene (20:11–18); then to a group of disciples in their hideout (20:19–23); then, eight days later, to Thomas "the twin," in company with the others (20:26–29). Then, after what looks like a conclusion to the narrative (20:30–31), we encounter a long resurrection narrative that occupies the entire final chapter. In this narrative we hear again of the disciple Jesus loved. The most significant sections of this narrative for our purposes are reproduced below (with summary indications of the connecting links). "There were together Simon Peter, and Thomas called the twin, Nathaniel of Cana in Galilee, the sons of Zebedee, and two others of his disciples. Simon Peter says to them, 'I am going fishing.' They say to him,

'We're coming with you.' They went out and embarked on the boat; but that night they caught nothing."

Then Jesus, incognito, gives them instructions from the shore about where to put their nets, with the result that they fill the nets. Then, "that disciple whom Jesus loved said to Peter, 'It's the Lord!' When Simon Peter heard that it was the Lord, he put on his clothes, for he was naked, and threw himself into the sea. But the other disciples came in the little boat" (21:7–8).

They then have a fish fry on the beach for breakfast. There follows a long dialogue in which Jesus asks Peter three times if Peter loves Jesus. Each time Peter responds affirmatively and is told to tend or feed Jesus' sheep. When Peter protests his love, Jesus talks about Peter having to be held up when he gets older, which the narrator tells us means that Peter also will be crucified. Jesus then tells Peter: "Follow me" (21:15–20).

> Turning, Peter sees the disciple that Jesus loved following them, who also was the one who leaned on Jesus' chest at the supper and had said, "Lord, who is the one betraying you?" Peter seeing this one says to Jesus, "Lord, and what of him?" Jesus says to him, "If I want him to remain until I come, what is that to you? You follow me!" The saying spread abroad among the brothers that this disciple is not to die. But Jesus didn't say that he doesn't die, but: "If I want him to stay until I come, what's it to you?"
>
> This is the disciple witnessing concerning these things and having written these things, and we know that his witness is true. (21:20–24)

The narrative ends with the notice that Jesus did many other things.

This final appearance of the disciple Jesus loved links up to the first appearance at the supper and echoes the word at the death of Jesus that he is a true witness. Here it becomes clear that the one referred to in 19:35 was probably the beloved disciple, because here the passage states explicitly that he is the faithful eyewitness whose testimony is somehow said to be basic to the text of the narrative.

I have cited these texts at such length so that the reader may see exactly the extent of the material with which we are concerned. I have also attempted to give a fairly literal rendering for the same reason. Interpretation of the texts and the consequences of a homoerotic interpretation are the subjects of the next five chapters.

Chapter 2

The Lover and His Beloved

While the question of the identity of the beloved disciple and his role in the text is a not uncommon feature of commentaries on the Gospel of John, little is written about the nature of the relationship between Jesus and this person. A conspiracy of silence seems to surround this question. Yet the Gospel itself places all the weight on the nature or character of the relationship between Jesus and his beloved, rather than the disciple's name or his "function."

The text makes clear that among so many to whom Jesus had strong personal ties, one particular disciple was Jesus' beloved. Along with Jesus' teaching concerning the nature of God's love and human love, and Jesus' demonstrating and awakening of this love, one person was simply "the disciple he loved" — the beloved one for whom Jesus was the lover. When all is said and done, the fact that the text does indicate that Jesus was in this most definite and concrete and intimate sense a lover with a beloved is itself quite remarkable, even apart from the added information that this beloved was also another male. However, this added information has served to "hide" the relationship wherever homophobic or heterosexist presuppositions have prevailed. Indeed the erotophobic presuppositions of much traditional exegesis would have made it difficult to see Jesus as a lover with a beloved even if the beloved were female. But the taboos constructed by homophobia and heterosexism have rendered a reading of the relationship between Jesus and his beloved virtually impossible.[1]

In this chapter, I attempt what may be called a homoerotic reading of the relationship between Jesus and his beloved. The aim of such a reading is to see what sense it makes of these texts to read them as suggestive of what we might today label a homosexual or gay relationship.

---

1. The taboo has not been absolutely effective, however, as we shall see in chapter 5.

19

Apart from the controversial nature of such a reading, two qualifications must be observed. First, I will not suggest what sexual practice, if any, served to mediate or express this relationship. As is true for other relationships, whether same-sex or cross-sex, the data in all but pornographic texts typically does not intrude into this sphere. In this chapter, the gay reading is not meant to foreclose the question of sexual practice one way or the other. This issue will occupy us in chapter 4.

The other qualification concerns the much vexed question of the "construction of homosexuality." The suppositions concerning homosexual relations that are present in contemporary society cannot simply be read back into other cultures or periods of history. The term "homosexual," as adjective or noun, is only a century old. As a noun, the term generally refers to persons who are disposed to find sexual fulfillment in relations with persons of the same biological sex as themselves. Cultural and historical study has shown that the classification of persons as either homosexual or heterosexual (or, more recently, bisexual) has virtually no precedent in premodern culture. Certainly knowledge of same-sex sexual attraction or sexual practice existed, but the way in which these were understood, thought about, poeticized, and so on was in quite different terms — whether same-sex sexual attraction and practice were regarded as obligatory, preferable, permissible, odd, or prohibited.

In the modern period, persons who are drawn to same-sex erotic relations are often presumed averse to "heterosexual" relations. This presumption clearly does not reflect the view of most cultures and historical epochs for which we have data. Moreover, the contemporary model of same-sex relationships in our society emphasizes relations between peers. But for Greek antiquity, medieval Japan, and tribal Melanesian society, cross-generational or pederastic structures were normative.

For our study, we should not read back into the sources stereotypes from our own culture concerning sexual structures, practices, or preferences. At the same time, we must use some language to identify the point of contact we wish to make with another epoch or culture. Extreme relativism can produce only the silence of cultural solipsism. The difficulty we face here is not different in kind from the difficulty of speaking about "marriage" or "family" or "the poor" or "justice." In each case, modern ways of understanding these categories differ markedly from those of other epochs and other cultures. Thus, without either ignoring or being paralyzed by cultural and historical differences, the "point of contact" with the text that we seek to illumine is the love of one man for another that is "more" than friendship and which does not foreclose erotic attraction or sexual expression.[2]

With these qualifications in mind, let us turn now to the texts to see how a homoerotic reading makes sense of the data that the Gospel of John presents.

Intimacy

The disciple Jesus loved makes his first appearance in chapter 13. The Gospel sets the scene: "Now before the feast of the Passover, when Jesus knew that his hour had come to depart out of this world to the Father, having loved his own who were with him in the world, he loved them to the end" (13:1).

With this begins the story of Jesus' last meal with his disciples ("his own"), which remains the setting of the narrative until the end of chapter 17. Five chapters (about 20 percent of the Gospel as a whole) are thus concerned with this farewell dinner and discourse of Jesus with his disciples.

The theme for this section of the Gospel is the love of Jesus for "his own." This theme is made concrete in the dramatic symbolic action of washing the feet of the disciples. In this action Jesus strips to perform this menial and intimate service, an action that runs against both class and gender roles.[3] Jesus offers this action as a pattern for the disciples' behavior toward one another (13:15ff). For Jesus, such an action is the concrete form of love.

Subsequently Jesus talks about the meaning of love in his farewell discourse to the disciples (chapters 14 and 15). Throughout this section of John's narrative, what is at stake is the love that binds Jesus to the disciples and binds them to one another.

Precisely in this context we meet "the disciple loved by Jesus." We do so in the only segment of this material that bears even superficial resemblance to the accounts of Jesus' last meal with his disciples in the other narratives of the New Testament, the so-called "Synoptic Gospels." In those texts,

---

2. A further caveat before proceeding: Homosexual attraction in classical antiquity and in early modern culture was sometimes articulated in a misogynist way, on account of the patriarchal and often misogynist cultural presuppositions of the culture as a whole. One of the insights of feminist hermeneutics is that Jesus deviated from his culture in overturning these patriarchal and misogynist structures. Thus, to read Jesus' relation to his beloved as a homoerotic relationship is not to read it as conforming to the sexist structures of some homoerotic rhetoric of classical (and modern) culture.

3. See chapter 9 below.

the emphasis falls on the bread and wine and the apparent institution of a commemorative meal by which the death of Jesus is to be remembered and his return anticipated. Nothing of this emphasis appears in John. In its place we have the action of foot washing and the discourses.

But this account is connected to the synoptic (and Pauline) accounts by the motif of Jesus' impending betrayal at the hands of "one of the twelve." The impending betrayal is already anticipated in 13:2 and is developed, following the foot washing, in 13:21–31. Here, for the first time, we encounter the figure of the beloved.

The context in which the man Jesus loved is introduced is striking. As we have seen, this whole section of the Gospel is devoted to the love of Jesus for his disciples and the way Jesus' love serves as a model of their love for one another. This love is expressed in intimate fellowship, mutual service, friendship, shared understanding, a common fate, and destiny, which together characterize Jesus' relationships to all these disciples and to those who through them are to become disciples.

That one disciple is singled out in *this* context as *the* disciple loved by Jesus is striking. Jesus loved all the disciples in the most intimate friendship and in sacrificial solidarity. The singling out of one who is loved by Jesus makes clear that some kind of love is at stake other than the love that unites Jesus to the rest of his disciples. The text itself suggests that we should recognize here some form of love that certainly does not contradict the more general love of Jesus for all, but which does set it apart from this general love. A reasonable conclusion is that this difference points us to a different sphere or dimension of love: love characterized by erotic desire or sexual attraction.

This impression is immediately strengthened when we consider how the narrative describes this love: "one of the disciples of Jesus — the one Jesus loved — was reclining in Jesus' lap.... Falling back thus upon the chest of Jesus, he said to him... "

In antiquity, the normal posture for dining together among friends was that of reclining on mats or pillows. Thus all the disciples — we are not to think here of just the twelve but of a larger group, perhaps including women[4] — are lying about in this way. But one of them is lying in (on) Jesus' lap — that is, snuggled up to Jesus. The disciple leans forward to

---

4. Other Gospels suggest the presence of the twelve, but this group is not given much credence by John. The exclusion of women from the meal may have been characteristic of both Jewish Passover tradition and of Greek symposium etiquette. Nevertheless our picture of Jesus' behavior should consider that he broke these and associated taboos.

hear Peter's question and then falls back (onto the chest of Jesus) to relay the question.

The text thus depicts the relationship of love in terms of physical closeness and bodily intimacy. This feature is expressed twice here (lap, chest) and is reiterated in the final scene of the Gospel when the beloved is pointed out as the one who had lain on Jesus' chest (21:20). The Gospel draws particular attention to this gesture of affectionate intimacy as the dramatic representation of what it means to say that this disciple was in some special way "loved by Jesus."

Jesus' love for all his disciples is a love to the end, an intimate friendship, yet at the same time Jesus has a different love for one of them. The mark of that difference is the posture of bodily intimacy. This physical intimacy differentiates Jesus' love for this disciple from the intimacy of friendship expressed in Jesus' discourse on love and even from the physical intimacy expressed toward all the disciples in the foot washing. The text marks one of the disciples as "more than a friend," though he is a friend as well. He is the beloved, one for whom the appropriate expression of love is that of physical closeness and bodily intimacy.

The narrative also suggests that this relationship is one that Peter accepts and acknowledges. Thus Peter assumes that the beloved would be privy to Jesus' intimate thoughts in a way that neither he nor the others would. Peter signals the beloved with a nod. The beloved leans forward out of his nest to hear Peter's question and then falls back on Jesus' chest to ask him in more privacy, "Who is it?"

Instead of responding directly, Jesus instructs him to watch who receives the piece of bread that Jesus dunks in the gravy. The scene appears as a small moment of intimate conspiracy and shared confidence. Hardly any other interpretation makes sense of the narrative as it stands.[5]

Consider: Peter assumes the beloved would know, if anyone did, the identity of the betrayer. Why should Peter assume this? Because Jesus is intimate with this disciple in a way different from his intimacy with the others, an intimacy depicted as that of bodily intimacy. Peter draws the understandable conclusion that this bodily intimacy entails a superior understanding of Jesus' meaning; but he is mistaken. That is, the physical intimacy of the beloved does not entail special knowledge. The beloved doesn't know so he falls back to ask.

---

5. Some commentators see here an insertion into the text that is poorly integrated into the narrative as a whole. However, our concern is not with hypothetical sources or redactions but with the interpretation of the text as it stands.

Now Jesus could simply answer the question, but this is something he does not often do in the Gospels. Instead Jesus plays a kind of game with the beloved.

But this game by no means gives esoteric knowledge to the beloved. He knows a short time before anyone else the identity of the betrayer.[6] This foreknowledge scarcely constitutes a theological "big deal." Indeed the only importance which the narrator attributes to the identity of the betrayer is that he is "one of the twelve," something already announced at 6:70. The interaction between Jesus and the man he loves simply underscores the intimacy of Jesus' relation to the beloved. Jesus tells him a kind of secret, but one that is unimportant. The secret is simply an expression of intimate affection, precisely the sort of thing that Jesus could share with his beloved without compromising the basic unity of this band of comrades.

Jesus discloses important concepts in the discourses that follow: the meaning of love, the destiny of Jesus and the followers, the role of the Paraclete, and so on. These topics are certainly weighty, but none of these are directed to the beloved. In these matters, he remains on exactly the same footing as the others. Jesus does not play favorites when it comes to theologically important matters.

The introduction of the beloved makes clear that Jesus' love for him is different from the intimate friendship that characterizes his relationship to all other members of this band. This love for the beloved is expressed in physical intimacy among friends. The least forced reading of the text is that in addition to loving his disciples, Jesus also had a beloved for whom he was the lover.

Acknowledgment

The beloved is not singled out again until Jesus' death on the cross. He is not identified as one who participates in the dialogue with Jesus concerning where Jesus is going (13:36ff), nor is he singled out from among the other disciples when Jesus discourses on the nature of love and unity with him, nor is he singled out at the scene of Jesus' betrayal in the Garden, nor does he seem to be identified as one of the disciples who witness Jesus'

---

6. Actually even this conclusion is in doubt since the narrator reports that "no one at the table knew" (13:28) the meaning of Jesus' subsequent words to Judas: "What you are going to do, do quickly" (13:27). Thus, if we take the text as it stands, we would conclude that the beloved was also mystified by what Jesus had said to him and only later recalled the incident when he, with others, knew that Judas had been the betrayer.

trial before the Sanhedrin (18:15ff).[7] When our attention is next drawn to him, Jesus is already on the cross.

The passages where we are reminded of the presence of the beloved are as significant as are the passages where we are not. He has no special role in terms of the handing on of Jesus' teachings; he is exactly on a par with all the others. His "specialness" lies elsewhere. Nor is he ever the only witness to any of the important events of this fateful twenty-four hours of Jesus' passion.

Even here at the cross he is not the only witness. He is present with a number of women.

Four of Jesus' followers witness his execution: His mother, his aunt, Mary Magdalene, and the beloved (19:25). Jesus' aunt is not mentioned before or after. His mother has been associated with him before (2:1–5). Mary Magdalene has not been mentioned earlier but will appear subsequently (20:1–18).

John's narrative of the cross is quite different from what we find in the other Gospels. Here we have three sayings of Jesus that are not found in the other Gospels. Two of these are quite brief. One, "I thirst," is treated as a fulfillment of Scripture. The last ("it is accomplished") serves to designate the end of Jesus' mission as well as the achieving of that mission's goal.

But before we come to these sayings so weighted with theological significance for the author and reader of this text, we find something quite remarkable. Jesus is said to notice the presence of the beloved and of his own mother. He addresses them each by directing them to one another: "Woman, behold your son," and to the beloved: "Behold your mother."

At a subsequent point, we will have opportunity to develop at greater length the question of the relation between Jesus and his mother in this text.[8] Here it should be noted that she is identified by the narrator as Jesus' "mother" but is addressed by Jesus only as "woman." This shift in terminology also agrees with what occurs in the earlier story of the wedding in Cana (2:4). Jesus uses for Mary exactly the same form of address that he uses for other women that he encounters: the Samaritan woman (4:21), the woman taken in adultery (8:10), and Mary of Magdala (20:15). That is, Jesus is not at all given to a kind of "Mothers' Day" sentimentality in the Gospel of John or, still less, in the other Gospels.[9]

---

7. Reasons for doubting that the "other disciple" of 18:15–16 should be included among the texts that contribute to our knowledge of the beloved are given below, pp. 47–53.

8. See chapter 10.

9. See Mark 3:32–35 and parallels and Luke 11:27–28.

But what is the true meaning of this scene at the cross? Some imagine that Jesus deflects attention from himself here in order to tell his followers that they are to care for one another. Whatever the merits of this edifying reflection, they have no basis in *this* text. For if the author wanted to make this point, leaving out Jesus' aunt and Mary of Magdala hardly seems appropriate. Surely a simpler approach would be to say to the group as a whole: Look after one another.

If we cannot read this episode either as an edifying reflection on the care of the disciples for one another or as depicting Jesus' sonly sentimentality, what does it mean?

If we assume that Jesus and the beloved are lovers, the action becomes a transparent acknowledgment of the special relationship between Jesus and the beloved, an acknowledgment that has the same effect as a kind of betrothal. Our interpretation would be easier if Jesus had singled out, say, Mary the Magdalene instead: "Woman behold your daughter," and to Mary Magdalene, "Behold your mother." Had Mary of Magdala been depicted as having a particularly close relationship to Jesus characterized by physical intimacy, we would read the text quite easily. Because Mary of Magdala is Jesus' lover, she is *therefore* his mother's daughter (in-law). Especially does this relationship come to the fore with the death of the son of the one and "husband" of the other. In such a case for the sake of the dead son, the mother takes as her daughter the one who had been closest to him in life. And the lover takes the husband's mother as her own mother. That is, they adopt one another. We already possess a beautiful model for this sort of relationship in the story of Jesus' ancestress, Ruth, and her mother-in-law, Naomi. That story of love and loyalty between two women has even become a staple of marriage ceremony texts (Ruth 1:16–17) in spite of the same-sex love that the story actually depicts.

The mutual adoption of mother-in-law and daughter-in law would be the natural reading of the text if Mary of Magdala were the other. But she is not. Instead the *man* Jesus loved is now placed in an adoptive relationship with Jesus' mother. So why should we permit the feature of the disciple's gender to hide the plain sense of the narrative?

The plain sense of this episode is to buttress our hypothesis that Jesus is to be understood as having a lover or, in the more precise terminology of antiquity, as being the lover of a beloved. The relationship is depicted by the text as a homoerotic one, which is here acknowledged as entailing a loyalty that has consequences even beyond the death of Jesus.

We should notice that the relationship of adoption that Jesus indicates is one of mutuality. His mother and the man he loves adopt one another on account of the love they apparently have for Jesus. The man does not simply adopt the mother in order to look after her and comfort her in her grief. The reverse could also be true. The mother is to "mother" the beloved. The character of this adoption makes clear that we are not simply dealing with a concern for the mother (as in Mothers' Day rhetoric) but a concern for the beloved.

This aspect of the episode is strengthened when we recall that the way of identifying this disciple stresses the fact that Jesus loves him. Thus this scene should be read as underlining not Jesus' love for his mother (which is suggested nowhere in this or any other Gospel) but Jesus' love for his beloved. The mother's role and responsibility is expressed first: "Woman: behold your son." Only then does Jesus relate the responsive role of the son: "Behold your mother."

Jesus' instructions are all the more striking given that the Gospel of John speaks of Jesus having "brothers" (2:12; 7:2–5, 10).[10] One would think that Jesus' mother is not alone in the world. She has other sons, not to mention the sister at her side at this moment. She has no need of relatives or kin, but now, in addition to those blood kin she already has, she receives another son — one who becomes her son because he is the beloved of her dying son. She is being charged with a responsibility here: being mother to this man for the sake of his lover who was (one of) her son(s).

The beloved thus receives a mother and in this way becomes the son of Jesus' mother. She adopts him first (as a parent must do) and then he adopts her.

The episode concludes that the beloved did in fact take her as his mother. The passage often appears translated as "took her to his home," but "home" is not found in the text. The word is added by the translator. He took her "into his own" is more literal. But specifying home or family or anything of the kind here is not necessary. According to the account, he indeed accepted the adoptive relationship, which began "from that hour."

"That hour" is the hour of Jesus' death. Thus the relationship between the beloved and the mother of Jesus begins from the death of Jesus. While before their relationship had been to Jesus, now it is to one another. The grief of the mother for (one of) her son(s) and the grief of the beloved for the man who loved him are to find consolation in their care for one another.

---

10. The other Gospels know this also. See Mark 6:3 and Matthew 13:55, where we also learn that he had sisters as well.

This scene is also consistent with what we noticed before concerning Jesus' relation to the disciple he loved, namely, that it was not clandestine. The relationship was apparent to those people who knew Jesus best.

But why should such a domestic scene be recorded here at this climactic moment in the Gospel? We have to deal with this question again in connection with all the texts concerning the beloved. Here the text itself suggests that the event is recorded because the beloved said it happened and that his testimony was accepted by the writer(s) of the narrative.

The beloved is here also for the first time identified as a source for the recollections that serve as the basis of the narrative (19:35). Specifically what the beloved witnesses is that Jesus' legs were not broken but that his side was pierced. This account is regarded by the narrator(s) as consistent with Scripture (19:36–37). But behind this fact is the even more important one that Jesus really and truly died. The beloved is certainly not the only witness to this fact, but he is a witness.

But another and more important reason exists for why the episode between Jesus, his mother, and his beloved may be recorded in connection with the account of Jesus' execution. One of the themes of this Gospel is that the "Word became flesh." Indeed, on account of the importance of this theme, John's Gospel came to be accepted as an antidote to gnosticism.[11] That Jesus really died was important for countering gnostic and docetic tendencies in the early church. The death of Jesus according to the flesh is the culmination of the incarnation (en-fleshing) of the Word. The scene of his death then is accentuated by the presence of his mother according to the flesh and of Jesus' beloved according to the flesh. The presence of Jesus' mother (who is certainly not regarded as an exemplary disciple) and the presence of Jesus' beloved (who is also not singled out as a model disciple) underscore the bodily reality that is crucial for the death of Jesus as well.

Put another way, the love that is so often the theme of this Gospel is not only "spiritual"; it is also physical, just as the death of Jesus (or his incarnation) is not only a theological symbol but also a physical, bodily reality.

In this way also, the scene at the cross connects back to the scene at the meal where we first encountered the beloved and where his relation to Jesus was marked precisely by physical, bodily intimacy.

---

11. This reading from Irenaeus was already established by the end of the second century.

The Tomb

The episode of the tomb does not add a great deal to our hypothesis concerning the nature of the relationship between Jesus and the beloved. Nothing here is inconsistent with the view that theirs was an erotic friendship. But because Jesus himself is not present, little in the tomb account supplements the nature of their relationship either.

The main figure in the account of the empty tomb is Mary of Magdala, whom we first met by name as a witness to Jesus' execution (19:25). She finds the tomb empty, and she is the one who first brings word of this event to the others. Although Peter and the beloved come running to the tomb and enter it, she rather than they encounter Jesus here.[12]

The hypothesis of an erotic friendship between Jesus and his beloved disciple at least serves to clarify the text and to "flesh out" some of the details of that relationship.

We notice first that Mary finds the beloved and Peter together. In the next chapter, we see that this piece of circumstantial evidence supports, though does not require, the view that the beloved is Andrew, Peter's brother. Whether or not they are brothers, they are clearly at least companions. The supposition that Jesus' relation to the beloved was an erotic one makes the relationship between Peter and the beloved more intelligible. According to the text, each has particular reasons to seek out the other's companionship. The beloved has witnessed the death of Jesus. He may be found here seeking consolation. Peter has denied one he followed and loved. Who else to turn to in order to unburden himself and seek forgiveness than the one who was the beloved of the one he had denied?

The race to the tomb tells us that the beloved is faster but that he waits for Peter before going in. One could suppose that he is faster because he is younger. One might suppose that he waits for Peter because here, as elsewhere, Peter is represented as the boldest (despite his cowardice at the trial).[13] One may suppose that the loved one hesitates also because he is still traumatized by the sight of the mangled bleeding corpse of his lover only some hours before.

---

12. Indeed the role of Mary here has even led to the suggestion that she had an especially close relationship to Jesus of the sort that this narrative in fact reserves for a man. This suggestion must be wholly based upon the account of Jesus' appearance to her in the garden, because at no other point is she represented, by name, as having an especially close relationship to Jesus. A displacement seems to be taking place from the beloved to Mary Magdalene, as if the reader recognizes that something more than ordinarily intimate seems to be signaled by the text and so constructs, from another figure in the text, a more acceptable recipient of this intimacy.

13. The Gospel of John is alone in identifying Peter as the one in the garden who has a sword with which he seeks to defend Jesus from the Temple police (18:10).

In any case, Peter enters first and sees the grave clothes. The beloved then also enters (seeing no disfigured body) and sees and believes.

Obviously the beloved is by no means the sole witness. Mary is the first, followed by Peter, and then the beloved. Thus the episode does not serve to establish the peculiar authority of the beloved, only his personal status as the beloved.

While the beloved believed, he is not necessarily exemplary of subsequent faith. Rather his status serves to make intelligible his reserve at the entrance to the tomb. The lover is dead, and nothing more was to be expected of him since "they did not yet know the writing that he must rise from the dead." What then is the object of this "belief"? Thus far simply that the body is not in the tomb. Mary supposes that the body has been stolen or hidden (vv. 11–15).[14]

Even if, on the basis of the empty tomb, we supposed that the beloved "believed" that Jesus had risen from the dead, this status would not make him a paradigm for the faith of the church which is subsequently identified, in the episode with Thomas, as the believing that proceeds without having seen (20:29).

The episode at the tomb serves to confirm that the beloved is neither an independent source of authority in the church nor a representative of the church as such but is a particular disciple.[15] The beloved disciple appears to have a noncompetitive relationship with Peter, the leader of the disciples. The final scene of the narrative confirms this.

Fishfry

We come now to the final episode of the Gospel of John. All of chapter 21 is concerned with a final resurrection appearance of Jesus.[16] Peter and several of his friends, a group we later learn includes the beloved, go fishing. A mysterious stranger gives them instructions from the shore concerning the placement of their nets. When the tactic meets with overwhelming success, the beloved recognizes the stranger as Jesus (v. 7) and relays this information to Peter. Peter puts on his clothes in order to swim to the shore while the others follow with the boat, now loaded with fish.[17]

---

14. We should notice that the assertion that the lack of understanding concerning the resurrection attributed both to the disciple and to Peter makes it difficult to suppose that the beloved is to be identified with Lazarus, who had already been raised from the dead.

15. The question of the role of the beloved disciple is addressed again in the next chapter.

16. The chapter is also regularly regarded as a kind of appendix to the Gospel, which seems to end naturally at the end of chapter 20.

17. A similar story appears in Luke 5:4–11.

The scene is consistent with the picture of the beloved disciple and Peter from the preceding material. They are regularly paired and appear as companions, as was also true in the dinner scene of chapter 13 and the tomb scene of chapter 20. As in the tomb scene, Peter acts precipitously (although oddly; he puts on his clothes in order to swim, though it may be more the arrival at shore than the swimming that motivates the putting on of clothes). The beloved defers to Peter in this case — as also at the entrance to the tomb — despite the fact that the beloved is said to be the first to recognize Jesus, as he was the first to arrive at the tomb.

Here, as in all the resurrection appearance stories, something is quite odd about the recognition of Jesus. That is, Jesus is never immediately recognized either in this Gospel or in any of the others. Inferring the identity of the mysterious stranger is always necessary. In the case of this narrative, this inference has been based on the calling of a name (20:16), the demonstration of his wounds (20:20, 27), or, in this final episode, with the result of his instructions. Therefore, that the beloved as well should not recognize Jesus directly but only inferentially is not out of keeping with this feature of appearance narratives.

A long dialogue follows, or rather an interrogation of Peter by Jesus, consisting of a thrice-repeated question: "Peter, do you love me?" Each time Peter replies in the affirmative, and each time he is charged with the care and feeding of Jesus' sheep. We subsequently consider the vocabulary of love that is used here and throughout the Gospel, but here we should notice that the question addressed to Peter concerns Peter's love for Jesus. (The triple question may correspond to Peter's triple negation of Jesus during the trial.) This approach contrasts with the designation of the beloved disciple, not as one who loved Jesus but as the one whom Jesus loved. In this final chapter, he is designated in this way twice (vv. 7, 20).

The dialogue between Jesus and Peter concludes with a proverb about growing old, which is reinterpreted by the narrator as foretelling the crucifixion of Peter. This death is the content of the final injunction to Peter: "Follow me."

It is here that we again encounter the man Jesus loved:

Turning, Peter sees the disciple that Jesus loved following them, who also was the one who leaned on Jesus' chest at the supper and had said, "Lord, who is the one betraying you?" Peter seeing this one says to Jesus, "Lord, and what of him?" Jesus says to him, "If I want him to remain until I come, what is that to you? You follow me!" The saying spread abroad among the brothers that this disciple is not to die. But Jesus didn't say that he doesn't die, but: "If I want him to stay until I come, what's it to you?"

Compared to Peter, the beloved clearly plays a very minor role in this episode. Indeed he is utterly silent and passive save for the initial recognition of Jesus and his "hanging around" while Peter and Jesus talk.

The final appearance of the beloved recalls his first appearance in the Gospel and reminds the reader of his intimacy with Jesus, as indicated by physical proximity and affectionate stance. Thus the cycle of texts concerning the disciple Jesus loved comes to a kind of closure.

Once again we are reminded of the relationship between this disciple and Peter. The beloved disciple had told Peter of the identity of the mysterious stranger. Here Peter expresses solicitude for the beloved of Jesus. In this way we may say that Peter is, in a sense, beginning the task that Jesus had set for him: caring for those whom Jesus had cared for. In any case the close relationship between Peter and the beloved is a constant feature of these texts.

But Jesus here interdicts this care of Peter for the beloved, making it clear that though Peter is charged with responsibility for the others (the sheep) he does not have the same responsibility for the beloved ("what is that to you?"). Jesus makes himself responsible for the fate of the man he loves. Once again the beloved is distinguished from the others who are entrusted to Peter's care. His special relationship to Jesus abides.

No commission is given to the beloved that would place him in competition with Peter, the beloved's fate is simply Jesus' concern.

"The brothers" thought it appropriate that the beloved, whatever might befall the rest, should remain alive until the return of Jesus — understood here as the consummation of Jesus' mission in the reign of justice and joy on earth. The text disputes their interpretation, but for our purposes, that "the brothers" should have imagined that the beloved might very well be protected from harm so as to be the one to welcome Jesus on his return is significant.[18]

The story again is perfectly intelligible from the standpoint of a homoerotic interpretation of the relationship between Jesus and the beloved.

---

18. At 2:12, the text clearly distinguished the brothers from the disciples, and this may also be the meaning of 7:3–10. If so, then "brothers" here does not mean disciples but specifically the siblings of Jesus who will misunderstand his words. How they come to concern themselves with the fate of the beloved is understandable, given that the beloved has become something of a sibling through the mutual adoption of Jesus' mother and his beloved at the cross.

The confusion on the part of the "brothers" concerning the meaning of Jesus' saying about the man he loved is a strong indication of the historicity of this figure. See chapter 4.

This personal relationship does not seem to be a relationship that entails any special mission or responsibility on the part of the beloved. The task of serving as Jesus' stand-in falls to all the disciples who have been sent, just as Jesus was sent (20:21). If anyone has an "official" capacity, that disciple is Peter, who is to "tend my sheep" (21:15–17). The role of the beloved is in no way "official." He is not "favorite pupil," still less designated successor. The "specialness" of the relationship is entirely "personal."

We have seen that this relationship is not a "hidden" relationship. Peter takes it for granted. The relationship is expressed by the public display of affectionate intimacy before all the disciples, and Jesus even publicly acknowledges it as he is dying. Precisely as the acknowledged object of Jesus' erotic love does it become plausible that the beloved has the personal role of waiting for the return of Jesus.

Indeed Peter's concern for the beloved is just the sort of thing we might expect if Jesus and the beloved were "lovers." Peter's much protested love for Jesus extends quite naturally to include the beloved of Jesus. In this way, Peter understandably can accept the relationship of Jesus and the beloved. The beloved is not a candidate for Peter's official position, and Peter is not a candidate for the role of the beloved. We should notice that this situation would be different if the "beloved" were simply, in a nonerotic sense, the "favorite" of Jesus. In that case, Peter would be expected to want not only to be the leader of the disciples but also the favorite of Jesus. But if the beloved is not the "favorite" in this general sense but rather in an erotic sense, then Peter's role is not threatened by the beloved. Peter has no need to challenge the place of the beloved but is free to accept and honor the relationship, as the text suggests that he does.

The concluding lines of the text serve to buttress the impression that the truthful witness of 19:35 is the beloved, as we supposed. Clearly the faithful witness appears to be the beloved, but this status does not confer on him any distinctive authority. Indeed he is a witness to Peter's authority and vocation. Nothing else is claimed for him.

The unnamed editors ("we") do, however, wish to claim that their text does in some way or other derive from the witness and even the writing of this same beloved. A community, then, apparently compiles a Gospel making use of the recollections and the testimony of the one called "the disciple Jesus loved." That the text, then, does not seek either to further identify this figure or to place him in a position of particular authority among the disciples is all the more remarkable. He is simply the beloved of Jesus.

Conclusion

A close reading of the texts in which the beloved disciple appears supports the hypothesis that the relationship between him and Jesus may be understood as that of lovers. As it happens, both Jesus and the beloved are male, meaning that their relationship may be said to be, in modern terms, a "homosexual" relationship. But the main emphasis falls simply on the relationship of being lovers, not on the gender of the lovers.

Nothing is made in the text of the specific form of sexuality that mediates this relationship, something that is quite normal in literature of this type. At stake here is simply that they were lovers. We are no more told whether or how they "had sex" than we are in other connections about the sexual practices, if any, of Peter and his wife, or those of Mary and Joseph. Whether lovers are of the same or of different genders, the specific practices that mediate and celebrate their personal and physical intimacy are strictly their own business, not a matter for literary display or scholarly curiosity.

That we are told nothing of this is thus not surprising. Nor does the homoerotic interpretation of this relationship entail anything one way or the other about the sexual practices that may have expressed the intimacy of these "lovers." The text is more concerned that we see what the public — at least the public of Jesus' intimate circle of friends and followers — would see: that Jesus was the lover of the beloved. In this way, this disciple is already distinguished from the many whom Jesus undoubtedly loved as followers and friends, the many for whom Jesus' love was so pronounced that he would abase himself for them or die for them.

This relationship between Jesus and the disciple he loved is expressed in terms of physical or bodily intimacy at the supper. This factor is underlined in the account so as to leave no doubt about its importance and meaning. At the same time, this bodily intimacy, the intimacy of lovers, is clearly by no means an expression of the sort of intimacy on the basis of which the beloved might claim an official preeminence among the disciples. He is privy to no special teaching. He is theologically and ecclesially on a par with the rest. Indeed the only "leader" recognized here is Peter not the beloved. The beloved must be understood in the sense, then, not as friend nor as colleague (something shared with the others) but as "lovers."

That Jesus goes to the extraordinary length of having his beloved and his mother adopt and care for one another further denotes the personal and "fleshly" character of the relationship. Jesus acknowledges his lover according to the flesh, before his mother according to the flesh, charging her to be mother to him and then charging the beloved to be son to her.

Jesus' beloved (or, as we would say, "lover") appears accepted in this role by Peter, by the other disciples, and finally by Jesus' own family. For them to conclude that Jesus had decided that his lover should await him until his return was apparently quite natural. In this way, the permanence of their relationship was brought to striking expression.

This reading can only claim to make sense of the data provided by the Gospel of John and to do no violence to that data. To be sure we must exercise care not to read into the text the specific features of homosexuality that are characteristic of the modern construction of same-sex relationships. Our reading of the text does, however, depend on finding some point of contact between what we mean by gay or homosexual relationships and the relationship depicted in the text. If the text means to suggest that the relationship between Jesus and his beloved was a relationship of lovers, present-day readers should not conclude that the text supposes that Jesus and his beloved were "homosexual" in the modern sense. This category (of persons) was not operative in antiquity. But antiquity does know of relationships between persons of the same sex that were erotic and that may have been given expression through specific sexual practices. Our reading is meant to highlight this point of contact.

Unquestionably the suggestion that Jesus and the beloved were lovers in this sense could raise in the mind of the reader a number of questions and objections, and to these we next turn in the attempt to further clarify this relationship and its meaning.

Chapter 3

The Identity and Role of the Man Jesus Loved

While little attention has been given to the question of the kind of relationship that Jesus had with the disciple he loved, considerable attention has focused on the question of this figure's identity and to his role in the Gospel of John. Accordingly we now turn to this set of issues.

Role of the Beloved

What is the role in the narrative of the one called the beloved of Jesus? Why should one be singled out as Jesus' loved one in this way? Some of the proposed answers to this question have served to deflect attention away from the erotic character of the relationship that we explored in the previous chapter. Accordingly we need to pay these answers particular attention if we are to substantiate the homoerotic reading of the relationship that we have proposed.

The Claim of Authority

The beloved is shown as the witness to Jesus' death and resurrection, and is said to be the one whose testimony undergirds in some way the narrative we call the Gospel of John (19:35; 21:24). Is the point of singling out this disciple to claim a certain authority for him and his teaching?

Although this suggestion has regularly been tacitly assumed, it does not bear up well under scrutiny. At no point is the beloved said to be privy to information not available to the others. He is one of at least four witnesses to the death of Jesus. He and Peter both go to the empty tomb. Unlike Mary of Magdala, they do not encounter Jesus. Indeed the presence of the beloved disciple at a resurrection appearance is found only in the last chapter where he is in the company of others, most of whom have

36

presumably seen the risen Jesus at one or both of the two previous group encounters.

What at first appears to be a significant role, that of eyewitness to the most important events, turns out to be less than crucial.[1] Insofar as special information is involved, it seems to be trivial. The beloved disciple knows a few minutes before the others the identity of Jesus' betrayer. This sort of detail is theologically insignificant.[2] Nothing beyond personal significance is here, nothing that would establish the reputation of a school, nothing that would make the beloved an authoritative teacher.

To be sure, the Gospel of John is filled — certainly more so than the other Gospels — with what appears to be esoteric teaching concerning the identity of Jesus and the conflict between the gospel and the world. None of this esoteric teaching is ever associated with the beloved disciple. Jesus explains far more to Nicodemus (3:1–21) or the Samaritan woman (4:1–42) than to him. Even in the last discourse, where so much of theological significance is said, the beloved plays no role whatever. Peter, Judas not Iscariot, Philip, and Thomas all figure in this discussion, but no mention is made of the beloved.

Had the aim been to establish the authority of a particular teacher, a better job could have been done. The beloved might at least have been unambiguously identified, for example, or made privy in some way to Jesus' teachings. At least his presence alongside the others might have been mentioned when a decisive theological issue was discussed.

The supposition that the character of the beloved disciple is introduced in order to make a claim for the authority of some or other teaching or school of Christian thought does not stand up to scrutiny.[3] At no point does the beloved play any such role. Indeed the text itself precludes anyone from such a role since all of Jesus' teaching, however esoteric it may seem, is nevertheless public. Furthermore, more revelations will come to all the followers from the Spirit (16:13).

---

1. This conclusion is true as well if we include the reference to "another disciple" who gets Peter into the trial of Jesus. Here, too, this "other disciple" cannot be the sole source for information regarding the trial since Peter is there; presumably also (if they are not the other disciple) Nicodemus and even Joseph of Arimathea should be there.

2. C. K. Barrett also recognizes this insignificance: "It is no special revelation which is accorded him but a plain statement of fact." See *The Gospel According to St. John,* 2d ed. (Philadelphia: Westminster Press, 1978), 447.

3. Raymond Brown, for example, suggests that "the claim to possess the witness of the Beloved Disciple enabled the Johannine Christians to defend their peculiar insights in Christology and ecclesiology." *The Community of the Beloved Disciple* (New York: Paulist Press, 1979), 31.

The most that can be made of the authority of the beloved is that he, like others, was one of Jesus' followers. He does not have authority because he was the beloved (for no special knowledge is attributed to him as beloved), but only the same sort of authority as other followers. Some commentators have supposed that even this minimal authority may have been important to the "community of the beloved disciple" (the "we" of 21:24), but this conclusion would hold up only if the teaching of the beloved were regarded by other communities as heterodox. Thus, a claim that his testimony, while not by any means supplanting that of Peter, was nevertheless not heterodox but had a foundation similar to that of Peter and other disciples would be important. To carry this view forward, however, one must cease reading rivalry into the relationship between Peter and the beloved and accept that the beloved's association with Peter rather than his special relationship to Jesus was the foundation of his authority.

Allegory of the Church

Some interpreters have maintained that the anonymity of the disciple Jesus loved makes him an allegorical figure representative of the ideal disciple, or the Church, or some particular community of Christians.

Certainly anonymity may function allegorically in the Gospels. Perhaps the most striking evidence of this device is found in the Gospel of Mark, where such figures as the Syrophoenecian woman (7:21–30) or the woman who anoints Jesus in Bethany (14:3–9) may serve, in their anonymity, as representatives of important features of a participation in the mission and ministry of Jesus.

But do any signs exist that the figure of the beloved in the Gospel of John fulfills this function? A superficially plausible case is made by remarking that the beloved is to remain until the return of Jesus in chapter 21. What but the church itself may be said to have this role? On this basis, then, one may also say that the beloved, as the community, is the faithful witness who bears testimony to the death and resurrection of Jesus and so is the "author" of this narrative exposition of the gospel. Similarly one may suggest that the beloved, as the community, is rightly placed both as witness to the cross and to the empty tomb. We might even link this to the notion of the Church as the bride of Christ and so as the beloved of Jesus. And to this strand of thought may be added the idea that just as Jesus is "from the bosom of the Father" (1:18), and the disciple reclines on the breast of Jesus, so also the community reclines in the bosom of Christ.

But the superficial plausibility of this view evaporates upon examination. Its point of greatest strength — that the beloved is to remain until the return of Jesus — is also its fatal weakness, for this view is clearly mistaken according to the text itself. Though some of the "brothers" had concluded that the beloved was to remain until Jesus' return, the text itself disputes this supposition. Are we then to conclude that the community will not remain on earth until the return? The only reasonable conclusion on the basis of this passage is that here at least the beloved is regarded as an individual. Moreover if anyone in this scene is regarded as tied to the church, Peter would be the one. Peter is asked whether he loves Jesus. Peter is to feed and care for the "sheep." Peter is summoned to follow, even to death. Peter thus represents the leadership of the community, *not* the beloved. Nor is Peter given a commission with respect to the beloved. What happens to the beloved is a matter between Jesus and the beloved unmediated by Peter (What is it to you?). If the beloved represented the community, then why is Peter's commission (to care for the sheep) not a commission to care for the beloved?

The identification of the disciple Jesus loved with the bride of Christ does bring to expression Jesus' special relation to that disciple but not in such a way as to make the disciple a type of the church. Rather, that identification (inadvertently) suggests that the relationship between Jesus and this disciple had the erotic character of a bride and bridegroom relationship, except that both are male.

The suggestion that the location of the beloved (lying on Jesus' chest) is meant allegorically also falls when we consider that the very passage that emphasizes the individuality of the disciple (chapter 21) also recalls that he was the one who reclined in this fashion.

In order to solve this difficulty, Bultmann made the interesting proposal that the beloved be regarded not as a type for the church as a whole but for the Gentile church. In order for this assessment to work, Bultmann first must simply dispose of chapter 21 as a later addition to the text, an addition that misunderstands the allegorical role of the disciple and mistakenly treats him as an individual.[4]

Once this and other passages that speak of the beloved as a witness are rejected as later and mistaken interpolations, then, according to Bultmann, seeing the beloved as the type of gentile Christianity becomes possible. Using Bultmann's approach, the interpretation of the scene at the cross between Mary and the beloved is as follows: the gentile church (represented by the beloved) is to acknowledge the Jewish church (represented

---

4. Rudolf Bultmann, *The Gospel of John,* trans. G. R. Beasley-Murray (Philadelphia: Westminster Press, 1971), 483.

by Mary) and to care for rather than reject her. Bultmann can also see the same idea in other passages where Peter takes on the function of representing the Jewish church.[5]

What can be made of this view? In the first place, nothing in the text suggests that the beloved has a gentile form of faith. He is as Jewish as Mary, Peter, or Jesus. The Gentile should not necessarily have advance knowledge of the identity of the betrayer, be regarded as an eyewitness to Jesus' death, nor be a believer in the empty tomb tradition (which seems no more gentile than belief on the basis of a resurrection appearance).

Apart from the lack of any internal evidence from the Gospel to suggest this reading, most commentators are less inclined to see incompetence in redactors than was Bultmann. To be sure, the question of the writing and the editing of the text of the Gospel is a much vexed one, and the last chapter of the Gospel does read like a later addition. But the idea that later redactors were so incompetent as to change an allegorical into an actual figure is difficult to believe. Scholars have thus not accepted Bultmann's view of the beloved as representing (in some episodes) a gentile as opposed to Jewish Christianity.[6]

Some wish to see in the beloved a type of ideal discipleship, which the reader is then called upon to emulate.[7] The difficulty with this view is that at no point is the beloved characterized by any other quality than his relationship to Jesus. He is never singled out for his insight, his faithfulness, his courage, his obedience, or his "hearing" or "doing" of the word. He is not noticed in the foot-washing scene. He is not noticed in the appearance of Jesus to the disciples which eventuates in their being commissioned to participate in his mission or in the forgiveness of sins (20:19–23).

The attempt to identify the role of the beloved either in terms of his peculiar authority in the community or as an allegory for the community itself does not stand up to scrutiny. The only feature of the disciple that is distinctive is that Jesus loves him. This status is distinctive because Jesus loves this disciple in a special way in which he does not love the other disciples, although he loved them too. The homoerotic features of this

---

5. Ibid., 671–73, 684–85.

6. Among those later commentators who agree in rejecting Bultmann's interpretation we may cite Brown, *The Community of the Beloved Disciple*, 31; Rudolf Schnackenburg, *The Gospel according to St John*, vol. 3, trans. Cecily Hastings (London: Burns and Oates, 1982), 375; Barrett, *The Gospel According to St. John*, 116; and Ernst Haenchen, *A Commentary on the Gospel of John*, chapters 7–21, trans. Robert Funk (Philadelphia: Fortress Press, 1984), 193.

7. Bultmann attributed this view to, among others, Dibelius and Loisy (in Bultmann, *The Gospel of John*, 484). But the commentators cited above (note 6) who reject Bultmann's own hypothesis also reject this one.

relationship cannot be "sublimated" into the claims of rival authorities (Peter and the beloved) or "spiritualized" into an allegory for the relationship between Jesus and the church. We are thus returned to the startling but increasingly unavoidable supposition that physical and emotional intimacy characterize this relationship. In short, the increasingly apparent conclusion is that we are dealing with a homoerotic relationship.

The Question of Identity

Who was the disciple that Jesus loved? Was he John, as tradition maintains? Or one of the other disciples we encounter in this text? Pursuing this question does not bring us to a definitive conclusion concerning the name of this disciple, but the pursuit does provide us with a window into the relation between Jesus and his disciples generally. This perspective will make possible some further clarification about the relationship between Jesus and the disciple he loved.

John

The standard answer to the question is that John the son of Zebedee is the disciple Jesus loved. We know a great deal about this son of Zebedee from other Gospels, where he is identified as one of the twelve and as brother to James, together with whom he is termed a "son of thunder." He is portrayed as a former fisherman who is called by Jesus to leave family and work in order to join in the mission of announcing and enacting the reign of God. This same John, together with his brother James and the brothers Simon and Andrew, form the inner circle of Jesus' band of disciples. James and John furthermore aspire to be throned with Jesus in glory. But all these details concerning this son of Zebedee come from other narratives. They are not found in the text known to us as the Gospel of John. In fact, in this Gospel, he is never mentioned by name! We have one reference in the entire narrative to "the sons of Zebedee,"in the list of the "fishing party" organized by Peter (21:2). We may even say that one of the ways in which this narrative differs from the "Synoptic Gospels" is that the sons of Zebedee (and John in particular) play no role in the text.

Since the internal evidence of the Gospel so strongly points away from the identification of the beloved with John the son of Zebedee, we may wonder how it happens that this traditional identification comes about. It is based upon conjecture that reaches anything like its current form only at the end of the second century, at least one hundred years after the Gospel was written and distributed. Even that traditional evidence is less than meets the eye.

Our main source for insight into the process of attributing authorship to the Fourth Gospel is Eusebius, a fourth-century church leader whose *History of the Church* was written in order to impress the emperor Constantine with the bona fides of that part of the Christian movement to which Constantine was becoming an adherent. The part of the Christian movement so favored was what was coming to call itself catholic in distinction from, for example, gnostic or Montanist versions of the same movement.

From Eusebius we receive the tradition that a certain Papias, a second-century bishop of Hieropolis, wrote an otherwise lost document claiming that in his youth he had learned from the "presbyters" of the preceding generation. In this connection, the name "John" occurs twice: once in a list of those who taught (past tense), which includes some names that appear to be from the "twelve" companions of Jesus (though Papias does not himself say this); and again, as "presbyter John" (in the present tense) in company with "Aristion," who is also said to be a disciple of Jesus.

From Eusebius we also have the Greek text of Irenaeus's claim that his own teacher Polycarp had heard the teaching of John in Ephesus. Neither of these texts associates this John of Ephesus with John the son of Zebedee.[8] Irenaeus at the end of the second century apparently makes this connection rather than either Papias or Polycarp earlier in that century. Nor do the earlier sources identify either John the presbyter (of Ephesus) or John the son of Zebedee (of Galilee) with the disciple Jesus loved.

I agree therefore with Sanders in supposing that a certain presbyter John in Ephesus was connected with the editing and publication of our present Fourth Gospel. This presbyter John was not John the son of Zebedee who appears to have been martyred early in the Christian movement (see Mark 10:39). The identification of presbyter John with the Son of Zebedee emerges later in the controversy with the gnostics who may have claimed this Gospel as an authority for their views. Irenaeus succeeds in rescuing the interpretation of the document from the gnostics and so accepts the pious legend that it comes from one of the twelve, named John — hence John the son of Zebedee.

The presbyter John who is associated with the publication of the Fourth Gospel is apparently not "the disciple Jesus loved" since at least the

---

8. This point is also noted by James N. Sanders in "Who Was the Disciple Jesus Loved?" *Studies in the Fourth Gospel*, 2d ed., ed. F. L. Cross (London: A. R. Mowbray, 1957), 72–82.

twenty-first chapter clearly indicates that that disciple, whoever he may have been, had already died at the time that the document was finally edited and published.

The "external evidence" concerning the "authorship" of the Gospel turns out to be late, slender, and equivocal. The Gospel comes to be attributed by the end of the second century to an elder or disciple known as John. As part of a process of narrowing apostolic authority to the twelve and their intellectual descendants, this John is subsequently identified with John the son of Zebedee. This process includes making similarly dubious attributions of authorship, and thus of "authority," to other texts. Thus the "first Gospel" came to be attributed to Matthew, an otherwise unknown tax collector who was one of the twelve. Another such exercise is the invention of the saga that the John Mark who accompanied Paul at one point became the secretary of Peter and wrote the second Gospel. Luke is identified as the author of the third Gospel on the basis of a conjecture derived from his inclusion with a number of other people in certain travel sections of Acts. In addition comes the production of a host of literature attributed to Paul. All of this is an attempt to stabilize legitimate authority in the second- and third-century churches under the leadership of "bishops" who understood themselves as deriving from the twelve.

Not only is the attribution of the Gospel to John the son of Zebedee almost certainly mistaken, a reading of the Fourth Gospel demonstrates that the beloved disciple is probably not even one of "the twelve." Although the group of twelve plays a significant role in other narratives, they play almost no role in this Gospel. In fact, their only appearance is a reference to them in 6:66–71:

> After this, many of his disciples drew back and no longer went about with him. Jesus said to the twelve, "Will you also go away?" Simon Peter answered him, "Lord, to whom shall we go? You have the words of eternal life...." Jesus answered them, "Did I not choose you, the twelve and one of you is a devil?" He spoke of Judas the son of Simon Iscariot, for he, one of the twelve, was to betray him.

From this text we learn the following. (1) that Jesus had many disciples besides the twelve, and (2) Jesus put little stock in this group since it included his betrayer. There is no possibility of supposing that when the document refers to "disciples," members of the group of twelve are specifically implied, especially since the Fourth Gospel does give prominence to disciples who are not of this group — Lazarus and Nathaniel, for example. The rather skeptical attitude toward the twelve is expressed in several ways in the text. The first method is the very paucity of reference to them as a group. Second is the way in which Judas is represented as one of this group. Third, Thomas the twin is identified as "one of the twelve" only when the text also reported that he did not yet believe (20:24). Thus, whatever may be the case with church tradition, the author of this text obviously did not put much stock in this group of twelve. In any case, this Gospel supposes that ongoing authority in the community is derivative not from the twelve, nor from the disciples generally, but from the paraclete sent by Jesus following his execution (16:7–15).

To this point, the disciple whom Jesus loved cannot with any confidence be identified on the basis of the text, either with one of the sons of Zebedee or with one of the twelve. Such identification is not necessarily ruled out absolutely, but the text provides us with no basis for such an identification and indeed points away from it.

If the disciple whom Jesus loved cannot automatically be identified as one of the sons of Zebedee or even as one of the twelve, who then are the candidates who, on the basis of internal evidence from the Gospel itself, might be identified as the disciple Jesus loved? In the following discussion, I attend to a number of possibilities. But here the issue does not focus, as it does in the commentaries, on the question of authorship of the Fourth Gospel. To be sure, some role in authorship is attributed to the disciple Jesus loved in the last reference to him (21:24). But our focus is on the disciple who is identified as the man Jesus loved. Thus, we take into account a number of alternative possibilities that the commentaries generally ignore on account of their one-sided concentration on the question of authorship.

Before turning to other possible candidates, the best approach may be to begin with who can be ruled out. That the beloved is Judas Iscariot does not seem possible. Although John does not report the death of Judas, thus removing him from the scene prior to the activity at the cross or the resurrection appearances, he is nevertheless clearly marked off as demonic. Already in 6:71, Judas is said to be "a devil," and Judas eats the morsel that shows to the beloved that Judas is the traitor. The scene then ends with Satan entering Judas. While one could construct a narrative that reconciled all this with the figure of the beloved, the result would not be the narrative that we call the Gospel of John.

That the beloved disciple is Simon Peter is also not possible because the beloved is regularly mentioned along with Peter. To him Peter's question is addressed (13:24); in company with him Peter runs to the tomb (20:2ff); and Peter inquires about his fate in 21:20.

Peter's Companions

This brief survey indicates not only that Peter and the disciple whom Jesus loved are different disciples, but also that a pronounced relation is present between them. They appear in the text as comrades, which suggests, in fact, the possibility that the beloved disciple may be Andrew, Peter's brother. In the Gospel of John, we are told that Andrew, who had been a follower of John the Baptist, is the first to follow Jesus and identify him as the Messiah. Andrew then brings his brother to Jesus (1:35–42), and together they are involved in recruiting Philip (from the same city, Bethsaida, as Peter and Andrew).

Andrew appears later as the one who finds a lad with loaves and fish that Jesus multiplies to feed the multitudes (6:8–9).

Finally Andrew is mentioned as one to whom Philip goes to introduce a group of Greeks who had come to see Jesus. Andrew then takes Philip to Jesus where they relay this information to him (12:22).

Let us now review this material to see what kind of a case could be made for identifying of the beloved disciple with Andrew.

1. As Peter's brother, Andrew would be expected to have the sort of relation to Peter that the beloved disciple is represented as having.

2. Relative to the other Gospels considerably more detailed interest in Andrew is available. He is given a "prehistory" as a disciple of John the Baptizer that also serves to account for the greater attention that this narrative gives to the baptizer.

3. This disciple is represented as having the role of greater access to Jesus. Andrew brings Peter to Jesus, brings the lad to Jesus, and brings Philip to Jesus with news of the Greeks. He appears to have a certain personal access to Jesus consistent with the depiction of the beloved disciple, which is especially suggested in the case of the beloved by the question addressed to him by Peter at the supper.

4. The mention of the beloved disciple coincides with the disappearance of Andrew from the text. Andrew last appears at 12:22, and reference to the disciple Jesus loved first appears at 13:22.

A case can thus be built for identifying the beloved disciple with Andrew. The difficulty that we encounter here is that the text does not provide us with more than this circumstantial evidence. Furthermore, this evidence is all formal in character; that is, it stresses the "role" of Andrew within the first half of the text as formally similar to the role of the beloved in the second half of the text.

One of the problems with the case for Andrew is that he is not named as a member of the fishing party organized by Peter in the last chapter of the text. This is, of course, not a crippling difficulty since two unnamed disciples are there as well, one of whom could be Andrew. In fact, this would correspond with the way in which we first encounter Andrew in the text. We are first told of John the Baptizer speaking to two of his (unnamed) disciples (1:37). They then follow Jesus. Only then we are told that one of these anonymous disciples of John (and now of Jesus) is "Andrew, Simon Peter's brother" (1:40). A certain symmetry would exist in Andrew's being present in the final scene of the narrative as one of two unnamed disciples, since that is in fact how he makes his first appearance in the opening scenes of the Gospel.[9]

The pairing of Peter with the disciple loved by Jesus in many of the texts that mention the latter have suggested the possibility that Andrew may be the disciple whom Jesus loved.

Another passage sometimes linked with the tradition concerning the beloved concerns an unnamed disciple with connections to the Jerusalem establishment who gains access for Peter to the trial of the Sanhedrin (18:15–16). He is twice identified as "known to the high priest." It seems most unlikely that Andrew, or for that matter any other Galilean disciple of Jesus, would have been known by the high priest in such a way as to gain access to the proceedings of the Sanhedrin for himself and for another of his company. But Jesus does not only have Galilean followers in the Gospel of John. Indeed one of the best-known passages in this Gospel concerns a dialogue between Jesus and a "Pharisee named Nicodemus, a leader [ruler] of the Jews" (3:1). The designation of Nicodemus as a ruler indicates that he was a member of the Sanhedrin and thus clearly in a

---

9. As far as I have been able to determine, the only traditional association of Andrew with the beloved disciple comes from the Muratorian Canon (a list of books received as authoritative by a Christian community perhaps from the late second century [cited by Sanders, p. 79]), which claims that the Gospel was written by "John, one of the disciples," after it had been revealed to "Andrew, one of the apostles, that John should narrate all things in his own name as they called them to mind." The text may be found in "Fragments of Caius," trans. S. D. F. Salmond, in *Ante-Nicene Fathers*, vol. 5 (Edinburgh: T. & T. Clark, 1885), 603. This external evidence would concord quite well with the supposition that Andrew was the disciple Jesus loved and that he entrusted the task of writing to a certain John who, though a disciple (in the sense of one who sought to follow the way of Jesus), was not an apostle (in the sense of one who had been with Jesus in the beginning). This assessment would agree then with the scenario that the Gospel is based in some way on the witness of Andrew/beloved but that it receives its current form from another hand (a disciple named John who, however, is not the son of Zebedee). Only later, for church political reasons and to separate the Gospel forever from suspicion of heterodoxy, does the association of John the disciple or John the elder with John the son of Zebedee come into play. Curiously, Sanders does not raise the question of the possible connection between Andrew and the disciple loved by Jesus.

position to gain admittance to the deliberations of that body. This status is also true of Joseph of Arimathea who, unlike Nicodemus, is known to the synoptic tradition, is a member of the ruling council, and is identified by the Gospel of John as a secret disciple of Jesus (19:38). In this Gospel, Nicodemus and Joseph share in the tasks of claiming, preparing, and burying the body of Jesus (John 19:38–42).

But from the text, a conclusion that the disciple known to the high priest is also the beloved is not necessary. In favor of such an identification would be that the "other disciple" known to the high priest does accompany Peter (something otherwise true of the beloved) and that the beloved then would be a witness to the trial as well as to the Last Supper, the execution, the empty tomb, and the risen Jesus' commissioning of Peter. However, no apparent reason exists for the Gospel's not identifying this disciple as the beloved in the text if the author wants us to suppose that he is. When Nicodemus reappears at the end of the story, he is reintroduced as the one "who had at first come to Jesus at night" (19:39), and Joseph is introduced as a secret disciple as though he had not previously appeared in the narrative. Moreover the beloved need not be a witness at the trial since Peter is, thanks to the work of another disciple. Thus, while we have one or two likely candidates for the "other disciple" who admits Peter to the scene of the trial (Joseph and Nicodemus), nothing connects this figure to the disciple whom Jesus loved.[10]

Fishermen

We have thus far pursued the clues in the text that place the beloved alongside Peter. Another clue more often pursued to discover the identity of the beloved is the makeup of the fishing party in the final scene of the Gospel where, we subsequently learn, the beloved is also found. Peter is here, as are (for the only time) the unnamed sons of Zebedee.[11]

---

10. Oddly, those commentators who try to link the beloved to Jerusalem and thus connect him to the one who gains admittance to the trial for himself and Peter do not think of identifying Nicodemus with the beloved, although this connection would seem obvious on the basis of their presuppositions. Sanders, who argues for Lazarus as the most likely identity of the beloved, does suppose that the beloved was "a man of the same class as Nicodemus and Joseph of Arimathea" (81), yet does not take the route of even entertaining the possibility that he was Nicodemus (or Joseph). He also cites (79–80) the tradition recalled by Eusebius of a certain Polycrates, bishop of Ephesus at end of the second century, that John, supposed to be the beloved, was or became a "priest wearing the petalon." As Sanders notes, this comment may be simply a guess based on John 18:15.

11. We know from the other Gospels that the sons of Zebedee were James and John. But we do not know this from the Gospel that bears John's name. No basis exists in this text for ascribing the Gospel to one of these sons rather than another. If the beloved disciple is one of the sons of Zebedee, it could as well be James as John. External evidence would allegedly count

Who else?

The first disciple listed here is Thomas the twin. Do we have reason to suppose that Thomas is the beloved?

In his favor we may mention the following:

1. He is placed at the final scene where we subsequently encounter the beloved.

2. He is called "the twin." What are we to make of this strange designation? Could this be because he is someone else's twin or because "twin" is used here as an allusion to his relationship to Jesus? In this case, he would not be a blood twin but a twin in the sense of the affectional other of Jesus.[12]

3. This possibility receives a certain amount of substantiation in that the twin is represented as having an especially fervent attachment to Jesus. In chapter 11, we have the dramatic story of Jesus' return to Judea on account of the death of his friend Lazarus. He has been camped out on the other side of the Jordan in order to escape the attempt on his life by the Judeans. When news comes of Lazarus's illness and then death, Jesus leaves his hideout to go into danger to the scene of Lazarus's death. Here for the first time in the narrative we encounter Thomas. "Thomas, called the twin, said to his fellow disciples, 'Let us go also, that we may die with him' " (11:16).

   They then proceed to Judea where the raising of Lazarus takes place. The determination of Thomas to die with Jesus is especially striking in view of Jesus' subsequent word that the greatest love is the willingness to die for one's friends (15:13). Thomas is thus represented as having this love for Jesus in a particularly striking degree.

4. Thomas together with Peter, Philip, and Judas (not Iscariot) are the interlocutors of Jesus in the long final discourse of Jesus with his disciples following the first appearance of the beloved. This discourse deals in part with the nature of love (13:36–14:24). But nothing can

---

against this since we know that James was an early martyr, while the author of this text seems to have lived to a long age. This knowledge is no help, however, for the internal evidence of the Synoptic Gospels suggests that John son of Zebedee was martyred with his brother, unless the saying of Jesus that the brothers would share his baptism and drink from the same cup (of execution) was mistaken (Mark 10:39).

12. The suggestion that Thomas is the twin brother of Jesus is emphasized in the claims to authorship of the Gospel of Thomas and in the identification of the hero of the so-called Acts of Thomas. The first document may go back to the first century while the second is from a significantly later period.

be determined from this passage since the question raised by Thomas, "Lord, we do not know where you are going. How can we know the way?" bears on the question of the destiny of the disciples rather than on the character of love per se.

While some suggestive details are present, no compelling reason exists to identify Thomas with the beloved. Some evidence even seems to count against such an identification. After the beloved sees the empty tomb (with Peter) and is said to "believe," Jesus appears to the other disciples except Thomas. The latter then refuses to believe the accounts of the others of the appearance of the risen Lord without seeing for himself the wounds of the cross. Subsequently Jesus does appear to him with the others and exposes his wounds to Thomas's inspection.

Reconciling the belief of the beloved with the subsequent unbelief of Thomas (20:25) is difficult even if not completely impossible. After all, the object of belief is somewhat different. In the first case, the belief addresses the emptiness of the tomb. In the second, the belief has to do with the appearance of the risen Jesus to the disciples. Some early traditions maintained that Jesus has been raised but that this resurrection is "enthronement in the heaven." Thus the empty tomb does not in itself lead to resurrection appearances. But the difficulty with this attempted reconciliation is that what Thomas believes is expressed as the recognition of Jesus as "my Lord and my God." Thus, what is focused by Thomas's confession is not that there are "appearances" but that Jesus is Lord and God — precisely the conclusion that would be reached on the basis of the empty tomb, if that had been combined with an enthronement view.

Thus that the author(s) of this text supposed that Thomas was the beloved disciple appears virtually impossible. Despite indications of a strong attachment to Jesus on the part of Thomas and the intriguing designation of him as "twin," the text makes his identification with the beloved very difficult, if not impossible. In this connection, remember that the designation of the beloved disciple does not emphasize his attachment to Jesus but Jesus' attachment to him. That is, the evidence of 11:16 concerning Thomas's attachment to Jesus does nothing to establish the converse: Jesus' preferential attachment to the beloved disciple.

The next disciple mentioned in the fishing party is Nathaniel. Can a case be made for his identification with the beloved disciple? In his favor, we may mention the following:

1. Nathaniel is singled out by Jesus for special remark when he is recruited in 1:44–51. He is called "an Israelite indeed, in whom there is

no guile"(47). He was known to Jesus before Philip called him (48). He acclaims Jesus as Son of God and King of Israel (48). And Jesus tells him that he will see "heaven opened and the angels ascending and descending on the son of man" (51).

2. Together with Philip, Nathaniel occupies the place that the other Gospels give to the sons of Zebedee, that is, as the second pair that Jesus recruited.

3. Nathaniel is mentioned only in the Gospel of John. Identification of the author of a text is sometimes made on flimsier grounds, as for example the identification of Matthew as the author of the first Gospel because of the use of this name in place of Levi or the identification of Luke as the author of the third Gospel because he is among those included in the "we" of certain passages of Acts.

Despite these hints, no reason is available for identifying the beloved disciple with Nathaniel. To be sure, Jesus is represented as having special regard for Nathaniel's character, as a man without guile. But this fact alone does not argue for the identification of the beloved with him since no stress is placed in the Gospel on the character of the beloved.

Of the disciples named as members of the fishing party, no strong candidates emerge for identification with the beloved disciple. Peter is ruled out. Thomas is unlikely. Nathaniel has no strong claim. The sons of Zebedee (whether James or John) have no case at all. But two unnamed disciples are in the party. Besides those we have considered, are there other candidates from John's narrative who could be one of these unnamed disciples and thus be a candidate for identification as the disciple Jesus loved? In fact, three additional possibilities are available: Judas not Iscariot, Philip, and Lazarus.

In order to be complete we should mention the Judas who is always identified as "not Iscariot" and to whom tradition ascribes the short letter of Jude. As we have seen, he is recalled as having been present at Jesus' final discourse (14:22), and he asks the final question in the series: "How will you reveal yourself to us and not to the world?" This scene presents his only appearance in the Gospel of John.[13]

---

13. In Mark 6:3 and Matthew 13:55, a Judas is named as one of Jesus' brothers (along with James, Simon, and Joses). Luke 6:16 (and Acts 1:13) indicates a Judas who is identified as "the son of James." Thus Judas is unlikely to be the one identified as the brother of Jesus, unless we suppose that Joseph had died and Mary had remarried. Finally the author of the book of Jude identifies himself as "a slave of Jesus Christ and brother of James" (Jude 1). Whether the Judas not Iscariot of the Fourth Gospel is to be identified with any of these other Judes or Judases is not clear. One possible reading would be that the disciple Jesus loved was Judas

Philip is mentioned as being recruited by Jesus immediately following Andrew and Peter (1:43–48). He is the link to the recruitment of Nathaniel.

Philip also appears in the discussion about how to feed the multitude. He remarks that "200 denarii wouldn't be enough," to which Andrew responds by bringing the lad with loaves and fishes (6:5–7).

Philip also is connected with Andrew in that he approaches the latter with news of the inquiry of the Greeks (12:21–22).

Finally, Philip is one of Jesus' dialogue partners in the last meal (along with Peter, Judas [not Iscariot], and Thomas) where we have previously encountered the beloved disciple. In the dialogue he asks, "Lord, show us the Father and we will be satisfied" (14:8).

Although Philip is mentioned several times, nothing in all of this suggests him as a candidate for identification with the beloved disciple.

Lazarus

That then leaves Lazarus. What makes Lazarus an intriguing possibility is that he is singled out as loved by Jesus. Let us see how this happens.

We are first told that the sisters, Mary and Martha, send a message to Jesus to inform him of Lazarus's illness: "Lord, the one you love is ill" (11:3). After the report of Lazarus's illness in chapter 11 we are told, "Now Jesus loved Martha and her sister [Mary] and Lazarus" (11:5). When Jesus finally arrives on the scene, Lazarus is dead. He is confronted by the grief and protest of Mary and the weeping protest of the Judeans. In the face of this grief we are told that "he was deeply moved in spirit and troubled." As he is led to the tomb we are told, "Jesus wept. So the Judeans said: 'See how he loved him!'" (11:35–36).

Here we have an account of Jesus being deeply moved. The narrative leaves open whether Jesus is more troubled by the death of his friend or the grief of those who mourn, or the protest against his tardy arrival — a tardiness that has led both to the death and the grief. The crowd in any case supposes that the weeping is an indication of Jesus' love for Lazarus.

Lazarus appears again in the narrative only in the following chapter when Jesus has a meal in Bethany with Lazarus, Mary, and Martha (12:1–2, 9–11). Here we learn that "the chief priests planned to put Lazarus to

---

not Iscariot who was also Jesus' own brother, indeed his favorite brother. Thus the special intimacy between them is that of an older for a younger brother. A difficulty with this view is that in the Gospel of John, as well as in other Gospels, Jesus is not regarded as being close to his own family (see chapter 10, below). Even more difficult is that the relation between Jesus' mother and the beloved is said to begin from the hour of Jesus' death, something not possible to reconcile with the identification of the beloved with one of Jesus' brothers.

death as well, since it was on account of him that many of the Jews were deserting and were believing in Jesus" (12:10–11).[14]

How are we to evaluate this evidence? Supporting the identification of Lazarus with the beloved is that Jesus in both cases is said to love them. This fact in itself seems to give Lazarus some claim. But is it a strong one? In the first case, the sisters say that Jesus loves Lazarus, but the opening of the story suggests that the sisters are better known than Lazarus. The next time Lazarus is said to be loved by Jesus is as the last member of a group of three siblings. The final time is because Jesus weeps as he goes to Lazarus's gravesite. When Lazarus next appears, nothing is made of his relation to Jesus, save as one who has been raised from the dead.

Another piece of indirect evidence is available, however. From the end of the Gospel we know that the "brothers" supposed that the disciple Jesus loved would not die (21:23). This supposition would have another explanation if the beloved were Lazarus who had already died. If Lazarus's resuscitation were the beginning of the resurrection of the dead, then no reason would exist for him to taste death again.

Clearly then Jesus has some emotional attachment to Lazarus and to his sisters. Indeed the attachment of Jesus to the sisters serves (together with Luke 10:38–42) as the basis for the speculation that Jesus was bonded with one or both of them. This view, which has been enshrined in some Mormon speculation, has a rather slender textual basis. But recalling it here is instructive in order to see how much stronger a case can be made for Jesus' attachment to Lazarus, even if he is not the beloved disciple.

Ruling out Lazarus as a candidate for the identity of the beloved disciple does not seem possible. The terminological link (Jesus reported to have loved him) and the conjecture concerning his death are both supportive. But beyond that, nothing is definite.[15]

Conclusion

Where then does this review of possibilities leave us? We have seen that a case can certainly be made for Lazarus on terminological grounds. An

---

14. We should note that this account makes impossible the connection that Sanders suggested between Lazarus and the "other disciple" who gained admittance for Peter to the trial of Jesus. If the chief priests intended to put Lazarus to death, then he could not have entered the trial with impunity, much less have gained admittance for another on the basis of his connections to the high priest.

15. At a later point, we consider the "external evidence" supplied by Morton Smith's much discussed fragment of a "secret Gospel" of Mark. This text strengthens the case for Lazarus.

intriguing case can be made for Andrew on the basis of his role in the narrative. Rather less compelling cases can be made for Thomas and Nathaniel, and even for Philip and Judas not Iscariot. If one supposes that the "other disciple" known to the high priest belongs in the relevant data, then a case can be constructed for Nicodemus or even Joseph of Arimathea. Nor can we exclude the possibility that the beloved disciple is a person not otherwise named in the Gospel of John. This option is, in fact, attractive because the references to the disciple Jesus loved insist upon not naming him. If this disciple is in some way connected to the authorship of some of the Fourth Gospel, he appears determined not to be named, or rather to be named only as the disciple that Jesus loved.

Only the external evidence of later tradition seems to point toward the name of John, and only an even later interpretation of that data points to the identification of such a "John" with the like-named son of Zebedee.

The upshot of this review of possibilities is that none of them are conclusive. This in itself is intriguing. Why are we are not told in the text which of the disciples is the beloved one? Why is it that so few of the disciples (Judas Iscariot and Peter) can be completely ruled out from this list of possibilities? What is the point of so strongly underlining a relationship to Jesus while leaving the one who occupies so important a role unidentified?

Despite the inconclusive result of our search for the identity of the disciple Jesus loved, our inquiry has by no means been in vain. This review of the evidence and of the possibilities has at least produced from the text an array of strong relationships to Jesus. To this list, if we were to attempt to make it complete, we should have to add the special relationship to the sisters Mary and Martha as well as the bond between Jesus and Mary the Magdalene (19:25; 20:11–18) and even the Samaritan woman of 4:7–42. We obviously have a series of strong and special relationships, any one of which would be remarkable in itself. Indeed one of the characteristic features of this narrative in comparison to the others we find in the New Testament is that so much is made of strong personal ties. In the other Gospels, we have nothing comparable to the number and intensity of personal relationships between Jesus and individual followers. The picture we have of Jesus from the Fourth Gospel is of one who had a gift for friendship and who awoke in others a strong bonding of affection and loyalty.

Therefore, that among so many powerful relationships one is singled out as the man Jesus loved becomes all the more striking. What makes this relationship so special among so many other remarkable relationships? We are left again with the physical and emotional intimacy of lovers as the most likely way of understanding the distinctive character of this relationship. But this increasingly plausible interpretation of their relationship opens up a number of issues and questions to which we must turn if our interpretation is to be accepted.

Chapter 4

Reconsidering the Gospel of John

In spite of the fact that the text is rendered intelligible by the suggestion that Jesus' relationship with the beloved disciple was that of "lovers," this hypothesis raises a number of issues with respect to the interpretation of the Gospel of John as a whole. In general the issue is whether the reading I have proposed is compatible with the apparent worldview of the Gospel.

To be sure, the reading I have proposed will be rejected out of hand by people who regard as blasphemous the suggestion of an erotic relationship between Jesus and the disciple he loved. Insofar as such a view springs from a deep-rooted antipathy to homosexual acts or to the persons who engage in such acts or to the desire that generates or is generated by such acts — an antipathy today called homophobia — then any textual evidence will probably not be regarded as persuasive.

The aim of this chapter is not to address directly the issue of homophobic interpretation but rather to clarify the way in which the reading I have put forward fits within the thought-world of the Gospel of John as a whole. We proceed by attempting to take into account various objections that may arise to the proposed reading.

Terminology

In the first place, we may wonder whether the Greek terminology employed in the designation of one of the disciples as the one that Jesus loved would preclude an erotic interpretation of the relationship. Does the Greek allow the meaning I have suggested?

We must first recall that Greek terminology for relationships is different in significant ways from similar terminology in modern English. We speak of lovers in a way that includes both partners of an erotic relationship, but

55

the terminology of the Greco-Roman world usually distinguishes between the lover and the beloved. In a heterosexual relationship, this distinction is usually applied so that the woman is the beloved while the male is the "lover." In same-sex relationships, the "lover" is typically the older of the pair, often associated with the one who takes the active part in wooing or in lovemaking. The beloved in such a case is the younger, the pursued, the object of desire, or the "passive" partner where sexual practices are specifically in focus. The ideal that stands behind this linguistic convention is that of a pederastic relationship. The point here is not that all relationships conform to this model. Far from it. But this model nevertheless informs the terminology. The only way to overcome the asymmetrical character of this terminology is through supplementing it with the language of friendship. In classical Greek, the terminology for asymmetrical love is *eros* while the terminology for symmetrical love is based on *philia*. In the Greek of the Septuagint and of the New Testament, the term *agape* substitutes for *eros* in designating the asymmetrical form of love. In English one word combines these different senses: lovers. That is, "lovers" may be characterized both by a relationship of desire (whether or not consummated by specific sexual practice) and by mutuality.

In general, I have to this point designated Jesus as the lover and the disciple as the beloved, in order to reflect what the text itself says. The relationship of the disciple to Jesus is generally not specified. Jesus' relation to the disciple is highlighted. Jesus is the lover, the disciple is the beloved. Such a construction is quite awkward in contemporary English; hence the tendency to designate both as "lovers." We shall have to see whether this approach is consistent with the perspective of the Gospel.

The readers of modern biblical scholarship are often under the impression that the New Testament distinguishes between three terms for love: *eros, philia,* and *agape*. On this view, *eros* can refer to sexual love, *philia* to friendship, and *agape* to the disinterested love of God (or the disinterested love we are to have toward our neighbor).[1] Those people who uncritically accept this distinction will conclude from the fact that the love of Jesus for this disciple is expressed as *agape* that the questions of particular friendship or erotic attachment do not apply.

The koine Greek in which New Testament texts are written use only two words for love: *agape* and *philia. Eros* does not occur either in the

---

1. The classical study is Anders Nygren, *Agape and Eros,* trans. Philip S. Watson (Philadelphia: Westminster Press, 1953). Nygren's argument is not so much about terms as about ideas or "motifs," but his work has introduced confusion about terminology.

New Testament or in the Septuagint, the Greek translation of the Old Testament made in the third century B.C.E.

While reference is made, for example, to the love of a husband for his wife or even to the illicit loves of inordinate desire, they are always referred to with the term *agape!* Some examples may be useful.

In the case of Samson, when he is in the NRSV said to "fall in love" with Delilah, the verb is *agape* (Judg. 16:4). The story of Delilah or of Samson and his other paramours never suggests anything other than sexual attraction. In the story of David, we are told that the people loved David (1 Sam. 18:16), that Jonathan loved David (1 Sam. 18:1), that David loved Jonathan (1 Sam. 20:17), and that Mical, Jonathan's sister and Saul's daughter, loved David (1 Sam. 18:20). The result of this last in that Mical becomes David's first wife. In every case the verb is *agape*. The Song of Songs, which is a prolonged description of erotic love, always uses a form of *agape*. That is, deciding on the basis of the term itself which of the kinds of love alleged by this modern theory to be so distinct is meant is never possible. Put another way, the situation with respect to the first-century Greek of the Old or New Testament is in this regard much like English. We require the context to determine whether the love between two persons is to be understood primarily as altruistic, as erotic, as friendship, as the love of siblings, of parents for children, and so on.

In the Gospel of John, even the terms *philia* and *agape* are treated as equivalent, or at least are used together to complement one another. Thus, for example, in the text we have referred to where Jesus asks Peter if he loves him, the terms are used interchangeably. Jesus asks using *agape* twice (21:15, 16). Peter responds using *philia*. The third time Jesus uses *philia* (21:17), and the narrator remarks that Peter was grieved because Jesus had asked three times if he loved (*philia*) him. The terms seem to be equivalent.[2] This usage is further exhibited in the story of Jesus' response to the death of Lazarus. Lazarus is identified as the one Jesus loved (*philia:* 11:3). We are then told that Jesus loved all three siblings (*agape:* 11:5). And the crowd concludes from Jesus' subsequent tears how much Jesus loved (*philia*) Lazarus. Again we seem to have equivalence.

The same trend seems to occur in the texts concerning the disciple Jesus loved. At 13:23, 19:26, and 21:7 and 20, the text uses a form of *agape*. But at 20:2 (the race to the tomb), a form of *philia* is used. Similarly,

---

2. Thus also C. K. Barrett: "The usage of these verbs throughout the gospel makes it impossible to doubt that they are synonyms," in *The Gospel According to St. John,* 2d ed. (Philadelphia: Westminster Press, 1978), 584.

although Jesus' teaching concerning love typically uses *agape,* he also uses *philia* to designate the new relationship with the disciples (15:13–15).

On the basis of this cursory review of the evidence, no objection to the supposition can be raised that Jesus and the disciple were lovers in the erotic sense on the basis of the terminology employed. A dictionary cannot decide this. Only attention to the context, the function, and the action of the text itself can contribute to the understanding.

The use of *agape* does not preclude what we would call the erotic dimension. Whether this dimension is present or not must be determined on other grounds. Variations of *philia* and of *agape* appear to be used interchangeably in the Gospel of John. Insofar as a distinctive nuance is entailed in *philia,* it may compensate for and correct the asymmetrical character of *agape* (a structure also present in the use of *eros* in classical Greek). In this sense then, the modern use of "lovers" to designate both beloved and lover has a certain warrant in the text's use of *philia* to correct the asymmetrical tendencies of *agape.*

Sublimation

Analysis may conclude that the relationship depicted in the text itself suggests a kind of homoerotic attachment. But does this mean that the relationship was sexually consummated? We cannot expect to find direct evidence for this conclusion from a text that is not itself sexually explicit. But we can look for indirect evidence that would make the suggestion of sexual expression unlikely. Certainly we know from antiquity, especially from Plato, of a tradition of sublimated love, especially in same-sex relationships. The term "platonic love" derives from this tradition of renouncing the bodily expression of same-sex desire and attachment.[3]

In our own day, a number of folk have come to the conclusion that homosexual desire is "natural" for some people and that the presence of this desire is not in itself a negative thing. But, they argue, it should be sublimated. That is, such persons should not "have sex."[4] This stance is a permutation of the notion of platonic love modified by the ascetic views of Christian monasticism. The view has gained some currency in contemporary church discussions of homosexuality.

---

3. That a heterosexual relationship could be "platonic" was not explicitly realized for more than a millennium.

4. This is the view, for example, of Helmut Thielicke, in *The Ethics of Sex,* trans. John W. Doberstein (New York: Harper & Row, 1964), 287.

For purposes of our discussion of the Gospel of John, we must ask whether the text as a whole exhibits views that would preclude the sexual expression of a relationship. That is, does the text demonstrate an ascetic view toward life generally or toward sexuality particularly? The answer is a definite no.

Traditions of sublimated sexuality existed among the Greek philosophical schools of the period.[5] These traditions come to play an important role in Christian theological-ethical reflection. They are usually found in connection with a more general ascetic view. But no demonstrable asceticism is apparent in the Gospels, still less in the Gospel of John.[6]

The Gospel of John has its own way of bringing to expression the anti-ascetic character of the Jesus tradition. In the first act of Jesus deemed by the author(s) to have theological significance, he is entreated by his mother to do something about the shortage of wine at a wedding party to which he and his disciples had been invited. Despite some initial reluctance, Jesus orders that the bath water be brought to him. The report states that the hundreds of gallons of water used for this purpose were transformed into wine of exceptional quality (John 2:1–12). Whatever else may be indicated by this episode, clearly no ascetic tendencies are to be found here. On the contrary, Jesus acts so as to make possible an extraordinary bout of celebrative drinking. (An ascetic would have replied that wine was unnecessary, the guests had evidently had enough, or that it was inappropriate to be partying in any case.)

When we turn to the more particular question of the attitude toward sexuality, we find nothing that would support an ascetic attitude. That Jesus is found at a wedding party and is complicitous in its celebration already shows the absence of a suspicion directed toward sexuality as such.

This attitude is brought to expression in other ways as well. On at least one occasion, Jesus is confronted with what we may call unconventional sexual mores. This episode concerns the Samaritan woman who, it turns

---

5. The texts from classical Greece that prize erotic relationships between males that are not brought to direct sexual expression typically entail no moral judgment on those that are expressed sexually. Plato's *Symposium* provides an illustration. However, the much later hellenistic interpretation of these ideas and texts does begin to stigmatize sexuality generally and, therefore, the sexual expression of male-male relationships.

6. The general principle is articulated in the Synoptic Gospels with the distinction between the movement of Jesus and that of John the Baptist. The latter was known for ascetic tendencies. But Jesus is distinguished from him in such a way that he has the reputation of being a "drinker and a glutton" (Matt. 11:19; Luke 7:34). This motif is carried forward by the Gospel texts in a number of ways. Jesus' teaching is often cast as a kind of "party etiquette." The setting for his teaching and action is often a banquet or feast. His followers are also notorious for their nonpractice of fasting along with their nonperformance of other aspects of religious observance.

out, has had several men (or husbands) and is now with one who is not her own (4:16–18). The word *andro* used here is simply "male," which can be understood as man or as husband. That she is currently with one who is not her own either means that she isn't married to him or, more probably, that he is another's man; that is, he "belongs" to someone else.

Whether we regard the woman as having had several lovers and now to have as a lover a man who belongs to another (is another's husband or lover), or to regard her as having had several husbands but now to be living with one to whom she is not married (the less likely reading), her sexual mores are in any case "unconventional." Yet Jesus makes nothing of this unconventionality. That he knows about it demonstrates his extraordinary knowledge. But this knowledge is not spoken or heard as an accusation. The woman marvels that he knows all this about her. But she is not, as conventional eisegesis would have it, moved to repent of her form of life.

Jesus is clearly not portrayed as in any way scandalized by her unconventional lifestyle. It is simply accepted as a fact whose only importance is that Jesus knows about it. Absolutely nothing here smacks of judgment or suspicion. Jesus' knowledge apparently provokes no alteration in the situation. What is important is that she uses this response as a theme for her proclamation to her village of the mysterious abilities of Jesus and that this report serves as the basis for the villagers coming to Jesus, inviting his presence among them and believing (once they know him for themselves) that he is savior of the world.

Far from being a problem, her unconventional lifestyle is an occasion for the evangelization of her neighbors. Nothing could be less compatible with an ascetic view of sexuality.

Another episode usually associated with the Gospel of John is that of the woman taken in adultery. This episode is not found in many of the most reliable early manuscripts of John. It is even sometimes found inserted in the Gospel of Luke. Now the story is usually printed as a footnote to the Gospel of John, and in other texts it is printed as John 7:53–8:11. It may also appear following Luke 21:38 or as a kind of appendix following the end of the Gospel of John.

While we cannot use this text as definitive of the attitude of the Gospel of John since its place here is so uncertain, the episode does suggest that Jesus protects an adulteress from the application of the legal penalty. This refusal to enforce the penalty is somehow made persuasive to the woman's accusers on the basis of their own sin and need for mercy. The text makes clear that despite her evident guilt, Jesus does not condemn her.

The weight of conventional exegesis is often made to fall upon the final saying of the episode: Jesus' words, "neither do I condemn you, go, from now on no longer sin." However, Jesus is not upset by the sexual mores of the woman. He is far more concerned with stopping the punishment of this "sin" than with condemning it. Indeed the text makes clear that he does not in any case condemn it.[7] Even if the text is understood to confirm that adultery (that is, having sex with the spouse of another) is a sin, Jesus refuses to condemn the one who is caught. She is urged not to return to sin, but no penalty is suggested.

This episode has in common with that of the Samaritan woman that Jesus is not especially worried about sexual irregularity. The adultery text is distinguished from the earlier episode in that here Jesus seems to accept the conventional view that her behavior is "sin," something that plays no role with the Samaritan woman. This difference may be regarded as a reason for disputing, on grounds of content, the place of this episode in the same narrative as that which also tells of the Samaritan woman. But perhaps, although Jesus has a relaxed attitude toward sexual impropriety, he either wants the woman to avoid the behavior that would result in her being stoned if he were not there to protect her in the future, or Jesus does disapprove of adultery but is not prepared to make a big deal about it.

Whichever way we regard the text, we have additional information that Jesus takes an anti-ascetic attitude taken toward sexuality. It is not regarded with suspicion. It is not supposed that sexual irregularity is an especially egregious form of sinful behavior. The Gospel of John, like the other Gospels, displays on this topic a view very much at odds with subsequent Christian tradition and even at odds with prestigious first-century forms of Jewish (Qumran) and pagan (philosophical) piety.

Negation of Bodily?

But if ascetic tendencies are not found in the narrative, we may still wonder whether we may discern an attitude that negates the significance of the bodily or physical in favor of the spiritual. If this attitude is indeed characteristic of the thought world of the Gospel of John, then a reasonable presumption would be that the author(s) could take for granted that Jesus' relationship to the beloved would be perceived as "platonic," receiving no

---

7. Presumably Jesus does not have the same reason for withholding judgment as the others; according to traditional exegesis, he is not himself a sinner.

carnal expression. We must therefore also consider this more indirect way of clarifying the character of the relationship.

At first glance, the Gospel of John does seem to emphasize spiritual realities at the expense of their concrete or bodily manifestations. Virtually anything may be allegorized, and impatience with those who are unable or unwilling to make this allegorizing move is often expressed. Thus, for example, in the case of the encounter with Nicodemus, we have a discussion concerning birth "from above" in which Nicodemus is portrayed as unable to understand what Jesus is saying in an allegorical sense: "How can you enter again into your mother's womb?" (3:4). Here the fixation on physical birth prevents an understanding of spiritual birth and so of the point of Jesus' teaching.

Similarly in the episode concerning the Samaritan woman, the dialogue begins with talk of a drink of water (4:4). Then the woman is led through a number of allegorical transformations of this theme. Thus she is challenged to move beyond the bodily or physical sense of water to a spiritual understanding. Subsequently the disciples are unable to understand Jesus' not needing the food he has sent them to acquire (4:31–34).

In the aftermath of the miraculous feeding of the multitude, Jesus expresses his exasperation that the crowds only want bodily food rather than being hungry for the spiritual food he wishes to give them (6:26–27).

In these ways, the text seems to suggest the view that a fixation on bodily or physical reality may serve as a hindrance to the reception of the spiritual truth that is mediated by these physical expressions. Translating this attitude into the domain of Jesus' love for the beloved would appear possible, in order to suggest that this love would have to be seen as platonic rather than as physically expressed or consummated.

But a closer reading of John's Gospel reveals a quite different dynamic at work, which is already evident at the very beginning in the well-known prologue to the Gospel that speaks of the word of God (1:14) becoming "flesh." The view that the divine word becomes flesh is a scandal for the philosophical turn of mind that regards the flesh as at best the sphere of mere appearance and illusion if not of downright sin. But for this text, becoming flesh is precisely the event of salvation. Far from celebrating a disembodied reality, the text insists on the becoming flesh, the em-body-ment of the truth.

Consequently, in addition to a tendency to allegorize, a marked tendency toward an emphasis on the body is also present. The healing stories emphasize physical detail. In the last healing narrative that occupies all of chapter 9, the mode of healing seems almost crassly physical: "When he had said this he spat on the ground and spread the mud on the man's eyes" (9:6). And this detail is recalled twice more in the account (9:11, 15). This same tendency is expressed also in the worry about the corpse of Lazarus: it stinks (11:39). Thus, those actions that express Jesus' concern for the other are not simply "spiritualized." They are, we may say, "physicalized" too, as expressed quite concretely in the foot-washing scene. Here Jesus' love of the disciples is expressed in the performance of menial and intimate service. Further, the disciples are specifically commanded to do for one another what Jesus does for them. Thus, intimate bodily service is regarded as indispensable to the expression of love.

This same tendency to draw attention to physical detail comes to expression as well in the account of Jesus' crucifixion (19:28, 34) and in the account of his resurrection where particular stress is laid upon the bodily wounds (20:20, 25, 27) and upon the physical location and placement of the grave clothes (20:5–7).

The Fourth Gospel then is characterized by a double movement: a very marked tendency to allegorize physical reality and, at the same time, a marked tendency to physicalize spiritual reality. Bodies are more concrete, more fleshly, and also more the bearer of spiritual meaning. In a remarkable way, the flesh is more fleshly, the spirit more spirited, and the two are one. Indeed, precisely this emphasis on both the body and the spirit serves to set the context for the development of orthodox Christology, and emphasis on the bodily reality persuades the church, through the arguments of Irenaeus, to accept this Gospel as the antidote to gnosticism.

Now with what view of sexuality is this most compatible? It appears to be incompatible with the view that physical expression is either insignificant or to be renounced in favor of a purely spiritual or "platonic" relationship. The domain of the flesh, the body, is specifically and repeatedly valued, but not in such a way as to sever it from meaning, from being the bearer of spiritual value.

Abstinence regards physical expression as distasteful, unnecessary, and polluting. Promiscuity may regard the bodily as autonomous of the sphere of meaning. In this way, certain kinds of promiscuity and asceticism are in a sense twins, as the history of gnosticism shows. But for lovers the flesh is the expression of the spirit. These domains are not opposed or separated but rather are intensifications of one another.

The worldview of the Gospel of John then turns out to be compatible with the view that if two persons are lovers they will naturally incarnate that love in attentive service to the body of the beloved. The worldview of the text is incompatible with the repressed sexuality of the moralist, the sublimated sexuality of the philosopher, or the surrender of sexuality to the merely physical characteristic of the hedonist. But the text's worldview does appear to be compatible with the celebrative sexuality of the lover.

We noted earlier that the fact that two persons are lovers may itself be a public fact without this knowledge entailing any special mention of the sort of practices that bring this relationship to expression. Whether and how lovers express their intimacy with one another remains "hidden" precisely because of its intimacy, unless some particular reason exists for drawing attention to this otherwise hidden sphere. One reason for doing so would be to make a point of the sublimated character of the relationship, which is what happens in some cases of platonic love where the lovers have in mind that they must refrain from the bodily expression of intimacy. Our investigation of the text has shown that not only is such a view never directly expressed, it is actually incompatible with the worldview of the text itself. We have not, though, lifted the veil of privacy that normally covers the intimate details of the practices of lovers. We have no idea how the love of Jesus for his disciple came to sexual expression. We do know the public fact: they were lovers. And we know that the text does not lead us to believe that this affection was limited in principle to nonbodily expression.

The Law

Even if the text suggests that the relation between lovers could, in certain circumstances, be expressed in sexual terms and would be so expressed quite naturally, does it not seem unlikely, given certain presumed Jewish views of homosexuality, that a same-sex relationship could be expressed in this way?[8] Does not the fact that Jesus' lover was also male not preclude the physical expression that might otherwise be taken for granted?

This objection has a number of elements, only some of which can be dealt with here. For example, we should have to inquire whether the attitude toward homosexual relations apparently expressed in Leviticus should be regarded as characteristic of Judaism as a whole. We would also have to inquire about what can be known about the attitude toward same-sex relations of hellenistic and rabbinic Judaism and whether these

---

8. We attend to the question of the presumed attitude of Judaism toward eunuchs in chapter 9, below.

views should be transferred to Jesus, to the Jesus tradition, or specifically to that aspect of the Jesus tradition represented by the Gospel of John.

For purposes of this discussion, however, we must limit ourselves to what can be learned from a reading of the Gospel of John. If we accept this restriction, then we are left with three aspects of this question. The first is: Does this text show that Jesus is typically disposed to accept without question the views of the legal code that appears to require the death of homosexual lovers? The second is: Does the text represent Jesus as supportive of the view of purity and uncleanness that is connected with same-sex sexual expression in Leviticus and at least some first-century interpretations of Judaism? The third is: Is Jesus represented in this text as generally supportive of the conventions of behavior that would include an unquestioning support for heterosexist institutions and conventions?

Simply to raise these questions is to answer them. Even if Judaism's attitude toward homosexuality were correctly deduced from the holiness code, Jesus would not feel himself bound by this. This conclusion is so obvious given what we know of Jesus that it scarcely requires argument. If the question bore on any other aspect of the holiness code (the attitude to be taken toward menstruating women, for example), we would see the answer without difficulty. But because *our* taboos are in question, because this discussion has to do with homosexuality, we have some difficulty in seeing the obvious. Accordingly some argumentation of this point may be in order.

What is the attitude taken by this text to the Torah or "law of Moses"?

In the first place, we may notice that this text, like the other Gospels, gives a certain authority to the Scriptures of Israel, especially wherever the events of Jesus' ministry and mission may be seen as fulfilling expectations raised by liturgical and prophetic texts. In the Gospel of John, this material is concentrated in the accounts of Jesus' passion (18:32; 19:25, 28, 36–37).

Several references to Moses, however, raise the question of the standing of the Mosaic law. Of the six references to Moses, two refer to Moses not as a lawgiver but as a prophet (1:45; 5:45). Here the concern is the way Moses anticipates, through his words and deeds, the expectation of final deliverance. Thus, the "literal" words of Moses are not at issue but rather Moses interpreted as a "type" of messianic expectation. The significance of Moses can also be expressly relativized. Jesus maintains that it was not Moses but "my Father" who gave their ancestors bread in the desert (6:31–32). The effect of this saying is to place Moses in a subordinate position relative to Jesus.

This relativizing of Moses is further expressed in the initial reference to Moses in the Gospel (1:17), in which Jesus and Moses are contrasted: the law came through Moses but "grace and truth" through Jesus. We should notice that the law here is contrasted not only with grace but also with truth.

Two other references to Moses continue the theme of Moses as a giver of the law. But here the law is understood as something that applies to Jesus' opponents, and not to Jesus and his followers. The most telling is the assertion that Moses gave the law to Jesus' opponents yet they don't keep the law (7:19–24). Their attack on Jesus is thus unwarranted. This passage seems to admit that Jesus does not himself keep the law, but that this fact places him in no worse condition than his opponents. What is at issue here is Jesus' nonconformity with the law regarding observance of the Sabbath. But Jesus' reply here is exactly parallel to his defense of the woman taken in adultery. How can you condemn her/me if you are yourselves guilty of disobeying the law?

Finally we may notice that Pharisees emphasize the contrast between being a disciple of Jesus and one of Moses (9:28).

Now whatever else may be made of the relationship exhibited in this text between Jesus and Moses, Jesus certainly could not be understood as being the exemplar of literal conformity to the law. He and his followers are "above the law." Thus, even if the law of Moses were correctly understood as proscribing same-sex relations, neither Jesus nor his followers would necessarily find that in itself a sufficient reason for applying this law to themselves.

Indeed the difference between Jesus and Moses is to be found even with respect to the most fundamental expression of the law as articulated in the Ten Commandments. Jesus is portrayed as disregarding the commandment regarding the sabbath, the commandment generally viewed as definitive of Judaism (5:9–10, 16; 7:23; 9:14). Moreover, Jesus is viewed as violating the first commandment, which protects the sanctity and uniqueness of God (10:30–31, 39). When Jesus is accused of blasphemy he does not simply pull rank by claiming divinity but, in effect, compounds the problem by referring to the biblical suggestion that all are gods (Psalm 82:6); hence for him to say that he is a god cannot be blasphemy (10:35). The two commandments that seem to bear most directly on religious identity are subjected to a thoroughgoing critique by Jesus. Thus his sovereignty with respect to suspending the penalty required by Moses for adultery (8:11) is consistent with the general view of this text that God is concerned more for human welfare than for religious rules.

Purity

Of course this critique of the law is carried even further in other New Testament texts. In the Gospel of Mark, for example, this critique is most clearly directed against the laws that were concerned with purity: fasting, washing, touching of corpses, menstruating women, lepers, and so on. The overcoming of the notion that observance of the law was the mark of Israel's special religious and ethnic identity was a life-and-death issue for Christianity as it reached out to include the Gentiles. Here critique of the laws regarding purity becomes especially acute, and the legislation regarding homosexuality is precisely found in the part of the law most radically rejected by early Christianity.

In the Gospel of John, Jesus is portrayed in ways that bring him directly into opposition to the views of purity that govern the levitical proscription of homosexual acts.[9] The water that he turns to wine in chapter 2 is water that is ritually impure since it had been used to wash the hands and feet of the party guests. His discussion with Nicodemus in chapter 3 associates the new life with birth, a process that renders the woman ritually impure. He breaks the taboo on association with the Samaritans in chapter 4. He speaks quite provocatively about eating his flesh — flouting another taboo — (5:51) and compounds this by speaking of not only eating his flesh but also of drinking his blood (5:53–58). The consumption even of animal blood was considered prohibited, and any contact with human blood rendered one ritually impure. The author(s) of the Gospel seem to have deliberately sought to select "impure" symbols for the activity of Jesus. This approach is consistent with the provocative notion of the word becoming flesh, as well as the emphasis upon washing the disciples' feet. None of this should be too surprising within a community that asserts that an executed man (the height of impurity) is the Messiah, the Christ, the Son of God.

The attitude toward Moses and toward sacred institutions of the law and toward purity in this text would not suggest a slavish acceptance of the legislation of Leviticus. Thus ample reason exists for doubting that the mere presence, in a code of national purity, of the prohibition of same-sex relations could conceivably have been felt to be binding on the author(s) of the Gospel of John. Thus the attitude taken toward the law, and toward

---

9. For further discussion of the following points, see William Countryman, *Dirt, Greed, and Sex: Sexual Ethics in the New Testament and Their Implications for Today* (Philadelphia: Fortress Press, 1988), 11–96.

issues of purity generally, far from undermining our thesis seems actually to support it.

Conventionality

If we turn to the more general question of the attitude shown toward what we may call conventional mores, the plausibility of Jesus being understood as disregarding or indeed flouting such conventions becomes even more marked. That is, not only is the attitude of Jesus toward the law not one of slavish acceptance and obedience, but his attitude toward conventional morality and lifestyle is even more one of insistent, persistent subversion.[10]

From the very beginning, Jesus' intention seems to be to drive the representatives of conventional piety crazy. He simply will not conform to any of their expectations regarding a holy man, a prophet, a messiah. His action is provocative throughout. He is contemptuous of conventional expressions of piety, especially as this concerns the observance of cult. Thus his attitude toward the temple expressed first in his assault upon the temple market, which in this Gospel opens his public ministry (2:13–16), his saying to the Samaritan woman that the all-important question of worship in Jerusalem or the holy mountain of Samaria was utterly beside the point (4:21), his contemptuous saying that he could rebuild the temple in three days (2:19) — all are calculated to awaken the outrage of the conventionally pious.

He seems utterly unconcerned for his own reputation. When he is accused of being religiously and ethnically illegitimate because he is a Galilean or a Samaritan, he doesn't even bother to reply (8:48). Nor does he reply when he is repeatedly called a sinner. None of this seems to matter to him. All that matters is that he acts as God acts: that he befriends those people rejected by conventional piety and those who are in distress. This activity of compassion rather than living up to conventional expectations is the mark of his relationship with God.

The persistent unconventionality of Jesus serves as a context within which an unconventional erotic attachment, while not necessary, would scarcely be unthinkable. Indeed such a relationship would be unthinkable today precisely for those who are the modern successors of Jesus' opponents: those people who set store by a literal adherence to laws, to codes of purity, and to conventional lifestyle and morality.

---

10. See Robert Goss, *Jesus Acted Up* (San Francisco: HarperSanFrancisco, 1993), esp. 61–86.

I do not suppose that Jesus' attitude toward the law or his unconventionality by themselves suggest that Jesus had a same-sex erotic relationship. The argument is only that since the text suggests that Jesus did have such a relationship, a consideration of his attitude toward the law and toward conventional behavior generally makes clear that this relationship would be entirely consistent with what else we are led to suspect about Jesus. So far from being out of the question from "John's" point of view, such a relationship fits with other critically important aspects of John's Gospel.

Origin

Even if the suggestion that Jesus had a beloved among the many whom he loved does fit well with the worldview of the Gospel of John as a whole, we may still be perplexed about the presence of this figure in the Gospel. How are we to evaluate the Gospel of John as a historical source? Why should the beloved appear here and not in other Gospels?

We must first address the question of the "historicity" of the depiction of Jesus as the lover of a beloved. Is this recollection to be understood as historical or as in some way or other "invented" by the author(s) of the Gospel of John?

To this point we have not argued that Jesus did in fact have such a relationship — only that the text suggests that he did. Now for many readers, the historicity of New Testament accounts is not in question. If a text says that something happened or was said, then that statement is sufficient to establish the fact. But other readers may have doubts. After all, the texts of the New Testament do not seem to agree concerning historical details, especially when we consider the relationship between the Fourth Gospel and the so-called Synoptic Gospels. We notice a strong disagreement between John and the others concerning a number of important "details" of this sort. The majority of the narrative and teaching material in the Gospel of John is simply not found in the other Gospels. And the overwhelming amount of material shared by two or more of the other Gospels is absent from John.

The Gospel of John is set apart from the others in a number of areas. The other Gospels have Jesus confine his early ministry to the area of Galilee and Syria, arriving in Jerusalem only in the final week of his mission. In John, on the other hand, the narrative of Jesus' ministry is organized around several forays into Jerusalem. In keeping with this presentation, John places Jesus' dramatic "cleansing of the temple" at the beginning of his public ministry as a whole, whereas the other Gospels place it in the final week of Jesus' ministry.

Great discrepancy also exists regarding the events of Jesus' final days. No elements are in common in the relation of Jesus' last words from the cross; no points are in common in the empty tomb or resurrection appearance stories or episodes.

On the other hand, the episodes basic to John's narrative — the changing of water into wine, the encounter with Nicodemus, the Samaritan woman, the raising of Lazarus, and so on — are not mentioned in other texts.

The point of mentioning these striking differences is not to decide the much vexed question of the relative historical merit of the Synoptics versus John. Scholars generally recognize that in all the Gospels we have to do with theologically constructed narratives from which attempting to draw inferences to the "historical" substratum lying behind them is extremely perilous.

One of the characteristics of John's narrative is the use of considerable "personal" detail not found in the other Gospels. Considerably more is made of the relationship between Jesus and John the Baptist. Andrew is given a prehistory as a disciple of John and then as instrumental in the calling of other disciples. Figures who only appear here are given prominence: Philip, Nathaniel, and Lazarus. Where parallels exist with the other Gospels, we notice a tendency to identify individuals. Thus in the scene of the anointing of Jesus, the one doing the anointing is identified as Mary the sister of Lazarus and Martha (not Mary Magdalene), and the one who protests is identified as Judas Iscariot, also identified as the treasurer of the group. In the scene in Gethsemane when Jesus is arrested, we are provided with the identity of the bystander who attacks the priest's servant (Simon Peter) and are even given the name of the servant (Malchus, 18:10).

Now what is the meaning of all this "personal" detail? Some readers argue that it demonstrates a personal familiarity with the actors and so lends credence to the historicity of the narrative as a whole. The detail has also been understood as demonstrating a desire to give the appearance of verisimilitude. This latter view is of the same order as the tendency of later tradition to provide names and biographies for the writers of the Gospels themselves. That is, the detail may show invention rather than recollection.

We need not decide this question here. But we can note that precisely in this context of what we might call biographical detail we meet with the figure of the beloved. Unfortunately, the tendency to identify persons otherwise not identified in other traditions does not hold here. The beloved is not named! On the one hand, his identity is etched clearly. He is given a role and a recognizable "profile." He is intimate with Jesus, he is a companion of Peter, he is taken into Jesus' family, and he is present at several critical points. But he is not given a name.

Why would such a figure be invented? What would be the motive for inventing an apparently homoerotic relationship where none existed? We may put it in another way. Why might this figure be present in this text but not in the other texts of a similar kind? Why in this Gospel and not in the others?

As it happens, a easier task is to suggest reasons for leaving this figure out of the other Gospels than for inventing him for the purposes of this one.

Imagining such a figure being left out or suppressed in the Gospel of Matthew is not too difficult, given that narrative's rather more stringent view of the applicability of the law to the community of Christians. Jesus is said there to fulfill and not abolish the law. Many scholars today suppose that Matthew was written in the context of a struggle with the emerging synagogues of Pharisaic Judaism concerning the correct interpretation of the Torah. If so, the author would not wish to draw attention to an aspect of Jesus' history that would justify excluding his followers from the synagogues and, indeed, appear to justify the death sentence carried out against Jesus.[11]

The Gospel of Luke seems to be addressed to "outsiders" (Theophilus) rather than to insiders of the community. In such a text, explaining the presence of a male beloved in the story of Jesus might be more trouble than it was worth. The attempt to "simplify" the apologetic task would certainly make explicable the nonappearance of that figure.

In the case of the Gospel of Mark, the text is so concentrated upon the theology of martyrdom as the application of a theology of the cross that room scarcely exists for any interest in merely biographical detail. Moreover, a follower of Jesus who was thought to be exempt from martyrdom (as the beloved [John 21:22]) would not play a significant part in a narrative concerned with martyrdom. However, as we shall see in chapter 7, traces of a figure like the disciple Jesus loved appear in this Gospel.

Giving a straightforward account for the elimination of the figure of the beloved from the other Gospels is thus possible. Is it possible to account for his presence in this Gospel?

---

11. We will return to the question of the attitude of this text to same-sex relationships in chapter 8.

The easiest explanation is the obvious one: The beloved is present in this text because the writer(s) knew a disciple who was the beloved of Jesus and they have in some way based their text on his testimony (19:35; 21:24). This claim would not in itself resolve the question of the historicity of the Gospel as a whole since its narrative structure and discursive strategy may still be theologically motivated either by the beloved or the writers/editors or both.

When the question of the composition of this Gospel is raised, scholars generally suppose the existence of a tightly knit community within which the teaching of the beloved disciple is developed.[12] This sort of community is mirrored in Jesus' farewell discourse. That the text is supposed to originate within such a tightly knit community of "insiders" also helps to account for the presence of the figure of the beloved in the text. Precisely in such a community would the recollection that Jesus had a same-sex lover be something that could be openly acknowledged without the need for complicated explanations.

Moreover, even if we suppose that Jewish Christians may have been influenced by the sort of antihomosexual (or rather, antipederastic) rhetoric that characterized some Jewish anti-Gentile propaganda, the Gospel of John was not written to or for such an audience. The text frequently explains Jewish customs and ideas in such a way as to make clear that its intended audience was unfamiliar with Judaism. Hence the writer(s) need not have been worried about the impression given of a contravention of Jewish law in the depiction of the relationship between Jesus and the beloved. An imagined audience unfamiliar with even the most elementary features of Judaism could scarcely be supposed to be acquainted with, still less governed by, the antipederastic rhetoric of some Jewish propagandists. Indeed the original audience may have regarded the presence of an erotic attachment between men as unproblematic. This audience is more likely to have had the rather relaxed attitude about sexuality characteristic of much of the hellenistic world.[13]

Now we could also ask whether assignable reasons existed even within such a relatively closed community for the invention of such a figure or relationship.

---

12. See Raymond E. Brown, *The Community of the Beloved Disciple* (New York: Paulist Press, 1979).

13. The only New Testament writer likely to have been influenced by Pharisaic traditions is Paul. His own views on sexuality are rather heterodox in that context since he rejects the obligation of marriage. He does appear to make some use of the typical Jewish propaganda about the characteristic impurity of the Gentiles in connection with homosexual acts in Romans 1, but his views need not have influenced the writer(s) of the Gospel of John.

The reasons that normally come to mind in such circumstances are (1) to buttress the claims for a particular theological point of view, (2) to buttress claims for ecclesial leadership, and (3) to claim personal importance. We have considered these possible motives in the previous chapter. We may briefly review them again here.

Does the claim of the text to be based on the recollections of Jesus' lover serve to lend authority for its particular theological point of view? To be sure, much is theologically distinctive about this Gospel. Most notably Jesus is represented as the Son of God in a way not found in the other texts. His identity with God is made much clearer here than in any of the other narratives. He is in many ways a more transcendent figure. But the theological claims made here seem not to be in need of buttressing within the Christian community as a whole. Even more to the point is the fact that the beloved is never even mentioned as present for these theological, Christological, and pneumatological discourses. In no way is he made to be their source. They presumably could as well come from any of the other disciples.

What then of ecclesial authority? Does this community have a certain preeminence among the Christian communities because of its relation to this disciple? The text itself makes this impossible. Preeminence is unquestionably given to Peter. The beloved has no official role, and the teaching that is yet to be supplied is given by the Spirit, not to the beloved, but to all. The beloved is not even specifically mentioned as present when Jesus commissions the disciples to be sent as Jesus himself had been sent (20:21).

But if the beloved has no theological insight or leadership role to set him off from the others, his community would seem to have no possible motive for inventing him.

Did he then invent himself? That is, did he claim a relationship to Jesus which (though it conveyed no special authority nevertheless) gave him at least personal importance? The whole idea seems impossible. Nothing is made of the beloved in any way beyond the fact that Jesus loved him. Even with respect to personal qualities, he does not stand out. Thomas would die with Jesus. Peter has the courage to defend Jesus in the garden and to enter the tomb; Peter must swim for Jesus. Nathaniel's character is especially praised. What personal importance does the disciple gain by claiming to be the one that Jesus loved? And if personal vanity reached the stage of inventing an intimate relation to Jesus, why stop at this? Why not suggest a certain special knowledge or position? Why not at least step out of the shadows so far as to give oneself a name?

The simplest explanation for the presence of the beloved in the narrative is that Jesus was the lover of a beloved, that this beloved was wholly identified with the one who loved him and so claimed nothing for himself, wanted only to "testify" concerning his lover.

Nor could he omit the fact that he was the beloved. The one whose message was love was also a lover, and the one who was the recipient of this gracious choice could not do otherwise than to remember it. He could not leave it out of his account because it was true. The relationship could not be erased without betraying the lover, without betraying the miracle of that love, the miracle that love is for those who are truly loved, always and everywhere.

One might also attempt a different approach. One could attempt to argue that this document suggests that Jesus had a homoerotic relationship precisely in order to bring to expression certain features of the worldview of the text itself. We have already seen that the gay-positive reading of the relationship between Jesus and the man he loved does in fact help us to see more clearly certain aspects of the Gospel. It underscores, for example, the anti-ascetic and antidocetic perspective of the text while also bringing to expression its oppositional stance to the law, to notions of purity and uncleanness, and to conventional mores.

One might take this argument a bit further in asking whether it would not be important to bring the insistence upon the enfleshment of the word into the human sphere of sexuality. In this way, the emphasis of this text upon love would receive concrete expression in the way in which love often comes to concrete expression: in the sphere of sexuality. And if this sphere were to be dealt with without falling back into the conventionality represented by "marriage and family values," would not the suggestion of a same-sex relationship be an appropriate vehicle? After all, such a relationship does not engage one in the perpetuation of social institutions of this world in the same way that marriage and progeny unquestionably do.

This interpretation of the place of the reference to the beloved in this document is certainly possible. And the interpretation opens a host of questions (like the relationship of the Jesus tradition in John and the other Gospels to the institutions of marriage and family) that will have to be addressed in a fuller discussion of the available evidence.

A number of ways are available to try to account for the presence in this text of the figure of the disciple Jesus loved. In the nature of the case, we cannot attain complete certainty in any attempt at historical reconstruction, but the simplest explanation for the presence of the beloved in this narrative is the obvious one. He and Jesus were lovers.

Chapter 5

The Hidden Tradition

The reading of the Gospel of John's treatment of the disciple Jesus loved that I have proposed may seem more novel than it in fact is. In this chapter, I wish to draw attention to the hidden tradition of what might be called a gay reading of the relationship between Jesus and the disciple he loved. Only in the last few years has it begun to become clear that such a hidden tradition even exists. The uncovering of such a hidden tradition has been one of the fruits of the renaissance of gay or queer studies. In what follows, I simply report and follow up on some of the results of that work. When I first wrote the preceding chapters, I was unaware of such a tradition. I am therefore indebted to those who have ferreted out that which has been so assiduously "hidden from history." I believe that further research will undoubtedly bring to light additional texts that reflect on the Gospel of John in ways that I have proposed. I expect this because I do not see how it would be possible for such a tradition not to exist given the self-evidence of the text as I have interpreted it.

Aelred and the Middle Ages

In his groundbreaking work *Christianity, Homosexuality, and Social Tolerance,* John Boswell does not himself discuss the relevant texts of the Gospel of John. Instead he contents himself with a passing (and rather coy) reference to the text: "Jesus was apparently celibate himself, and the only persons with whom the Gospels suggest he had any special relationship were men, especially Saint John, who carefully describes himself throughout his gospel as the disciple whom Jesus loved" (115). But in a footnote to this, Boswell adds: "This was not lost on gay Christians of later ages: see below, pp. 225–26."

When we turn to the indicated discussion, we find ourselves in a discussion of the views of the twelfth-century British abbot Aelred of Rievaulx, as expressed in his classic works *The Mirror of Charity* and *On Spiritual Friendship*. Here Boswell quotes a passage from *The Mirror of Charity* that he interprets as expressing Aelred's view that the relation between Jesus and the man he loved is one of deep homoerotic but virginal attachment. The passage as quoted in Boswell is as follows:

It is in fact a great consolation in this life to have someone to whom you can be united in the intimate embrace of the most sacred love; in whom your spirit can rest; to whom you can pour out your soul; in whose delightful company, as in a sweet consoling song, you can take comfort in the midst of sadness; in whose most welcome friendly bosom you can find peace in so many worldly setbacks; to whose loving heart you can open as freely as you would to yourself your inmost thoughts; through whose spiritual kisses — as by some medicine — you are cured of the sickness of care and worry; who weeps with you in sorrow, rejoices with you in joy, and wonders with you in doubt; whom you draw by the fetters of love into that inner room of your soul, so that though the body is absent, the spirit is there, and you can confer all alone, the more secretly, the more delightfully; with whom you can rest, just the two of you, in the sleep of peace away from the noise of the world, in the embrace of love, in the kiss of unity, with the sweetness of the Holy Spirit flowing over you; to whom you so join and unite yourself that you mix soul with soul, and the two become one.

We can enjoy this in the present with those whom we love not merely with our minds but with our hearts; for some are joined to us more intimately and passionately than others in the lovely bond of spiritual friendship. And lest this sort of sacred love should seem improper to anyone, Jesus himself, in everything like us, patient and compassionate with us in every matter, transfigured it through the expression of his own love: for he allowed one, not all, to recline on his breast as a sign of his special love, so that the virgin head was supported on the flowers [sic] of the virgin breast, and the closer they were, the more copiously did the fragrant secrets of the heavenly marriage impart the sweet smell of spiritual chrism to their virgin love.

Although all the disciples were blessed with the sweetness of the greatest love of the most holy master, nonetheless he conceded as a privilege to one alone this symbol of a more intimate love, that he should be called the 'disciple whom Jesus loved.' "[1]

---

1. John Boswell, *Christianity, Social Tolerance, and Homosexuality: Gay People in Western Europe from the Beginning of the Christian Era to the Fourteenth Century* (Chicago: University

In Aelred's later work *Spiritual Friendship* — toward the end of his reflections, just before recounting something of the relationship he had had with his two closest friends — he again returns to the image of the relationship between Jesus and "St. John."[2]

> Nor should anyone say that he is held in contempt for the reasons that he is not promoted, since the Lord Jesus preferred Peter to John in this respect; nor did he, on that account, lessen his affection for John, because he had given Peter the leadership. To Peter he commended his Church; to John, his most beloved Mother. To Peter he gave the keys of the kingdom; to John he revealed the secrets of his heart. Peter therefore was the more exalted; John, the more secure.... Peter, therefore was exposed to action, John was reserved for love, according to the words of Christ: "So will I have him remain till I come."[3]

Now we can see that, to a significant degree, Aelred's view of the relationship between Jesus and the disciple Jesus loved corresponds to what we have found: the love for the beloved sets him apart from the others that Jesus doubtless loved with special intimacy. The mark of Jesus' love for his beloved is to be seen in the physical posture of the beloved: "for he allowed one, not all, to recline on his breast as a sign of his special love" (*Mirror,* p. 299). Aelred interprets the scene at the cross with Jesus and his mother and his beloved in terms of that intimacy: "to Peter he commended his Church; to John his most beloved Mother' (*Friendship,* p. 125). The closing episode from the Gospel further is taken to underline the unofficial status of Jesus' relationship to the one he loved: "Peter exposed to action; John reserved for love" (*Friendship,* p. 125).

Of significance also is that Aelred supposes that the sort of love he discovers between Jesus and his beloved is to be understood as a parallel to the relationship between David and Jonathan. He cites this comradeship as a model of "spiritual friendship" in the *Mirror of Charity* 3.29.69–71 and in his treatise on *Spiritual Friendship* (2.63 [p. 84] and 3.92 [pp. 115–16]).

---

of Chicago Press, 1980), 225–26. This is Boswell's translation of the passage from Aelred's *Mirror of Charity* 3.109–110. Since Boswell wrote, the *Mirror* has been translated in full by Elizabeth Connor and is published by Cistercian Publications, Kalamazoo, Michigan, 1990. The passage I have quoted from Boswell is on pp. 298–99 of that edition. The translations are different in style but not in content. All subsequent references are to the Cistercian edition.

2. Aelred of Rievaulx, *Spiritual Friendship* (Kalamazoo, Mich.: Cistercian Publications, 1977).

3. *Spiritual Friendship* 3.117, p. 125.

Aelred is quite clear that the relationship between Jesus and his beloved is to be understood as a kind of marriage, indeed as the very model of marriage. In the passage we have cited at length from the *Mirror*, Aelred speaks of the friendship which is modeled on that between Jesus and his beloved as the "two become one." Now this is the way in which Genesis describes the relationship between the first male and female, a relationship that church tradition has taken to be the paradigm for marriage. Nor is this an isolated instance. In *Spiritual Friendship*, Aelred also describes the relationship of most intimate (male) friends as the two becoming one (3.48, p. 103). Indeed Aelred takes the model of mutual intimate friendship, a model derived from biblical descriptions of Jesus and his beloved and David and Jonathan, to be as well a paradigm for the originally intended relationship between the sexes! He writes:

> It was from no similar, nor even the same, material that divine Might formed this helpmate, but as a clearer inspiration to charity and friendship he produced the woman from the very substance of the man. How beautiful it is that the second human being was taken from the side of the first, so that nature might teach that human beings are equal and, as it were, collateral, and that there is in human affairs neither a superior nor an inferior, a characteristic of true friendship.[4]

Thus the equality that Aelred takes to be essential to true friendship is here transposed into the marriage relationship across sexes. Homoerotic relationships as exemplary of love produces the view that men and women should be equals! We return to this concept in the next chapter when we reflect on the significance for all erotic relationships (regardless of gender or sexual orientation) of the homoerotic interpretation of the beloved disciple texts.

At this point, when Aelred refers to the "fragrant secrets of the heavenly marriage" (*Mirror*) in describing the relation between Jesus and the beloved disciple, he is really supposing that this relationship was in every way a "perfect marriage."

The sharing of "secrets" in Aelred takes the place of sexual practice. What makes a relationship intimate then is primarily the sharing of secrets. Aelred therefore reads this into the relationship between Jesus and his beloved, taking his cue from the scene at the Last Supper. This substitution of secrets for sex is understandable for Aelred. It is the way of expressing

---

4. Ibid. 1.57, p. 63.

intimacy under conditions of virginity/chastity. But we have seen that the Gospel of John by no means requires this substitution.

What are we to make of this appropriation of the image of the beloved? Aelred is making use of this image in order to insist upon the appropriateness of a friendship that attaches itself to a particular person in desire and delight as opposed to the view of love that insists that no special or particular attachments are appropriate for the sort of love that models itself upon the divine love. That Aelred feels it necessary to defend such deep attachments itself indicates that they were suspect, if not on sexual grounds then, at least, on theological grounds.

Aelred clearly supposed from other texts that the sort of relationship he was contemplating was compatible with some erotic practices but not with others. Aelred was in agreement with others of his epoch who valued same-sex relationships in supposing that kissing and hand holding, at least under certain circumstances, were appropriate expressions of the special spiritual friendship he was advocating. His biographer, writing soon after Aelred's death, recalls that he, unlike other abbots, accepted his monks expressing special friendship in public by holding hands.[5] On the other hand, he would not disagree with the view that anal penetration between males would be an unacceptable practice. In this sense the relation was "virginal." But between the clearly included (kissing and caressing) and the clearly excluded (anal penetration), a number of erotic practices exist of whose place in Aelred's perspective we may be less certain. What, if any, other erotic practices were to be permitted, expected, or prohibited? The important thing about this question is that it draws our attention to the view of Aelred that some but not all erotic practices appropriate to marriage in the general sense were taken to be appropriate mediations or expressions of the "heavenly marriage" that he envisioned for himself and those who were beloved of him, and that he saw the model of Jesus and his beloved as paradigmatic for himself in these relationships and for those he counseled to emulate this pattern.

Furthermore to raise the question in this way is to remind ourselves that the configuration of erotic practices varies enormously from culture to culture, from epoch to epoch, and, indeed, from person to person. In his own context, the erotic practices that Aelred values would be regarded

---

5. "He did not treat them with the pedantic imbecility habitual in some silly abbots who, if a monk takes a brother's hand in his own, or says anything that they do not like, demand his cowl, strip and expel him. Not so Aelred, not so." Walter Daniel, *The Life of Aelred of Rievaulx*, trans. F. M. Powicke (Kalamazoo, Mich.: Cistercian Publications, 1994), 40; cited in the introduction to *Spiritual Friendship*, 13.

as inappropriate for mere acquaintances and would likely be regarded as prohibited for cross-sex relationships outside of courtship and marriage. In Aelred's view, the sensual pleasure of physical intimacy is appropriate to the "spiritual friendship" he saw expressed between Jesus and the disciple he loved.

The erotic practices approved of by Aelred would, in other contexts, be regarded as repugnant. Thus that men would kiss and caress one another is viewed with loathing by at least some subcultures within the domain of homophobia. Indeed some persons whose sexual experience is entirely with persons of their own sex would, for personal reasons, regard this sort of affectionate display with repugnance. Thus they might think nothing of anal penetration but regard kissing as "unmanly." Gayle Rubin observed that whatever our erotic practices, a segment of the population regards that practice with horror.[6]

The point of this reflection is to note that, for Aelred, the relationship between Jesus and the man he loved was self-evidently mediated by some erotic practice. But the way in which erotic practice is organized on a grid as expressive of the appropriate, the permissible, the repugnant, or the prohibited varies enormously. The point then is neither to adopt nor to reject the way in which Aelred may have structured erotic practices, but only to notice that, however structured, we are still dealing with erotic practices — that is, with practices that grant bodily pleasure in the presence of the object of desire and delight.

As I have repeatedly indicated, the text of the Gospel of John does not suggest which erotic practices mediate the relation of Jesus and the man he loved. The text, taken as a whole, does not point us away from any such mediation; this Gospel is not ascetic in orientation. Similarly Aelred supposes the appropriateness of erotic mediation of this relationship and of those modeled upon it. His suppositions about what erotic practices were appropriate were those shaped by his own experience and by the range of meanings associated with such practices in his culture or subculture, especially as shaped by the conventions of monasticism. This stance may be no less true of the reader of today. Given the great variation in personal tastes and cultural norms of modern society, readers accordingly vary considerably in the sorts of erotic practices they deem fitting for the sort of relationship depicted in the Gospel of John and recognized under very different cultural conditions by Aelred of Rievaulx.

---

6. Gayle S. Rubin, "Thinking Sex: Notes for a Radical Theory of the Politics of Sexuality," in *The Lesbian and Gay Studies Reader*, ed. Henry Abelove, Michele Aina Barale, and David M. Halperin (New York: Routledge, 1993), 15.

Marlowe and the English Renaissance

The second indication of a hidden tradition of homoerotic readings of the relationship between Jesus and the beloved disciple comes from the period of the English Renaissance and the accusations against Christopher Marlowe.[7] Marlowe was England's most famous poet and dramatist next to Shakespeare and has sometimes even been said to have written Shakespeare's plays. His plays *Dido, Hero and Leander, Tamerlaine,* and *Edward II* all employ homoerotic themes.

Marlowe, who had also been something of a spy, was killed, probably assassinated, in a tavern brawl. At the inquest into Marlowe's death, one of those who had been involved in the plot against him, Richard Baines, accused Marlowe of atheism and blasphemy. Karlen quotes from the deposition as follows:

He affirmeth that Moyses was but a Juglar, & that one Heriots being Sir W. Raleighs man can do more than he.
That the first beginning of Religioun was only to keep men in awe.
That Christ was a bastard and his mother dishonest.
That if there be any god or any good religion, then it is in the papistes because the service of god is performed with more Ceremonies, as elevation of the mass, singing men, Shaven Crownes & cta. that all protestants are Hypocriticall asses.
. . . that all the new testament is filthily written.
That St. John the Evangelist was bedfellow to Christ and leaned always in his bosome, that he used him as the sinners of Sodoma.
That all they that love not Tobacco & Boies were fools.[8]

The point of this testimony seems to have been that the assassination of Marlowe was justifiable homicide! Here it matters little whether Marlowe actually did say that the disciple Jesus loved "was bedfellow to Christ" or that Jesus "used him as the sinners of Sodoma." What is most important is that the recognition of the possibility of this interpretation was just below the surface of cultural consciousness.

A further indication of the same view came from the testimony, extracted under torture, of Marlowe's friend and fellow poet, Sir Thomas Kyd. Alan Bray quotes Kyd's testimony: "He would report St. John to be

7. "One of them, Christopher Marlowe, was accused of atheism and blasphemy for saying, among other things, that Christ and saint John the evangelist were bedmates." Quoted in David F. Greenberg, *The Construction of Homosexuality* (Chicago: University of Chicago Press, 1988), 349.

8. Arlo Karlen, *Sexuality and Homosexuality* (New York: W. W. Norton, 1971), 116–17.

our Saviour Christ's Alexis. I cover it with reverence and trembling that Christ did love him with an extraordinary love."[9]

The reference to Alexis is to Virgil's second Eclogue, a poem from Rome's most famous poet of the first century B.C.E. This poem was devoted to the same-sex (pederastic) love of Corydon for Alexis:

> The shepherd Corydon with love was fired
> for fair Alexis, his own master's joy.

This poem served as a pattern for many poems of the English Renaissance, including Marlowe's own *The Passionate Shepherd to His Love*.[10] Bray's judgment is that this reference to Alexis rather than the reference to "Sodoma" is more likely to be what Marlowe actually said, since it places the love of Jesus for his beloved not in the context of the homophobic interpretation of Sodom but in the context of hellenistic valorization of same-sex desire and delight.

The inquest into Marlowe's death serves both to indicate the possibility of a reading of the relationship between Jesus and his beloved (whether in the inflammatory terms of sodomy or the classical conventions of pederasty) which recognized the same-sex love there portrayed, and, as well, the horror with which such a reading was received — even justifying the homicide of one of England's most distinguished men of letters. The extrajudicial execution of Marlowe serves as a graphic reminder of the way in which the text's own suggestion of homoerotic relationship was policed not only by the traditions of interpretation but also, if need be, by the use of terror.

Crompton and Bentham

The third clue that I wish to pursue in this discussion of the hidden history of a gay reading of the relationship between Jesus and the disciple he loved comes from Louis Crompton in his book *Byron and Greek Love: Homophobia in Nineteenth-Century England*.[11]

In this study, Crompton devotes a chapter to a discussion of an unpublished manuscript of Jeremy Bentham written around 1816 and tentatively

---

9. Alan Bray, *Homosexuality in Renaissance England* (London: Gay Men's Press, 1982), 64. See also Alan Bray, "The Homosexual Heresy," in *Chaucer Review* 6 (1971): 44–63.

10. For a discussion of this poem and its cultural ambience, see Bruce R. Smith, *Homosexual Desire in Shakespeare's England* (Chicago: University of Chicago Press, 1994), 89–115.

11. Louis Crompton, *Byron and Greek Love: Homophobia in Nineteenth-Century England* (Berkeley: University of California Press, 1985).

titled *Not Paul but Jesus.* As the title indicates, the manuscript anticipates a nineteenth-century genre which opposes the more human Jesus to the allegedly more doctrinaire or dogmatic Paul.

Bentham (1748–1832) was one of the most important political philosophers of the late eighteenth and early nineteenth centuries in Britain. He wrote copiously, although he published reluctantly. His work *The Principles of Morals and Legislation* was finally published in 1789. The three-volume *Traites de legislation,* collated and translated from Bentham's writings, was published in France in 1802, making Bentham's ideas exceedingly influential in the development of the reform of law associated with the Napoleonic Code. In England, Bentham's association with John Stuart Mill eventually resulted in the Reform Bill of 1832 (published shortly after Bentham's death) that significantly democratized the British form of government.

An extraordinary amount of Bentham's considerable energy was spent on the question of the decriminalization of homosexual relations, for he regarded the existing law as an unwarranted intrusion of government in the private life of its citizens. To a significant degree, Bentham was indirectly successful — outside of England. The Napoleonic Code did decriminalize "sodomy," as did the legal codes that Bentham also influenced in Brazil.

In connection with this interest in abolishing "victimless crimes," Bentham undertook his extensive review of the biblical materials related to sexuality generally and to homosexuality in particular, which is the theme of *Not Paul but Jesus.*[12]

In this work, Bentham anticipates much of the groundbreaking work of D. S. Bailey undertaken a century and a half later in connection with the belated consideration in England of the decriminalization of homosexuality. But Bentham goes even further. Bentham supposes that the story of David and Jonathan described a relationship that would have fallen under the then existing legislation against "sodomy." Even more surprisingly, Bentham also anticipates many of the suggestions that I have made concerning the interpretation of the "disciple Jesus loved."

Crompton reports:

Examining the Gospel of St. John with the same attention with which he had analyzed Genesis . . . he excerpts all the passages in the story of the Last Supper, the Crucifixion, and the Resurrection in which

---

12. Discussed in ibid., 278–83.

the "beloved disciple" speaks of the special fondness Jesus bore him. Could John have meant to imply that he and Jesus were lovers? Bentham admits that "good taste and self-regarding prudence would require us to turn aside" from this "topic of extreme delicacy." But "a regard for human happiness and important truth and the sound principles of penal justice compel him to go over it." (Crompton, 278)

Given the fate of Marlowe more than two centuries before, Bentham's view that a "self-regarding prudence" would argue against treating this relationship to close scrutiny seems more than justified. The same "self-regarding prudence" likely prevented the publication of the work and its virtual suppression by Bentham scholars until Crompton brought it to light in 1985.

Crompton quotes Bentham's interpretation of the text as follows:

If the love which in these passages Jesus was intended to be represented as bearing towards this John was not the same sort of love as that which appears to have had place between David and Jonathan, the son of Saul, it seems not easy to conceive what can have been the object in bringing it to view in so pointed a manner accompanied by such circumstances of fondness. That the sort of love of which in the bosom of Jesus Saint John is here meant to be represented as the object was of a different sort from any of which any of the other of the Apostles was the object is altogether out of dispute. For of this sort of love, whatever sort it was, he and he alone, is in these so frequently recurring terms maintained as being the object.

[As to] any superiority of value in his service in relation to preaching of the Gospel — no such foundation could the distinction have had; for of this nothing is to be found in Saint John by which he can stand in comparison with Saint Peter, and on no occasion is the rough fisherman to be seen "leaning in the bosom of Jesus" or "lying on his breast." (Crompton, 278–79)

Now, like Aelred, Bentham recognizes the distinctiveness of the love of Jesus for this one disciple. But unlike Aelred, Bentham (though himself a life-long bachelor, and apparently celibate) has no difficulty supposing that the physical intimacy represented by "such circumstances of fondness" includes the sexual practices that were then criminalized in England.[13]

---

13. It should be clear that Bentham at any rate is proposing that the relationship between Jesus and the disciple he loved should be viewed as sexual since he considers this in relationship to the issue of the decriminalization of same-sex relationships.

According to Crompton, Bentham makes clear that Jesus, like the prophets but unlike much Christian tradition, certainly did not suppose that the story of Sodom could be used to cast suspicion on same-sex relationships. And he further argues that the "Mosaic" law against such relationships (i.e., Leviticus) could have no bearing on Jesus' attitude. Bentham writes:

> As to the law of Moses — to him who has resolution enough to keep his eyes open to it nothing can be more manifest than that in the eyes of Jesus the law of Moses was but a mere human law so ill-adapted to the welfare of society that on no occasion is it ever spoken of as coming under his cognizance without being taken by him more or less expressly for the declared object of [his] scorn.[14]

Crompton's own assessment of Bentham's views is rather circumspect:

> A Christian to whom homosexuality is abhorrent will of course reject Bentham's reading of the Gospels out of hand and with vehemence. Certainly the evidence he builds on is fragile and inconclusive, surprisingly so when we remember that Bentham was his age's leading authority on legal evidence. But what people believe, especially in matters of religion and morals, is rarely determined by evidence. Personal or cultural bias is much more important. A Greek ignorant of Paul or Leviticus who read the Gospel of St. John in the first or second century might very well have interpreted it as a homosexual romance, just as, with little more evidence, he interpreted the story of Achilles and Patroclus in the *Iliad* as a homosexual love affair. Bentham's interpretation is neither probable nor impossible. Most responses to Bentham's theory, however, will be less a response to the evidence than an indication of one's feelings about homosexuality or, for that matter, about ascribing sexual feelings of any sort to Christ."[15]

The reserve with which Crompton expresses himself here follows on a discussion of Bentham's remarks concerning what I call the "Nude youth in the Garden" (see below) which is admittedly less compelling in terms of evidence (a mere three verses in canonical Mark) than the evidence concerning the disciple Jesus loved. Moreover Crompton does not attempt an independent reading of the Gospel of John. Still it is striking the degree to which the regime of homophobia, as late as 1985, makes it prudent to

---

14. Ibid., 279.
15. Ibid., 283.

distance oneself from Bentham's views. But it may be that, as "his age's leading authority on legal evidence," Bentham has simply seen what the text presents to the unbiased reader.[16]

Groddeck and Psychoanalysis

Georg Walther Groddeck (1866–1934) was an Austrian psychoanalyst and contemporary of Sigmund Freud's.[17] Unlike Freud, Groddeck was inclined to make positive use of the Christian symbol system for analytical purposes, in contrast to Freud's preference for Greek myths as ways of illuminating psychic processes (the Oedipus complex, for example).

In 1923, Groddeck published his *Das buch vom Es*,[18] which dealt with the "it" or, as Freudian terminology came to be standardized in English, the "id." The book is a series of letters in which Groddeck seeks to understand himself and the psychoanalytic process itself.

In "Letter 27," Groddeck discusses the theme of homosexuality that he takes to be basic to human affectional life. He supposes that our first erotic attachment is to ourselves and that this is reenforced for the woman in that her initial "significant other" is a person of the same sex, namely, her mother. He believes, therefore, that what requires explanation is not how some persons are "homosexual," but how it is that many forget this and become "heterosexual."

Groddeck finds modern Western culture's ignorance of the primacy of homosexuality to be astonishing, as if willful ignorance prevented the West from seeing what is right before its eyes. This culture, he writes:

> ...must be at least surprised at that curious phrase in the Gospel concerning Christ's disciple, "whom Jesus loved," and who lay upon the Lord's breast. We make nothing of it at all. To all this evidence we are blind. We are not to see what is there to be seen.
>
> In the first place, the Church forbids it. Obviously she derives this prohibition from the Old Testament, the whole spirit of which was

---

16. In at least one respect, Crompton is decidedly right: the possibility of seeing the sexual implications of the relationship between Jesus and his beloved does indeed largely depend on the possibility of attributing sexual feelings or actions of any kind to Jesus. We discuss this in the next chapter.

17. Groddeck was first brought to my attention by James Creech through reference to another work, by Dominique Fernandez: *Le Rapt de Ganymede* (Paris: Bernard Grasset, 1989), which refers to Groddeck's work on pp. 98–99. Fernandez cites Groddeck's illustration of the disciple Jesus loved (98). Such are the circuitous ways by which a hidden tradition must be reconstructed.

18. Georg Walther Groddeck, *Das buch vom Es* (Vienna: Psychoanalytischer Verlag, 1923).

directed to bringing all sexual activity into direct association with the begetting of children, and, as a result of priestly ambition, she purposely made this inherited human instinct into a sin in order to lord it over the stricken conscience. This was particularly opportune for the Christian Church since it was able to deal with the root of Hellenic culture in its execration of male love.[19]

Groddeck supposes that the prohibition of same-sex love serves both to undermine Greek cultural superiority to the ideological advantage of the Church and to place people in the position of being guilty about what is natural and inevitable, thereby making the services of the church in forgiving sin essential to the guilty.

Now it is certainly true that the church has tended to deflect attention away from the biblical view of sin as injustice, which has made it easier for the Church to get along with wealthy and powerful patrons. And the focus on the domain of sexuality as the primary locus of sin means that those who are victimized by injustice may nevertheless be made to feel that they are the true sinners in need of forgiveness.[20] The erotophobia of much of hellenistic culture served the Constantinian church well in this regard. But Groddeck is also suggesting that homophobia has a privileged place within this erotophobic system of control. For Groddeck, the primacy of homosexual attraction makes the prohibition of homosexuality especially useful for systems of domination.

But for our purposes what is perhaps most interesting in Groddeck's position is that he regards the homosexuality of the relationship between Jesus and the beloved disciple to be *self-evident*. This relationship does not require argument: it is there before the reader's eyes. This outlook corresponds to what we have encountered in this "hidden tradition." Certainly for Marlowe or Bentham, the relationship between Jesus and the beloved was clear, but they were reading the text without the blinders provided by church tradition.[21]

---

19. Georg Walther Groddeck, *The Book of the It,* trans. V. M. E. Collins (New York: Vintage Press, 1949), 263–64.

20. For a discussion of the ways that the church has misused the doctrine of sin in this and other ways, see my essay, "Reconstructing the Doctrine of Sin," in *The Other Side of Sin: Woundedness from the Perspective of the Sinned-Against,* ed. Andrew Sung Park and Susan L. Nelson (Albany: State University of New York Press, 2001), 109–22.

21. I have had this verified anecdotally in that when I mention to Christians the sort of reading of the Gospel of John in which I am engaged, they are typically aghast (unless they are gay). But when I speak of it to intellectuals who are "post-Christian," their reaction is usually something like, "But of course; that's obvious, isn't it?"

Contemporary Voices

As the "question of homosexuality" becomes indeed more of an open question in the church, the power of tradition to hide the obvious is weakened. Still, many contemporary voices of gay interpretation or of antihomophobic interpretation are either silent regarding this aspect of John's Gospel or appear to dismiss it without argument. Thus, neither Edwards nor McNeill even mention this possibility, and Horner mentions it only to dismiss it in favor of some version of Bultmann's hypothesis and the edifying reflection that we are all beloved disciples.[22] Nelson also makes rather oblique reference to the possibility we have been considering:

> There are clear biblical affirmations of deep love between same-sex adults. I am not implying genital relations in these instances. I simply note that in the instances of David and Jonathan, Ruth and Naomi, Jesus and the "beloved disciple," and others, the scripture seems to hold strong emotional bonding between members of the same sex to be a cause for celebration, not fear.[23]

In its document "Towards a Christian Understanding of Sexuality," the United Reformed Church (of Great Britain) referred in 1984 to the suggestion that Jesus "may have... been homosexually inclined" and refers to the disciple Jesus loved.[24] To be sure, the document notes that this suggestion is one to which Christians "have tended to react with horror," but the document places this horror in company with that which people may have toward the suggestion that Jesus had "women lovers." Although the popularity of *Jesus Christ Superstar* and the discussion of *The Last Temptation of Christ* are likely sources for the latter suggestion, the document is, alas, silent concerning the sources for the suggestion of homosexual inclination.

One of the sources may well have been the suggestions of Canon Hugh Montefiore. In a sermon preached at Cambridge's Great St. Mary's in August 1967, Montefiore made the suggestion that Jesus was celibate because he was "not the marrying kind." Although the sense of this sug-

22. Tom Horner, *Jonathan Loved David: Homosexuality in Biblical Times* (Philadelphia: Westminster Press, 1978), 120–21.
23. James B. Nelson, *Body Theology* (Louisville, Ky.: Westminster/John Knox Press, 1990), 60.
24. Quoted in J. Gordon Melton, *The Churches Speak On Homosexuality* (Detroit: Gale Research, 1991), 245.

gestion may seem innocuous to the American reader, Montefiore himself feels compelled to insist that he does not mean to impute sin to Jesus, admits that the hearer may "have been filled with repugnance at all this," and goes on to suggest that this repugnance may be compared to that of Jews in reaction to "the scandal of the cross."[25] This very tentative proposal, it turns out, had been made more directly in a paper delivered the previous month at Oxford titled "Jesus the Revelation of God" but not published until later.[26] In this paper Montefiore also begins with the issue of Jesus' celibacy. After considering other possible interpretations of this fact, Montefiore suggests:

> Men usually remain unmarried for three reasons: either because they cannot afford to marry or there are no girls to marry (neither of these factors need have deterred Jesus); or because it is inexpedient for them to marry in light of their vocation (we have already ruled this out during the 'hidden years' of Jesus' life); or because they are homosexual in nature, in as much as women hold no special attraction for them. This homosexual explanation is one which we must not ignore. According to the gospels, women were his friends but it is men whom he is said to love. Possibly the hearer may shrink from this idea in disgust. If so let him consider that these are the very same emotions with which the Jews of Jesus' day received the idea that the Messiah of Judah died a criminal's death upon a Roman cross.[27]

Montefiore goes on to note:

> If Jesus were homosexual in nature (and if this is the true explanation of his celibate state) then this would be further evidence of God's self-identification with those who are unacceptable to the upholders of 'The Establishment' and social conventions.[28]

In a footnote, Montefiore responds to the outrage that his remarks evidently aroused:

> The furor that followed the sensational publicity which the national press accorded this speculation prompts me to add a note to what I

---

25. Hugh Montefiore, ed., *For God's Sake: Sermons from Great St. Mary's* (Minneapolis: Fortress Press, 1969), 182, 183.
26. Norman Pittenger, *Christ for Us Today* (London: SCM, 1968), 101–16.
27. Ibid., 109.
28. Ibid., 110.

said. The word 'homosexual', when applied to human nature, does not imply any moral connotation whatever. It is simply descriptive of a certain type of personality. It in no way implies or attributes any kind of sinfulness to Jesus.[29]

The suggestions of Canon Montefiore only obliquely refer to the role of the disciple Jesus loved: "it is men whom he is said to love." Here Montefiore may have in mind not only the beloved disciple but Lazarus as well and perhaps even the "rich young ruler."

In 1990, in an article in the *Advocate*, Malcolm Boyd asked "Was Jesus Gay"?[30] As it turns out, however, he concentrates his attention mostly on the issue of Jesus' sexuality generally and refers to the disciple Jesus loves only allusively and in the context of quoting the oral communication of other people. This editorial essay does more to establish the reluctance to interpret the relationship between Jesus and the beloved disciple in a homoerotic sense than it does to promote such a reading.

In 1992, Robert Williams in his *Just As I Am* (Harper) devotes considerable attention to the same question and answers in the affirmative, citing the accounts of the disciple Jesus loved (pp. 116–18) and the material in Secret Mark (pp. 118–21) to build up a composite picture of the disciple Jesus loved as Lazarus. This is, by far, the most detailed contemporary discussion of the possibility of a gay reading of this relationship to date.[31] What Williams does not provide is any careful rereading of the biblical texts or argumentation for his perspective.

While not specifically basing itself on the Gospel of John, mention should also be made of Terrence McNally's play *Corpus Christi*, which portrays a Jesus-like figure growing up gay in Corpus Christi, Texas, and subsequently becoming a healer and preacher with disciples, many of whom are also gay. The subsequent persecution and execution of this figure make clear that what is at work here is a reimagining of Jesus as gay. Understandably the play has been controversial but seems to have a strong appeal to younger audiences, including church audiences.

---

29. Ibid., 109. Montefiore is careful not to say here whether he would regard the practice of homosexuality as sinful or not. The reserve with which judgment is here expressed owes in part to the controversy concerning the decriminalization of homosexuality then raging in Britain. But Nelson was even more circumspect in 1990! See above n. 23.

30. Malcolm Boyd, "Was Jesus Gay?" *Advocate*, no. 565 (December 4, 1990).

31. I discuss this proposal more at length after the discussion of the Markan material to which Williams refers in his reconstruction of a kind of "gay romance" based on these texts.

The possibility of a gay reading of the disciple Jesus loved is being opened up by the willingness of theologians (and others) to reconsider biblical materials from a fresh perspective. I hope this discussion contributes to this process. Perhaps one day, even those who have been steeped in the Christian tradition can read with open eyes the story of Jesus and the man he loved.

Chapter 6

Theological Significance

When analyzing a text from the New Testament, one must not only ask what the text says or what interpretation it will bear, but also raise the question of the significance of a particular reading of the text for the Christian community that understands itself to be in some way answerable to the text. Our reading of the text has shown that the episodes concerning the disciple Jesus loved are best understood on the supposition that the relationship between Jesus and this disciple was a homoerotic one that may be supposed to include sexual expression. Not only does this reading of the text not do violence to the passages concerned, and not only does it illumine much that had been made obscure by ignoring the erotic character of the relationship, but it is also consistent with the overall worldview of the text as a whole.

But if what might be termed a gay reading of these texts does make sense of them, and does illumine the text in ways that other readings do not and cannot, what then might such a reading mean for the community of readers who understand these texts to be in some way revelatory of the human situation before God?

This reading of the text obviously makes it impossible for any who imagine themselves to be adherents of the Jesus depicted in this text to perpetuate heterosexist and homophobic institutions and attitudes. Although a wide cultural gulf separates first-century same-sex relations from those in the early twenty-first century that we call gay or even queer, the text of the Gospel of John suggests that Jesus had a relationship with another man that today might be called "gay."

The continued posture of many churches that oppose the inclusion of gay, lesbian, and bisexual Christians and which deny to these not only the dignity of openness about, and celebration of, their relationships, but also exclude them from the ministry of the Christian community is a particularly striking example of the way in which the church may come into

92

direct opposition to Jesus himself. Such opposition, of course, is nothing new for the church. In its history, the church has often enough sided with the wealthy and powerful and against those whom Jesus called his sisters and brothers. The church has been a bulwark of institutions of slavery and racism that others recognize as contrary to the way of the Galilean. In the majority of instances, the church continues to bar the door to women who would serve on an equal footing with men, despite the evidence from the Gospels of the opposite attitude on the part of Jesus.

The tragic history of the church offers plenty of examples of the church finding itself in clear opposition to the way of Jesus as that way is attested in the Gospels. But the marginalization and denigration of persons who engage in same-sex sexual relationships in the church is especially ironic, given the clear tendency of the Gospel of John to suggest that Jesus was himself involved in an analogous relationship.

Gay, lesbian, and bisexual Christians may find a certain validation in the suggestion that Jesus may well have experienced the sort of attraction and desire and delight that they also find to be a part of their experience, especially when they have known their own experience to be invalidated and denigrated by the church itself. But gay, lesbian, bisexual, or trans-gendered Christians need not suppose that Jesus was gay in order to find in him a sympathetic champion. After all, despite the racist and slave hold-ing ideology through which Jesus was presented to African Americans, many of them still recognized in Jesus an ally in the struggle against dehu-manization. The clear tendency of the Gospels' portrait of Jesus is to give aid and comfort to those who struggle against injustice and victimization, even when this injustice and victimization is sanctioned by the official inter-preters of the Jesus tradition. Thus, that many gays and lesbians have been drawn to the figure of Jesus should not be too surprising, even given the painful experiences of many such people within the churches that claim to worship and follow him. Still, many gays and lesbians have been persuaded by the indifference and faintheartedness of "liberal" Christians as well as by the homophobic rhetoric of "conservative" Christians that Christianity is hostile to their own quest for justice and love. The reading I have pro-posed of the relationship between Jesus and the man he loved may open the way to a reconsideration of Jesus and the "good news" concerning him, even if not of Christianity as a whole.

But is the reading of the Gospel of John that I have proposed "good news" only for gay and lesbian Christians? Or does it in fact also helpfully illumine our existence regardless of our sexual orientation? I believe that in important respects the reading of the text that I have proposed casts an important light on the relational life of all people, regardless of sexual orientation or preference.

Thus we ask: Is there any significance beyond the possibility of historical remembrance that can be assigned to the presentation of Jesus as the lover of a beloved in this text? At first glance certain difficulties may appear.

First, we may suppose an inappropriateness for one who is said to be the lover of all to be made out to be in this intimate sense the lover also of one in particular. Is Jesus as lover of one in particular at odds with Jesus as lover of all? That issue confronts us here.

Another issue deals not with the character of love (as general and particular) but with the possibility of a specifically sexual love. Does this possibility not invalidate the "purity" of the love we deem appropriate for one who manifests the divine love? Even if a particular affection should not be incompatible with the divine love, should a love that does not rule out in principle the expression of this love as specifically sexual be thought of as theologically suspect?

But even if we find good reasons for not shrinking from attributing sexuality as such to the one who is claimed to embody the divine love, surely the presentation of this relationship as involving a same-sex relationship is inappropriate. If Jesus were to be portrayed as having what we call a sex life, surely this activity might better take the form of a more conventional relationship. And wouldn't the suggestion of a same-sex relationship serve to marginalize the (presumed) heterosexual majority? Feminist theologians have asked the question: Can a male Christ save women? We might ask as well: Can a gay Christ save "straights"?

We deal with such issues here in an attempt to discover the significance that a theological reflection can find in the suggestion that Jesus was a lover and, in particular, the lover of another male. I maintain that this suggestion actually serves to illumine the significance of Jesus for all followers, whatever their relational or sexual orientation.

Love as General and Particular

We begin with the more general question concerning the relation between loving all and loving one in particular.

In another connection, we have to explore one of the ways in which the Gospel traditions do make clear that Jesus rules out explicitly one sort of affectional particularity. Jesus denies that the members of his family — his mother, brothers, and sisters — have, by virtue of kinship, any special claim to relationship with him, any special privilege. Ironically, the one sort of affectional preference that traditional piety claims for Jesus (his special relationship with his mother) is ruled out by Jesus himself. For Jesus, no relationships are, so to say, ex officio. The only relationships are those of adoption and of shared commitment. People who do as he does — announce and enact the coming of the divine reign — are truly his "mother, brothers and sisters."

But if Jesus' own "flesh and blood," his birth-kin, have no special claim on him, does this outlook not hold all the more for the possibility of the kind of preference entailed by loving one person differently from all others? Or does this stance not preclude the sort of preferential option that is characteristic of lovers, of husbands and wives, even of best friends?

A strong tradition in the church maintains that a love that seeks to make itself available to all, that seeks the good of the neighbor, which loves the neighbor indiscriminately and even loves the enemy, is incompatible with a love for just one. The vocation of celibacy is often explained that way. The one who takes this vow does so in order to be free to love all equally. What is at stake is not sexuality in the first instance but "preference."

Should one who represents the divine love be free of even the suspicion of preference, of choosing to love one above all others?

Now in a certain sense, this reflection corresponds with what we in fact find in the Gospel of John. Whatever Jesus' relation may be to the beloved, the relationship is not put forward as something that limits Jesus' love for the others. Instruction is given equally to all. Jesus abases himself to wash everyone's feet. He dies for the sake of all equally. The commission, "As the Father sent me so I send you," is given to all the disciples.

Jesus' love for all is certainly given expression in the text. But precisely in that connection is it also intimated that Jesus loved one of the disciples in a special way.

We notice that no motive is given for this love. No mention is made of any special traits of the beloved. He is simply the beloved. We are not told he is handsome, courageous, bright, remarkable for his devotion to Jesus. Nothing of the kind. He is loved because...he is the beloved.

Our experience of loving often occurs in precisely this way. Love itself — falling in love, being in love — is always in a sense inexplicable by reference to something else. Usually one could imagine a more comely "other," a more courageous or wise or virtuous "other." But one "falls for" or is "in love with" this particular beloved.

Is this characteristic of love — that it is adventitious and particular — incompatible with the love that loves all humanity, with the love that disregards its own self-interest and its own self-preservation in order to love all equally?

Is it not precisely in this way, as the gratuitous choosing of or being chosen by an other, that the most characteristic feature of love comes to expression? Is this not what in the Bible is thematized as grace? Precisely this arbitrary, and thus gracious, election is said to underlie the existence of Israel as the "chosen people." At its best moments, Israel knew that being thus chosen did not mean that Israel had some special virtue or special privilege. At its best, Israel knew that it was simply one of the peoples of the earth, neither more strong nor more good, nor in any other way more deserving. Israel was simply chosen. And this choice as the later prophets tried to make clear was to be the very instrument of Yahweh's gracious love for all the nations of the earth. Even at this level of collective election the choice of one was by no means regarded always as precluding love for all.

If the settling upon one in particular as the object of one's affections is something central to being human, then such action should not be understood as contrary to being divine. For the human as human has no other vocation than to represent the divine, as both Genesis and John make clear.

That Jesus is represented as having one beloved is then not incompatible with the representation of Jesus as loving either the world or the community. Rather, it serves instead as the concrete representation of the very character of love, which is, in some ways, always gratuitous.

The representation of Jesus as having a beloved then serves to make clear that he is the expression of divine love and the model for a transformed human love. Jesus' love of the beloved by no means severs the equality of the fellowship of his love. The beloved is not loved simply "more" nor does his status as beloved interfere with the equality of the community. On the other hand, the relationship to the community and indeed to the world does not prevent Jesus also from loving one, from being a lover, from this most human form of love.[1]

The Flesh

But even if we begin to see how a special friendship does not contradict the character of love for all but rather serves to clarify it and deepen it,

---

1. This argument is precisely anticipated by Aelred (see the previous chapter) in his reflections on the character of friendship for which Jesus and his beloved (as well as David and Jonathan) serve as models. And Aelred is at some pains to demonstrate the ways in which it is possible to work out the relationship between special friendship and general friendship in the daily life of the monastery. *Spiritual Friendship* 3.111–27, pp. 123–29.

we may still shrink from being able to affirm that this special friendship could also be or be interpreted as being a sexual friendship.

Even if we could suppose, for example, that Jesus had a lover (let us suppose Mary Magdalene in order to make clear that we are concerned here with sexuality and not yet with "homosexuality"), still we might be inclined to imagine that this could not be a consummated relationship.

Is sexual expression as such incompatible with the most fundamental character of love? Or is it instead the clearest expression of love among human beings called to represent the love of God?

Again much in the Christian tradition articulates a suspicion of sexuality itself, calling not only for celibacy but even more for chastity. Can a case be made for the opposite view, a case that takes into account some of the themes of the Gospel of John? We are reminded in the beginning of this text that the one who is Jesus is also the one who is thought of as involved in the act of creation at the beginning of all things. It is thus that it is said that he comes to his own. Is not sexuality a part of that which is created? Is it only a part of fallen nature, or is it instead known to be part of the creature created by and for love?

And if the creative word does not remain separated from the creature in transcendent splendor but actually becomes flesh then must this not entail the created flesh, inclusive of the sexuality appropriate to the creature created by and for love?

Could John really imagine an incarnation that took on flesh without taking on the sexuality represented as integral to that creature according to Genesis 1 and 2? Would this really be incarnation? Would this even be embodiment?

I am not maintaining that the incarnate one must have sex in order to be human or flesh. I am only saying that sexuality cannot be precluded in principle without vitiating the incarnation. The only way sexuality could be excluded in principle without eliminating the incarnation is to adopt an ascetic ethic. But neither John, nor the other Gospels, nor any other text of the New Testament can accept this ethic. They all seem resolutely opposed to asceticism, for they know that asceticism conceals the hatred of the real, of the human, and of the flesh — and thus a hatred of the creator and even a hatred of the human as such. Despite all their differences, the Gospels are united in maintaining that the good news concerns the affirmation of life, of the life of the creature created by God, and that this creature — not some imaginary substitute — is loved by God, redeemed by God, and made whole by God.

Sexuality, then, should not be ruled out in the presentation of Jesus as the incarnate word of God, as the expression of the perfecting of human love under the conditions of human being.[2]

Same Sex

But even if we could assign some theological significance to the depiction of Jesus as being the lover of a beloved in which relationship sexual intimacy is not ruled out but even suggested through physical intimacy and the portrayal of a "marriage-like" relationship, still we might suppose that the depiction of this relationship as homoerotic is inappropriate.

Again some representatives of the Christian tradition have regarded same-sex erotic relationships as being especially out of the question. We deal with some of these perspectives in another connection later. We inquire whether anything supports the conventional view that sexual relations must be correlated with procreation or be in some other ways expressive or supportive of what are called traditional family values.

But here we only ask whether the presentation of Jesus as engaged in a presumably sexual relationship with another man that is, in some sense, unconventional has positive theological significance.

Not just any kind of unconventionality is at stake here. We are not concerned with the expression of an obsessive sexuality that is frequently understood as "fornication," nor are we concerned with the sort of sexuality that betrays one's commitment to another or which leads another person to abandon or betray a person to whom one had been previously chosen or bonded. This last is usually termed "adultery." The relationship depicted here is neither adultery nor, in the correct sense, fornication. The unconventionality here is of quite a different order.

While the love depicted here expresses loyalty and trust and intimacy and is in this respect like the love often associated with the love between husband and wife, Jesus' love for the disciple is nevertheless different from marital love. It is not conventionally "heterosexual" but unconventionally "homosexual."

---

2. Here, as elsewhere, erotophobia clearly works as a powerful ally of homophobia. The significance of a gay reading of these texts is that it confronts an erotophobia which distorts the life of Christians whether they are gay or straight. Thus the extent to which a gay reading opens the way to a confrontation and critique of this erotophobia benefits not only gay but also straight readers.

To see what may be at stake here, consider what would be the case if the relationship were conventional. In that case, Jesus would be portrayed as a kind of conventional "family man" who therefore embodied the conventional mores of his and all human tribes.

But the Gospel of John, like the other Gospels, represents Jesus as unconventional in every way. His very unconventionality serves to bring into question the theological-social assumptions of his contemporaries. Thus Jesus does not conform to the conventions of pious respectability. He does not observe the sabbath in ways marked by conventional piety. He does not exemplify the practices of piety: fasting, ablutions, and temple worship. He does not accept the conventions of biblical interpretation. Still less does he accept the conventional ways in which the pious and respectable separate themselves from the sinners. His eating and drinking are regarded as notorious; he associates only with the most disreputable elements: prostitutes and collaborators. He has no regard for his own ritual purity: freely touching lepers, corpses, menstruating women. Nor is he in the least careful of his reputation: he is called a Galilean, a Samaritan, a sinner, even "in league with Satan." Indeed his words and deeds seem to court these opinions of himself.

What is the significance of all this? Clearly a central aspect of the gospel is that Jesus appears precisely as one who overthrows the conventional structures of social life so as to establish a new social reality in which the values of justice and generosity and joy may come to expression.

Nikos Kazantzakis represented as the "last temptation" of Jesus precisely the allure of conventional domesticity. The temptation was to turn away from radical confrontation with social structures and, instead, to embrace the most basic of social structures: marriage and family life.

Part 3 examines the message and mission of Jesus and how central to them is the notion that the conventions of marriage and family life must be brought into question. After all, these institutions are basic to the perpetuation of the world as it is. But Jesus was concerned with the inauguration of a new world, a new and radically different social reality. Thus for Jesus to be depicted as giving expression to sexuality not in the sphere of marriage and family but in relation to a person of the same sex makes a certain sense.

However, leaving the matter here will not do. For not only is this relationship distinguished from relationships of heterosexual marriage; Jesus' relationship with the beloved disciple may positively illumine them. We find this anticipated in the medieval reflections of Aelred of Rievaulx, who regards the relationship between Jesus and his beloved as a kind of marriage and for this very reason is able to use it as a way of speaking about the appropriate relationship between male and female, husband and wife. To be sure, Aelred supposed that such relationships would be best lived out without sexual expression. The husband and wife though lawfully permitted to have sexual relationships might nevertheless abstain. But Jesus' relationship did not speak primarily to abstinence from sexual relations in the relationship between man and wife. Rather the importance of the relationship for Aelred was the embodiment of true friendship, in the expression of true mutuality. Hence he writes:

> How beautiful it is that the second human being was taken from the side of the first, so that nature might teach that human beings are equal and, as it were, collateral, and that there is in human affairs neither a superior nor an inferior, a characteristic of true friendship.[3]

Now it seems to me that the apparently rather quaint notion that the relationship between Jesus and his beloved or that between David and Jonathan (which Aelred also cites in the connection) might serve as a true pattern for relationships between the sexes is of great importance. In Aelred's day as in the first century (or the tenth century B.C.E.), the relationship between male and female was largely governed by economic necessity and by patriarchal control. Heterosexual relationships were hedged about by the rule of social and biological necessity. Same-sex relationships, on the other hand, have the potential of representing freedom and something like mutuality.

The emergence of the theme of courtly or romantic love about the time of Aelred usually found it necessary to speak even of heterosexual relationships that embodied this ideal as outside the bounds of marriage. Thus the emergence of the themes of mutual desire and delight usually had their place over against marriage in an adulterous relationship. The relationship between Arthur and Guinevere, in contrast to that between Lancelot and Guinevere, is perhaps the best-known example.

Through various transformations of this tradition, what we have come to regard as an ideal for heterosexual relationships — mutual desire and delight, mutual and faithful companionship and friendship — was possible under conditions of patriarchy primarily for same-sex relationships.

For this reason, Aelred uses the relationship of Jesus and his beloved, as well as the relationship between David and Jonathan, to point to a

---

3. *Spiritual Friendship* 1.57, p. 63.

mutuality in the relationships between persons of the opposite sex which was otherwise not thinkable or was thinkable only as adultery.

In our own time, this tradition of using same-sex relations to represent an ideal of mutuality for cross-sex relationships is continued in the use of Ruth's words to Naomi ("I will never leave you nor forsake you...") as a biblical text for cross-sex marriages!

The point of this reflection is not that same-sex relationships are always in fact more mutual or free or liberating than cross-sex relationships. The structuring of human relationships by the forces of self-interest, of violence, and violation is no respecter of sexual orientation. But same-sex affectional and sexual relations may serve to represent the domain of freedom and mutuality in ways that are in tension with the way in which these structures govern heterosexuality.

We know that in Greek and hellenistic worlds, same-sex relationships were in fact regarded as indicative of freedom and mutuality in ways denied to cross-sex relationships. This point is usually made in dialogues between those people who prefer same-sex and those who prefer cross-sex relationships. But in that literary tradition, these different structures were simply regarded as alternatives. What Aelred suggested at the outset of the tradition of courtly love was that same-sex relationships might actually serve as a model for cross-sex relationships — that, in modern terms, homosexuality might positively transform heterosexuality.

Thus the suggestion that Jesus is portrayed as having a same-sex relationship is not limited in significance to those who find themselves drawn to erotic relationships of this kind. Instead the suggestion anticipates an erotic relationship freed from the constraints of social, biological, and economic necessity and which is therefore capable of transforming heterosexual relationships as well.

In a subsequent section, we return to this theme when we attend to the ways in which the Gospels set Jesus over against the patriarchally determined institutions of marriage and family and the linking of sexuality to procreation. The critique of these institutions found in the Jesus tradition is consistent with the supposition that the relation between Jesus and his beloved may serve as a paradigm for a new sort of sexual relationship also between men and women that is freed from the constraints of heterosexism and patriarchy.

Part Two

THE JESUS TRADITION

WE HAVE SEEN THAT THE RELATIONSHIP between Jesus and the disciple he loved in the Gospel of John lends itself to a homoerotic interpretation. Does this mean that the Gospel of John is entirely idiosyncratic in this regard or are there other aspects of the Jesus tradition that also lend themselves to homoerotic interpretation? I argue that in a number of places as registered in the canonical Gospels (and closely related texts) the Jesus tradition points in the direction of a positive view of same-sex love. Even though we do not seem to have additional explicit references to "the disciple Jesus loved" in the canonical Gospels, we do have a number of episodes that point in the direction of a positive view of same-sex erotic relationships. This fact further substantiates the plausibility of the gay reading of the beloved disciple texts that I have proposed.

In this discussion I turn first to the Gospel of Mark together with the fragments of so-called "Secret Mark." Canonical Mark contains the episode of the naked youth in the garden of Gethsemane, while "Secret Mark" suggests another encounter between Jesus and the same or another "naked youth." While not possessing the clarity of the beloved disciple texts, these references do offer another perspective on a potentially homoerotic relationship in the Jesus tradition.

I then turn to the story in Matthew (and Luke) of the centurion's boyfriend, which strongly suggests that Jesus was open to the same-sex erotic relationships of others. This discussion places the case of the centurion within the framework of a wider tradition of Jesus' generally accepting attitude toward the sexually marginalized.

Among the sexually marginalized we also encounter the case of the eunuch. Here we look at a saying in Matthew regarding eunuchs and an episode narrated by Luke (in Acts) concerning an African eunuch. A discussion of eunuchs leads to the issue of gender role expectations and nonconformity. This review of the Jesus tradition concludes with texts, including two from the Gospel of Thomas, that seem to encourage gender nonconformity. The interpretation of these texts leads us again to the setting of the texts concerning the disciple Jesus loved.

The point of this review is to show that all the narrative texts that may be regarded as sources for traditions concerning Jesus contain elements that lend themselves to a gay-affirmative reading. Thus the reading I have proposed for the references to the beloved disciple in the Gospel of John do not stand alone. Indeed the representation by the author of the Fourth Gospel of Jesus as the lover of a beloved is only the most open declaration of a much wider phenomenon: all the monuments of the Jesus tradition in varying degrees depict him as sympathetic to same-sex erotic relationships.

Chapter 7

The Gospel of Mark

Mark is generally regarded as the earliest of the Gospels and as one of the bases for the Gospels of Matthew and Luke. Indeed, about 90 percent of Mark is incorporated into the Gospel of Matthew. Mark is written in a popular style, often brash in expression and breezy in tone. In the last century it has become clear that several distinct versions of this Gospel circulated in the first and second centuries. One of the most controversial discoveries of alternative versions of this Gospel was that of the so-called "Secret Gospel of Mark," which adds certain episodes to the narrative we have in the Bible.

In this chapter, I consider first two episodes in canonical or biblical Mark, giving attention to the encounter with the one known to tradition as the "rich young ruler" and to the curious episode of the nude youth in the garden of Gethsemane. I then turn to a consideration of Secret or Clementine Mark and to the episodes there which lend themselves to a homoerotic interpretation as well as to the suggestion of the existence of a Carpocratian Mark, which was, apparently, even more homoerotically explicit.

This examination and interpretation of Mark seeks to clarify that the earliest of the Gospels contains material which, when examined closely, is also suggestive of a homoerotic relationship in the traditions about Jesus. The review of Mark then serves as independent confirmation of what we discovered in the Gospel of John: the early transmitters of the Jesus tradition contended with the "dangerous memory" of Jesus as erotically attached to other men.

The Look of Love

One episode in the Gospel of Mark that has seldom been the subject of a "gay" reading of the New Testament, yet which does have certain

105

resonances with what we have found in the Gospel of John, is the account in Mark of the encounter between Jesus and the one known to tradition as "the rich young ruler." Recounting the story in full may be helpful.

> As he was setting out on a journey, a man ran up and knelt before him, and asked him, "Good teacher, what must I do to inherit eternal life?" Jesus said to him, "Why do you call me good? No one is good but God alone. You know the commandments: 'You shall not murder; You shall not commit adultery; You shall not steal; You shall not bear false witness; You shall not defraud; Honor your father and mother.'" He said, "Teacher, I have kept all these since my youth." Jesus, looking at him, loved him and said, "You lack one thing; go, sell what you own, and give the money to the poor, and you will have treasure in heaven; then come, follow me." When he heard this he was shocked and went away grieving, for he had many possessions. (Mark 10:17–22)

What has occasionally drawn the attention of a gay reading of this encounter is the notice that "Jesus...loved him." This is the only occasion in the Gospel of Mark when Jesus is said to love anyone. The impact of this episode is much diminished if it is read from the traditional perspective that Jesus loved everyone. But this perspective, though common in homiletical tradition, cannot be derived from the Gospel of Mark where Jesus is depicted as extraordinarily abrupt, often rude, and usually irritated. In the context of *this* narrative, the assertion that Jesus loved this (or any) individual is quite startling. Recall, too, that this passage is the only place in the canonical Gospels outside the Gospel of John where Jesus is said to love anyone!

Now one could still dismiss the homoerotic reading of this episode with the observation that Jesus' love for this person appears at first sight to be motivated by the latter's assertion that he has kept all the commandments enumerated by Jesus from his youth (*neotatos*). In this view, the love of Jesus is provoked by the keeping of the commandments. Such a reading would produce theological problems, of course (Jesus loves those who keep the law rather than those who don't), and would seem to contradict the picture from the same narrative of Jesus as one who especially seeks out those whom the upholders of the law regard as sinners (Mark 2:15–17).

Another possibility, more palatable theologically and defensible exegetically, is to suppose that what provokes Jesus' love here is that one who has kept the law nevertheless comes to Jesus sensing the need for something more in order to "inherit eternal life." This aspect, together with the urgency of the request (running, kneeling), may be seen as exemplifying the humility and yearning that Jesus does not otherwise encounter among those people who keep the commandments.

This interpretation is certainly attractive, but the text itself has an odd way of pointing in another direction as well. The text interjects another element between the exemplary character of the petitioner and Jesus' love. This additional element is the relatively rare verb *emblepein,* translated here as "looking." What is this gaze that is interposed here between the saying of the petitioner and the love of Jesus? The verb occurs in two other contexts in Mark. First in 8:25, the verb appears in the story of the healing of blindness which at first does not succeed ("I see men as walking trees") and requires a second application of Jesus' healing power, after which the man "*looked intently* and his sight was restored." In the second occurrence, a woman who notices Peter outside the place where Jesus is on trial "*stared at* him [Peter]" (Mark 14:25) and thereby recognizes him as one of Jesus' companions.

As the translation in these other contexts suggests, what the verb indicates is an extraordinarily concentrated or focused gaze. This looking is not casual, but rather an intense beholding. Moreover, this gaze by no means looks "behind appearances" but precisely sees what is visible. Thus the woman recognizes Peter's face as the face of one who accompanied Jesus, and the healed blind man is now able to distinguish people from trees. Jesus is here not looking "into the heart" of the petitioner but rather directly at him, at his appearance, and this gaze serves as the proximate cause for the extraordinary love of Jesus. Here the good character of the petitioner serves as the precondition rather than as the sufficient cause of the love that ensues.

An erotic reading of this episode then would recognize in this gaze the beholding which awakens desire and anticipates delight.[1] This response to the combination of exemplary character and physical appearance would

---

1. The supposition that eros enters through the eyes was one of the standard conventions of hellenistic romance novels. Thus in Achilles Tatius's *Leucippe and Clitophon:* "It is through the eyes that Love's wound passes" (1.4 [p. 175]). The writer can even suppose that the exchange of visual contact "is a kind of copulation at a distance" (1.9 [p. 183]) and, in the same passage, speaks of the eyes as "ambassadors of love." Similarly Heliodorus in *An Ethiopian Story* speaks of "the genesis of love which originates from visually perceived objects, which, if you will excuse the metaphor, shoot arrows of passion, swifter than the wind, into the soul by means of the eyes" (3.7 [p. 416]). The page references are to *Collected Ancient Greek Novels,* ed. B. P. Reardon (Berkeley: University of California Press, 1989).

be entirely consistent with the literary traditions of same-sex eroticism in the Greek and hellenistic worlds where inward and outward, moral and physical beauty were supposed to coincide in the beloved.[2]

To say that Jesus' love is provoked by the conjunction of moral and physical beauty is not to say that Jesus is committed only to those who exhibit these characteristics. The text makes clear his commitment to all who need and seek his help. The attachment to this person is by no means a model of his attachment to all persons in need. Indeed the homoerotic character of this attraction is precisely what distinguishes it from other responses to people in the Gospel. Put another way, the homoerotic interpretation of this episode is virtually required if we are to account for the singularity of Jesus' love for just this person in the Gospel of Mark. Insofar as this attachment is homoerotic, Jesus' relationships either to the poor who come to him for help, or to the understudies (disciples) who accompany him, are not put in question.

To be sure, Mark's narrative does not insist on a recognition of this gaze as homoerotic in character. But the episode is sufficiently suggestive that one is entitled to ask: if the object of this intense gaze and the exceptional love were identified by the narrator as female, would the reader more readily recognize the erotic character of the encounter? I am confident that at least many readers would wonder, and many more would do so were it not for the erotophobia with which tradition blinkers our reading of the New Testament.

But the text indicates another male as the object of this intense gaze and this unique love. Thus to the erotophobic narrowing of vision is added homophobia, so that the possibility of recognition is all but foreclosed. But neither this erotophobic blinkering nor this homophobic blinding could reasonably be attributed to Mark's gentile readers of the first century.

By itself we might pass over this episode without giving it a second look, or with only a raised eyebrow. But the far more explicit indication of Jesus' love for another man in the Gospel of John makes it seem apparent that some of those who passed on the traditions concerning Jesus were aware of same-sex erotic attachment in this tradition.

We may note also certain vicissitudes in the rewriting of this episode in the records of the first century. I noted at the outset that the one who comes to Jesus here is known to tradition as the "rich young ruler." However, in the Gospel of Mark we are not given this information concerning the petitioner. All we are told is that he had "many possessions." Other elements

---

2. See, for example, Plato's *Symposium* 206b.

of description are supplied from the versions of this episode found in Matthew and Luke. Matthew 19:20 tells us that he was a youth (*neaniskos*). Luke does not say that he was young but does tell us that he was a "ruler" (18:18) and that he was "very rich" (18:23).

Perhaps most interesting is that Luke and Matthew each omit both the intense gaze and the saying that Jesus loved him! That both are omitted adds to the impression that the gaze and the love are connected to one another as I have suggested.

The traditional telling of the story then combines elements from Matthew (young) and Luke (ruler and rich) while agreeing with both of them in omitting Mark's troubling gaze and startling love. That is, the homoerotic undertone of the story is eliminated in its retelling. Already we can see the eyes of tradition closing themselves against the homoerotic elements of the Jesus tradition. Only if we follow Mark's stage instructions and "look intently" do we succeed in overcoming this blindness.

The Nude Youth in the Garden

In our discussion of the hidden history of a gay-positive reading of the relationship between Jesus and the disciple he loved, we considered the views of Jeremy Bentham, which in significant respects anticipate my own reading of that relationship. In his work on Jesus, Bentham himself indicated another incident in the Jesus tradition that suggested to him a homosexual relationship, or at least the inclusion of something like a gay interest. The incident is that of the youth who escapes naked from Gethsemane after the arrest of Jesus, as briefly described in the Gospel of Mark. In order to examine the scene more closely, I quote the text in full:

> And they all forsook him and fled.
> And a youth (*neaniskos*) accompanied him, clothed in a linen cloth (*sindona*) over his nudity (*gymnou*). And they seized him. And he, leaving the linen cloth (*sindona*), fled nude (*gymnos*). (Mark 14: 50–52)

Bentham's own suggestion regarding this youth is that he was a *cinaedus* (*kinaidos*) or boy prostitute.[3] What are we to make of Bentham's suggestion? In 1817, Bentham makes inexact reference to

---

3. As reported by Louis Crompton, *Byron and Greek Love: Homophobia in Nineteenth-Century England* (Berkeley: University of California Press, 1985), 280–83.

a terse paragraph in the *Monthly Magazine,* in which an anonymous writer, commenting on the odd grammar of the King James translation [of Mark 14:51–52], referred cryptically to the passage as the "episode of the cinaedus" (i.e., boy prostitute). Now Bentham recalls and, in effect, endorses this theory. He prefers the translation "stripling" as closer to the Greek than "young man" and suggests that the boy may have been a "rival or a candidate for the situation of rival to the Apostle" (i.e., to John). Bentham argues that the passage is intelligible only if the boy is indeed a "cinaedus" and the "loose attire," the badge of his profession. Bentham interprets the *sindona* or "linen" that the stripling wore as a fair and costly garment and thinks that the men who laid hands on him and it regarded both the boy and the cloth as a prize. . . . [4]

Here the accent falls on the makeshift covering (*sindona*) that both hides and discloses the nudity (*gymnos*) of the youth. The *sindona* is not properly clothing at all but a kind of sheet. It is a piece of linen that is wrapped about, or draped over, the body. In the Gospel of Mark it is used also to wrap the corpse (*ptoma*) of Jesus (15:46) prior to burial.

The suggestion of Bentham's correspondent appears to rely on a connection between the *sindona* and the profession of the *cinaedus* or *kinaidos.* In this case, the young male prostitute would be informally wrapped in a *sindona.* The very wrapping of the *gymnou* in this informal way is a sort of display that is meant to entice the would-be "john."

Read in this way, the *sindona* that covers while drawing attention to the nudity of the youth and which is subsequently left behind, exposing the nudity of the youth to the readers' gaze, not only suggests that the youth is the object of homoerotic attention but also serves to place the youth in relation to the institution of prostitution, which was one of the principal ways in which homoeroticism was legalized and institutionalized in the Roman Empire. So important was this institution that male prostitutes had their own public holiday and the taxes derived from brothels were a significant source of revenue even for the Christian emperors of the later empire.[5] However, I have been unable to substantiate any regular association between wearing a *sindona* and being a prostitute or *cinaedus.* Unless that association can be demonstrated, the suggestion of Bentham's

---

4. Ibid., 281.

5. John Boswell, *Christianity, Social Tolerance, and Homosexuality: Gay People in Western Europe from the Beginning of the Christian Era to the Fourteenth Century* (Chicago: University of Chicago Press, 1980), 77.

source must be suspended. But this still leaves Bentham's suggestion that the text solicits a homoerotic interpretation.

What are we to make of Bentham's suggestion? First, a return to the story from Mark may be useful. This incident is one of the few in Mark that are not reported in other Gospels.[6] The oddity of the episode together with the fact that it is recounted only in Mark has led many commentators, from rather early in the church tradition, to suppose that the incident is recounted as a way of placing the author (allegedly John Mark) in the narrative. Modern exegetes no longer accept this suggestion but remain puzzled by the episode.

The episode is puzzling because it associates an unnamed youth very closely with Jesus. Alone among Jesus' followers, he is said to accompany Jesus even after Jesus is seized by the mob sent by the rulers of Jerusalem. Unlike the others, he escapes not before Jesus is captured but only after he is subjected to something like the same fate as Jesus.

Not only is this youth (or young adult)[7] closely associated with Jesus and distinguished from Jesus' other followers in his apparent courage, the description draws particular attention to his nudity. The narrative, in effect, undresses him even before the mob does by referring to his nudity first as covered and then as uncovered. The term for nudity here is *gymnos,* which refers not simply to body (*soma*) or flesh (*sarx*) but to the nudity that gave its name to the gymnasium (or nuditorium) where hellenized youth honed and displayed their athletic prowess in the nude. In classical Greece and in the subsequent hellenistic world, the gymnasium is the privileged site for homoeroticism and for the making of pederastic liaisons. The nudity (*gymnou*) of the youth (*neaniskos*) is the focal point of the homoerotic gaze of men.

None of this could have been lost on Mark's hellenistic, gentile readers.[8] Moreover we may be sure that it would have scandalized Mark's more conservative Jewish readers. The allusion to *gymnos* and hence to

---

6. Recall that Matthew contains something like 90 percent of the Gospel of Mark.

7. Eva Cantarella shows that, at least in classical Greece, the term *neaniskos* refers to a young adult male, generally from eighteen to twenty-five or even thirty years of age. Cantarella, *Bisexuality in the Ancient World* (New Haven: Yale University Press, 1992), 28–48.

8. Thus Cicero, writing in Latin, and Plutarch, writing in Greek, could both maintain that the love of youths was created and disseminated through the institution of the gymnasium. Cicero's comments are cited by Cantarella in *Bisexuality in the Ancient World*, 97. Plutarch's view is found in his *Dialogue on Love (Erotikos)*, 751F. More recently, William Armstrong Percy has elaborated extensive grounds for the association of pederasty and the gymnasium in *Pederasty and Pedagogy in Archaic Greece* (Champaign-Urbana: University of Illinois Press, 1996), 98–116.

the gymnasium is a clear way of associating this youth with the temptations of hellenistic culture. In 1 Maccabees we are told that the beginning of the policy of hellenization under the notorious Antiochus Epiphanes (167–164 B.C.E.) was the desire of many in Jerusalem to be allowed to build a gymnasium as a symbol of acceptance of hellenistic culture:

> In those days lawless men came forth from Israel, and misled many, saying, "let us go and make a covenant with the gentiles.... " This proposal pleased them, and some of the people eagerly went to the king [Antiochus Epiphanes]. He authorized them to observe the customs of the gentiles. So they built a gymnasium in Jerusalem, according to the gentile custom, and removed the marks of circumcision, and abandoned the holy covenant. They joined with the Gentiles and sold themselves to do evil. (1 Macc. 1:11–15)

This account is elaborated upon in 2 Maccabees in which the political scheming of Jason leads to the establishment of the gymnasium:

> In addition to this he promised to pay one hundred and fifty [talents] if permission were given to establish by his authority a gymnasium and a body of youth for it, and to enroll the men of Jerusalem as citizens of Antioch. When the king assented and Jason came to office, he at once shifted his countrymen over to the Greek way of life.... For with alacrity he founded a gymnasium right under the citadel, and he induced the noblest of the young men to wear the Greek hat. (2 Macc. 4:9–10, 12)

The establishment of a gymnasium in Jerusalem was one of the outrages perpetrated by Jews who sought to come to terms with the ascendancy of hellenistic culture — an outrage because it symbolized the cult of the nude youth. The overtones could scarcely have been welcome to more conservative upholders of Jewish tradition, whose representatives here seize Jesus and the nude youth.[9]

Does the nude youth then represent the hellenized Jews who adopt the mores of the pederastic culture so despised by the heirs of the Maccabean revolt? And does he then also represent precisely those hellenized Jews who

---

9. We may also note that the nudity of those who participated in the gymnasium made them acutely aware of the difference in the appearance of their penises owing to circumcision. Thus they seek to undo circumcision ("removed the marks of circumcision") in such a way as to conform more clearly to Greek concepts of bodily beauty (1 Macc. 1:15a). Similarly the disciples of Jesus in Mark are accused of abandoning the distinctive customs of Judaism in such a way that they seem to become Gentiles. (Mark 2:18 on fasting; Mark 2:28 on Sabbath observance; Mark 7:2ff on ritual washing.)

ultimately come to accept and announce the gospel concerning Jesus? Here we should recall that a *neaniskos* is encountered at the tomb of Jesus when the women come to anoint Jesus' corpse. Instead of the corpse they find a *neaniskos* "clothed in a white robe" (16:5) who announces the gospel concerning the resurrection of the crucified (16:6–7).

Now the nudity of this youth may be meant to suggest to the reader the rite of baptism which, at least in some places in the third century, involved stripping off the clothes of those who are to be baptized, their entering naked into the water and their being clothed in white as they emerge from the waters. This possibility exists, even though certain difficulties must be addressed. First, the Gospel of Mark does not interest itself in ritual baptism. The only baptism with which it is concerned is that of shared martyrdom with Jesus. Thus the martyrdom of Jesus is anticipated in Jesus' remarks to James and John about being baptized with his baptism or drinking from the cup from which he drinks (Mark 10:38–39). Both actions point not to sacramental acts but to martyrdom. The youth in the Garden does, at least in a token way, share in the fate of Jesus even though he escapes, and the youth at the tomb is found in the place of the crucified. So long as we are aware that Mark is interested in martyrdom rather than cultic baptism, we might interpret the episode concerning the nude youth in these terms. But why then, if Mark emphasizes martyrdom as the meaning of baptism, should Mark use the term *gymnos* rather than, for example, *soma*, as Paul does in speaking of baptism? Why is the emphasis here placed on nudity?

The other issue to be addressed here has to do with the origin of the custom of naked baptism. We know from Hippolytus that this custom was practiced in the third century.[10] But do we know about the first century? Do we have good reason to suppose that nudity was associated with ritual baptism 150 years before Hippolytus (ca. 235) of Rome?[11]

If the baptismal practices cannot be established, then we are left with an apparent allusion to the typical recipient of homoerotic attention (the nude youth) in hellenistic pederastic culture at a decisive moment in the passion of Jesus, and with the suggestion of a particularly close relationship between Jesus and this youth.

This scene rather precisely parallels the situation of the disciple Jesus loved in the Gospel of John. He too is introduced within the structure of

---

10. *Apostolic Tradition* 21.3, "And they shall put off their clothes" [for baptism], and 21.11, "And let them stand in the water naked." See *The Treatise on The Apostolic Tradition of St. Hippolytus of Rome*, ed. Gregory Dix and Henry Chadwick (London: SPCK, 1968), 33–35.
11. Clement appears to have been unaware of this practice. See n. 21 below.

the passion narrative. In John he is at the cross; in Mark the youth is nearly arrested with Jesus. And in both cases he is described in ways that suggest homoerotic attachment within the world of hellenistic pederastic culture. Of course, in canonical Mark this figure is present far more "fleetingly" and allusively than in the more intimate account of John. This variation may have to do with the quite different audience of the two works; after all, Mark is a quasi-public account whereas John was apparently written for a more close knit company of readers.

In the text of the Gospel of Mark we seem to have two allusions to homoerotic elements in the traditions concerning Jesus. But as the text stands, these episodes seem unrelated to one another. They do no more than offer partial echoes of the material we have previously encountered in the Gospel of John.

Secret Mark: The Nude Youth in the House

The brief episodes in the Gospel of Mark, despite the tantalizing clues they afford, may seem too tenuous to some readers to permit any definite conclusion regarding their meaning. Indeed they are passed over in silence by virtually all contemporary attempts to provide a gay reading of the New Testament. However, the text of so-called "Secret Mark" has at least been alluded to in this connection.[12]

Morton Smith discovered the material called "Secret Mark" in an eighteenth-century copy of a previously unknown letter of Clement of Alexandria (ca. 200 C.E.) found in 1958 in the Orthodox monastery of Mar Saba outside Jerusalem. Subsequently Smith published the letter together with extensive analysis and commentary. Although the text has been the subject of intense scholarly debate, many scholars (including those of the Jesus Seminar), take it to be authentic and even to represent an earlier version of the Gospel of Mark than the one that is found in the New Testament. Scholars have long known that the Gospel of Mark was circulated in several different versions. For example, the earlier translations of the Gospel of Mark had the so-called long ending after 16:8, adding verses 9–20. However, other versions of the Gospel of Mark were found that had a two-verse ending (following verse 8), and the oldest and most reliable manuscripts were found to end with verse 8. Thus, most contemporary translations end with verse 8 and add the alternative versions

---

12. See, for example, Tom Horner, *Jonathan Loved David: Homosexuality in Biblical Times* (Philadelphia: Westminster Press, 1978), 118–21; and Robert Williams, *Just As I Am* (New York: HarperCollins, 1992), 118ff.

(short ending and long ending) as footnotes. Clearly we have to contend with three different versions of the conclusion of Mark's Gospel. But this letter of Clement suggests the existence of at least two new versions of this Gospel distinguished not by the endings but by the presence of provocative material regarding a relationship between Jesus and a nude youth (*neaniskos*).

The letter of Clement is written to warn its reader against yet another version of the Gospel of Mark that includes some especially scandalous material concerning this youth and Jesus' relationship to him. This other version is attributed by Clement to the Carpocratians, a group of Christians who seem to have rejected the growing asceticism and even erotophobia of mainline or catholic Christianity and who were consequently denounced for their libertine views and practices.[13]

Clement admits that in Alexandria they use a version of Mark that contains more material concerning this youth than is commonly known, and that this version is used in esoteric instruction of those "who are being perfected." But it does not include all the material that Clement's correspondent has been shown, and certainly not the "shameless lies" that the Carpocratians presumably have introduced into the text. In order to eliminate the pornographic parts, Clement goes on to indicate what is in the text as he knows it. This is the material:

> And they came into Bethany, and a certain woman, whose brother had died, was there. And, coming, she prostrated herself before Jesus and says to him, "Son of David, have mercy upon me." But the disciples rebuked her. And Jesus, being angered, went off with her into the garden where the tomb was, and straightaway a great cry was heard from the tomb. And going near Jesus rolled away a stone from the door of the tomb. And straightaway, going in where the youth was, he stretched forth his hand and raised him, seizing his hand. But the youth, looking upon him, loved him and began to beseech him that he might be with him. And going out of the tomb they came into the house of the youth, for he was rich. And after six days Jesus told him what he was to do and in the evening the youth comes to him, wearing a linen cloth over [his] naked [body]. And he remained with him that night, for Jesus taught him the mystery of

---

13. See Morton Smith, *Clement of Alexandria and a Secret Gospel of Mark* (Cambridge, Mass.: Harvard University Press, 1973), 266–78, for a discussion of the Carpocratians. Also see *Alexandrian Christianity*, ed. Henry Chadwick, Library of Christian Classics (Philadelphia: Westminster Press, 1954), 24–29.

the kingdom of God. And thence, arising, he returned to the other side of the Jordan.

After these [words] follows the text, "And James and John come to him," and all that section. But "naked [man] with naked [man]" and the other things about which you wrote are not found.

And after the [words], "and he comes into Jericho," [the secret gospel] adds only "And the sister of the youth whom Jesus loved and his mother and Salome were there, and Jesus did not receive them."[14]

We may first note the connection between the one who comes to Jesus seeking to inherit eternal life and the youth whom Jesus raises. The notice in Clementine Mark that "he was rich" links the resurrected youth to the one who went away sad "because he had many possessions."

We should also note that the episode of resurrection has yet another terminological link to the story of the one who sought to inherit eternal life. The same phrase that arrested our attention in that narrative — "looking intently at him, loved him" — is found here also in the resurrection narrative. But here the youth gazes intently (*emblepein*) at Jesus and loves him rather than the other way around.

The youth who is raised then returns the gaze and the love that in the immediately preceding narrative Jesus had directed toward his petitioner. In Clementine Mark, these two gazes are interrupted only by didactic material that follows from the theme of possessions introduced by the encounter with the one who went away sadly (v. 22). Thus verses 23–31 deal directly with possessions while verses 32–34 deal with the fate of the one who will be rejected by religious authorities and handed over to the State (the passion prediction) and subsequently be raised (10:34). In Clementine Mark this passage is immediately followed by the resurrection of the youth. Thus the two encounters follow one another in close proximity. The admiring gaze of Jesus and the grateful gaze of the youth answer one another. Jesus' love is now answered by the love of the one who had had possessions but who now has tasted death and the loss of everything, and has been restored to life beyond death by the one from whom he had sought the way to inherit eternal life, life beyond death.

In Clementine Mark the account of the resurrection is followed by the account of the further relationship between Jesus and the youth.

---

14. Morton Smith, *The Secret Gospel: The Discovery and Interpretation of the Secret Gospel According to Mark* (New York: Harper & Row, 1973), 16–17.

But the youth, looking upon him, loved him and began to beseech him that he might be with him. And going out of the tomb they came into the house of the youth, for he was rich. And after six days Jesus told him what he was to do and in the evening the youth comes to him, wearing a linen cloth over [his] naked [body]. And he remained with him that night, for Jesus taught him the mystery of the kingdom of God. And thence, arising, he returned to the other side of the Jordan.

This episode connects the story of the one who is raised to the story of the nude youth in the garden that we found in canonical Mark: "the youth (*neaniskos*) comes to him wearing a linen cloth (*sindona*) over his nudity (*gymnos*)." The three key terms, *neaniskos, gymnos,* and *sindona,* which we noted in the canonical account, are here in a single phrase. Clement's version of the Gospel of Mark then gives to the nude youth in Gethsemane a prehistory as one who was taught "the mystery of the reign of God" alone with Jesus at night while his nudity was draped in a linen wrap. The location (outside of Bethany) and the timing (at night) correspond exactly to the subsequent episode in Gethsemane.

If anything, the homoerotic elements are even more pronounced in the version of Mark preserved in Alexandria according to Clement. For the love which has now become mutual between Jesus and the youth results both in Jesus going home with the youth and the subsequent coming of the youth to Jesus at night. In this latter encounter the reader is pointed to the nudity of the youth draped by the *sindona.* The homoerotic aspect that we noted in the canonical story seems even more clear here.

Moreover the episode in the garden now acquires a greater plausibility: the loyalty of the youth to Jesus that results in his being arrested with Jesus is grounded in the singular attachment that has grown between him and Jesus. The intimacy of their relationship serves to explain the loyalty exhibited at the scene of Jesus' arrest. This loyalty between homoerotically attached friends was a staple of pederastic romance, at least in its idealized literary expressions. It was already inscribed in the homoerotic interpretation of the relationship between Achilles and Patroclus that had become a commonplace of hellenistic literature.[15]

According to the letter of Clement, another episode is excluded from canonical Mark but was known in Alexandria:

---

15. We should also note that Bentham's suggestion of an allusion to the institution of prostitution would be excluded if the incident of the youth in the garden were read in connection with the material in Secret Mark.

And after the [words], "and he comes into Jericho," [the secret gospel] adds only "And the sister of the youth whom Jesus loved and his mother and Salome were there, and Jesus did not receive them."

This passage is separated from the earlier material concerning this youth (his resurrection and his instruction) only by the issue raised by James and John concerning places of honor in the reign of God. In this brief episode, we are told only that the sister of the youth who had implored Jesus to help her dead brother now comes to find Jesus in Jericho where she is accompanied by "his mother and Salome." Deciding whether we are to assign this mother to Jesus or to the youth is difficult, but it seems plausible to suppose that Jesus' mother is meant since the sister has already acted on behalf of the youth as though there were no mother to seek help and because we have a similar episode concerning Jesus' mother in the Gospel of Mark (3:31–35). We are not told why "Jesus refused to see them," but Jesus' repudiation of family ties is well established in canonical Mark.[16]

In any case the sister appears to have followed Jesus and the youth to Jericho. That the youth is with Jesus may be inferred from the petition of the youth to accompany Jesus (apparently ready now to meet the conditions earlier rejected of selling his possessions and distributing the proceeds to the poor) and the apparent granting of that petition by Jesus in first going to his home and then instructing him at night in the "mystery of the reign of God."

Does the sister follow Jesus in a vain attempt to reclaim her brother, who had been restored to life but now lost to her again through his companionship with Jesus? Or does she sense another danger here—that her youthful brother may share the fate of martyrdom that Jesus by his own words seems to be courting?

We may also pause over the presence of Salome with the youth's sister and (Jesus') mother in Jericho. Salome is mentioned in the canonical Gospels only in Mark, where she is present along with many other women at the execution of Jesus (Mark 15:40) and is one of the three witnesses to the empty tomb (Mark 16:1) and to the words of the mysterious youth (*neaniskos*) who is encountered there in place of Jesus.

---

16. For a full account, see part 3 below. We may also note Smith's view that Clement is here not quoting the text but offering a summary that eliminates a possible encounter and conversation between Jesus and Salome. Morton Smith, *Secret Gospel*, 69–70.

We do know however that, in the second century, Salome was identified as the source of the libertine interpretation of Christianity whose best-known second-century representative was Carpocrates.[17] Thus Salome, the alleged apostle of sexual freedom, is here connected to the youth Jesus loved.

Thus far we have been considering the version of the Gospel of Mark known to Clement and others in Alexandria, which was distinct from the publicly distributed version of the Gospel of Mark. But Clement's letter is written not to inform his reader about this version but to warn against another version that he assigned to the Carpocratians.

Carpocratian Mark

Clement only obliquely refers to the content of Carpocratian Mark, saying,

But "naked [man] with naked [man]" and the other things about which you wrote are not found.

Morton Smith, the discoverer of these fragments, speculates:

Freedom from the law may have resulted in completion of the spiritual union by physical union. This certainly occurred in many forms of gnostic Christianity; how early it began there is no telling. (*Secret* pp. 113–14)

The suggestion of consummation of spiritual union by physical union has been noted by others who have attempted a gay-friendly reading of the Jesus tradition.[18] The explicit suggestion of physical consummation belongs not to Clementine Mark but to Carpocratian Mark — that is, to the version of Secret Mark that Clement is warning his inquiring reader against. Clement tells us that in Carpocratian Mark a number of additional passages appear, including the "nude with nude" which presumably belongs in the description of what happens when the nude youth wrapped in a *sindona* spends the night with Jesus. That is, the *sindona* comes off,

---

17. Thus Origen in *Against Celsus* Book 5.62: "Celsus knows, moreover, certain Marcellians, so called from Marcellina, and Harpocratians [*sic*] from Salome" (*Ante-Nicene Fathers,* 4:570). In the Gospel of Thomas we have a strange episode of a dialogue between Jesus and Salome which may be suggestive of an erotic encounter: "Jesus said, 'Two will recline on a couch; one will die, one will live.' Salome said, 'Who are you mister? You have climbed onto my couch and eaten from my table as if you are from someone'" (The Gospel of Thomas 61:1–2). The translation is from Robert J. Miller, ed., *The Complete Gospels* (Sonoma, Calif.: Polebridge Press, 1992).

18. See Horner, *Jonathan Loved David,* 120, who seems to reject the implication of sexual union.

and so too with whatever it was that Jesus had been wearing. Smith here suggests that the togetherness of nude youth with nude Jesus might be related to "physical union." In a more detailed study, Smith not only does not advance this suggestion further but actually seems to take it back:

> Since the Carpocratians had a reputation for sexual license (see Appendix B) and this section of the longer text reported that a youth came to Jesus [wearing a cloth over his nakedness] and stayed with him all night, it is easy to suppose that the Carpocratians took the opportunity to insert in the text some material which would authorize the homosexual relationship Clement suggested by picking out [naked with naked]. . . .
>
> However, Clement does not explicitly say that the additional material was sexually offensive, and he would hardly have missed a chance to say so if it had been.[19]

Here one wonders if Smith is simply being coy with his more academic reader. The letter of Clement in which Secret Mark is incorporated itself describes the additions in Carpocratian Mark as added by those "who wander from the narrow road of the commandment into a boundless abyss of carnal and bodily sins," and states this material has been "interpreted according to his blasphemous and carnal doctrine and moreover, polluted, mixing with the spotless and holy words, utterly shameless lies."[20]

Clement, who was one of the first to introduce homophobia into Christian biblical interpretation, seems here to be spluttering in exasperation at the Carpocratian suggestion of carnality in the story of the nude youth with Jesus.[21]

As we have seen, however, the material in canonical Mark is already suggestive of homoerotic associations. The material in Clementine Mark is further suggestive of a homoerotic attachment between Jesus and the youth. What we know of Carpocratian Mark is distinguished from these only in that it may make the homoerotic relationship even more explicit and so more difficult to explain away in the instruction of those "who are being perfected." We are dealing here not with differences of kind but with differences of degree.

---

19. Smith, *Clement of Alexandria,* 185.

20. Smith, *Secret Gospel,* 14, 16.

21. If the practice of nude baptism as reported in Hippolytus's *Apostolic Tradition* 21.11 had been known to Clement, why he would have rejected "nude with nude" rather than reinterpreting it in terms of this practice of baptism is unclear.

In his discussion of Secret Mark, Morton Smith rightly and helpfully points to the existence of a "libertine" tradition derivative from Jesus which was increasingly marginalized and eventually erased as Christianity came inexorably under the influence of ascetic traditions within the hellenistic world. One of the chief proponents of an asceticizing tendency was Clement.

Smith cites a number of passages, especially from the letters of the New Testament, that appear to be combating a more libertine view of Christianity. This antilibertine tradition stands in growing tension with the Jesus tradition contained in the Gospels, and, eventually, even with the letters of Paul, which still straddle the divide between ascetic and libertine versions of Christianity.

In the late second and early third centuries, the libertine version(s) of Christianity came to be associated with the Carpocratians, the group that Clement alleges has tampered with the longer version of the Gospel of Mark known in Alexandria.

If the reading of the episodes concerning the disciple Jesus loved is correct then, along with the memory of Jesus as a "wine bibber and a glutton" enshrined in the Gospels, the memory of Jesus as the lover of a man or youth may also have existed. These memories would lend credence to the "libertine" interpretations of the Jesus tradition and discomfit the ascetic and legalistic interpretations of the same tradition. The upholders of the latter views would seek to eliminate or reinterpret the textual grounds that seemed to support the libertine views.[22]

The Carpocratian Mark appears, at least from Clement's perspective, to have contained traditions that linked Jesus to same-sex erotic practices. This connection would have been unacceptable to Clement, who had also gone so far as to introduce into the Ten Commandments a prohibition against at least some forms of same-sex desire and practice.[23]

Now to this point I have accepted the view that a libertine version of Christianity took root in certain aspects of the Jesus tradition. Libertinism, however, is often in the eye of the beholder. That is, what a legalistic, moralistic, or ascetic interpreter sees in another position as leading not only to liberty but to license, as "anything goes," may rather be an insistence that love and justice rather than rules and regulations are the

---

22. Indeed, for this reason perhaps as much as for any supposed connection to gnostic views, many churches resisted the inclusion of the Gospel of John into the canon.

23. "Thou shalt not kill, thou shalt not commit adultery, thou shalt not seduce boys, thou shalt not steal, thou shalt not bear false witness," in "Exhortation to the Heathen," chap. 10, *Ante-Nicene Fathers,* 2:202.

governing principles in moral life.[24] Thus the Carpocratians, like despised groups often in Christian history, may have been accused of wild debauch only because they did not abide by the strict moralism or asceticism of their accusers.

In any case I do not suppose that the interpretation I have suggested for the episode(s) concerning the nude youth supposes an abrogation of any love ethic that may be otherwise fairly derived from the Jesus tradition.

Fitting Mark Together

We may conclude our reflections on this Markan material with some observations concerning its appropriateness in relation to the whole of the Markan narrative and its themes.

The material in canonical Mark that we have seen to be suggestive of homoerotic interpretation (the look of love, the nude youth in the garden) has been shown to be sufficiently suggestive as to have been left out of Matthew and Luke. Yet how is the material as it stands to be explained within Mark as a whole? Without the awareness of the tradition of "the disciple Jesus loved," one might find these episodes only vaguely disturbing.

The phrase "Jesus, looking intensely at him, loved him" does seem to become more intelligible when placed within the conventions of homoerotic attachment. However, as it stands, seeing how this advances Mark's own themes in the narrative is difficult. At most it serves to connect the "adventure story" style of narration employed by Mark with one of the tropes of such narration: a homoerotic attachment of the hero to someone met in the course of the adventure.

Thus, even if we were to suppose that Jesus develops a strong and even homoerotic attraction to the man, the relationship, in the canonical Gospel, doesn't go any further. Moreover, canonical Mark gives us little reason to link this man (only referred to with the pronoun "he") with the nude youth in Gethsemane.

The episode of the nude youth in the garden remains puzzling, although more readily explicable in terms of its possible relation to the beloved disciple tradition in John — that is, as an echo of that tradition. But it does place a possible object of homoerotic interest in the passion narrative in

---

24. There is evidence for this in the attack upon the Carpocratians in Irenaeus's *Against Heresies,* where he not only charges them with teaching the transmigration of souls but also with licentious behavior. Still he notes that their teaching is that "We are saved, indeed, by means of faith and love; but all other things, while in their nature indifferent, are reckoned by the opinion of men — some good and some evil, there being nothing really evil by nature" (Book I. xxv.5) *Ante-Nicene Fathers,* 1:351.

such a way as to bracket the whole of that part of the Gospel. In this case, the nude-youth episode must be complemented by the story of the empty tomb and the (re)appearance there of the *neaniskos*.

The material from Clementine Mark not only serves to link and interpret these episodes in canonical Mark, but also to anchor them more securely in the narrative development of Mark as a whole. For now the encounter with the petitioner comes to be positively related to the themes of this final section of Mark's narrative. Thus the inability of the youth to surrender possessions sets up the death of the youth as involuntary destitution, in comparison with which voluntary poverty is seen as more palatable. In the teaching of Jesus in this section, the relinquishment of property (and family ties) is a stage in preparation for undertaking the strategy of martyrdom, which necessarily includes a willingness to die.

In this context, the "instruction in the mystery of the reign of God" serves to bring the youth up to speed in terms of the instruction that Jesus has already given the other disciples and that Mark has given the reader (e.g., Mark 4:11ff).

Now the loyalty of the nude youth in the garden becomes explicable in terms of the loyalty that is appropriate between partners in homoerotic attachment while also facilitating the Gentile reader's capacity to identify with the narrative as in part reflective of the conventions of homoerotic romance. The picture of Jesus thus acquires a psychological attractiveness otherwise lacking in Mark's exceedingly brusque portrayal of Jesus' character.

The relationship between Jesus and the youth then makes the narrative more capable of connecting to readers who are aware of, and sympathetic to, the conventions of homoerotic relationships (by no means restricted in the hellenistic world to "gay" readers) and at the same time uses these conventions to bring home the themes of death and resurrection, loyalty and martyrdom, and commitment and courage, which are the main burden of Mark's narrative.[25]

On this reading, the material in Clementine Mark actually is better integrated into the narrative of canonical Mark than the remaining fragments of this tradition still to be found in canonical Mark itself.

---

25. For related readings of the basic message of canonical Mark, see Ched Myers, *Binding the Strong Man: A Political Reading of Mark's Story of Jesus* (Maryknoll, N.Y.: Orbis Books, 1988), and Herman Waetjen, *A Reordering of Power: A Socio-Political Reading of Mark's Gospel* (Minneapolis: Fortress Press, 1989). Also see Theodore W. Jennings, *The Insurrection of the Crucified* (Chicago: Exploration Press, 2003).

The relation of Clementine to canonical Mark also casts doubt on the interpretation of the Clementine fragments that Morton Smith, the discoverer of these fragments, gave. Smith's own interpretation of Secret Mark emphasizes the role of initiation and of baptism.[26] His interpretation is as follows:

> Thus from the differences between Paul's baptism and that of the Baptist, and from the scattered indications in the canonical Gospels and the secret Gospel of Mark, we can put together a picture of Jesus' baptism, "the mystery of the kingdom of God." It was a water baptism administered by Jesus to chosen disciples, singly and by night. The costume, for the disciple, was a linen cloth worn over the naked body. This cloth was probably removed for the baptism proper, the immersion in water, which was now reduced to a preparatory purification. After that, by unknown ceremonies, the disciple was possessed by Jesus' spirit and so united with Jesus. One with him, he participated by hallucination in Jesus' ascent into the heavens, he entered the kingdom of God, and was thereby set free from the laws ordained for and in the lower world.

As I noted, Smith is most interested in the issue of initiation into secret knowledge. And this may have been Clement's agenda as well. Certainly Clement was concerned with gnosis (knowledge) as the hallmark of the truly instructed Christian. Moreover, Smith is interested in possibilities of magic in the tradition and discerns here the possibility of a magical initiation rite.[27]

Serious questions may however be raised about Smith's interpretation of Secret Mark when we consider it within the context of canonical Mark where it allegedly belonged.

We have already had occasion to note that Mark is in no way concerned with the ritual of cultic baptism. Mark seems far more interested in the question of baptism as an imitation of Jesus' martyrdom (Mark 10:38–40). The episode of "instruction in the mystery of the reign of God" in Secret Mark does not contradict this emphasis. Indeed it is placed in such a way as to be most naturally interpreted in terms of Jesus' own sayings concerning the fate of the "son of man" who "will be handed over to the chief priests and the scribes, and they will condemn him to death; then they will hand

---

26. Note that the text of Clement's letter makes no reference to baptism, nor is it even possible that baptism is intended since the text of Secret Mark is reserved for those who are being perfected, according to Clement, not to those who are merely baptized.

27. Morton Smith, *Jesus the Magician* (New York: Harper & Row, 1978).

him over to the Gentiles; they will mock him and spit on him, and flog him, and kill him; and after three days he will rise again" (Mark 10:33–34).

The "secret of the reign of God," moreover, does not appear in the Gospel of Mark to presuppose esoteric instruction. Rather it is a device for disclosing to the disciples and to the reader the connection between Jesus' ministry and mission in Galilee and the mission and ministry of his followers in the altered circumstances of the hellenistic world known to Mark and the readers of Mark. Again the most natural reading of Secret Mark is provided by the framework of canonical Mark. In this case, the new companion of Jesus, met only near the end of Jesus' mission, is being brought up to speed in the same way that the first disciples have already been instructed.

Finally the suggestion of magical practices here seems out of place if these episodes of Secret Mark are read in the context provided by canonical Mark. The latter seems to actually "spoof" magical practices in the stories concerning Jesus. For example, in the story of the resurrection of Jairus's daughter, we hear what at first sounds (and must have sounded to Mark's hellenistic readers) like a magical incantation: "Talitha cum." But this is followed by a translation so mundane "little girl, get up" as to produce a comic effect. Like any good hellenistic adventure story, Mark makes use of conventions of, among other things, stories of magic. But Mark does so not in order to portray Jesus as a magician but in such a way as to caricature magic. Thus Smith's use of categories of magical initiation seems beside the point here compared to the far more recognizable situation that two people who are attracted to one another come to understand one another before going to bed.

Although these reflections suffice to show that Smith's interpretation of Secret Mark is inadequate, they do not discredit Secret Mark. To be sure, some scholars at first supposed that Smith might have invented the letter of Clement with the fragments of Secret Mark in order to bolster his own views of baptismal initiation into magical identification with Jesus. But, as our reflections show, if this had been Smith's intention, then the material in Secret Mark is singularly ill suited to further Smith's own interpretive strategies. The critique of his interpretation then only serves to strengthen the credibility of Secret Mark itself.

Relation to Matthew and Luke

We have already seen that Matthew and Luke eliminate from their narratives the homoerotically suggestive episodes in canonical Mark. But do they betray any familiarity with the additional material in Secret Mark? Two interesting pieces of evidence surface here from reference in these later narratives to a *neaniskos*. This term is rather rare in the New Testament. In Mark it occurs only in material that fits within the reconstruction of a homoerotic romance based on canonical and Clementine Mark.

In Matthew this term only occurs in the retelling of the one who comes to Jesus inquiring about eternal life (Matt. 19:16–30). As we saw, the term does not occur here in canonical or Clementine Mark but is supplied later when we encounter the youth as the object of resurrection.

Why does Matthew identify the petitioner as a youth despite the fact that Matthew nowhere else uses this term? One possible explanation is that Matthew knew the tradition of Secret Mark and transfers this designation from that narrative to the retelling of the story of the petitioner. Thus Matthew may bear inadvertent testimony to the tradition of Secret Mark in the very process of expurgating traces of this narrative tradition.

The term *neaniskos* also occurs only once in Luke's Gospel, strikingly in a story of the resurrection of a youth told in Luke 7:11–17. Here, as in Secret Mark, a woman relative's (here a mother rather than a sister) grief draws Jesus into action on behalf of the one he addresses as *neaniske*. Moreover, the end of the episode is apparently placed in Judea (7:17) rather than in Galilee where the story otherwise locates Jesus at this stage of his ministry. This placement corresponds to the location of the resurrection episode in Secret Mark. Many differences are apparent in the narration. In Luke, the youth is not yet in the tomb but is being carried to burial, and Luke tells us nothing of any ensuing relationship between Jesus and this youth. Nevertheless this resurrection narrative might be based in part on the expurgated narrative of Secret Mark.[28] Again perhaps Luke bears unwitting testimony to the tradition of Secret Mark concerning Jesus' homoerotic attachment to a youth.

John

Clementine Mark's description of the resurrection of the youth strongly parallels that of the resurrection of Lazarus in the Gospel of John. Of course, there are also differences: in Mark we are not told of Mary and Martha or of Lazarus. In Secret Mark, a great cry comes from the tomb, whereas in John, Jesus is the one who utters a loud cry; in John, Lazarus

---

28. We may also note that Luke's resurrection episode is placed next to the story of the centurion's slave, which has been the object of a "gay reading" (see chapter 8).

comes out; in Secret Mark, Jesus goes in and raises the youth by his hand (as with Jairus's daughter [Mark 5:41] and Simon's mother-in-law [Mark 1:31]). In this story, we are told that the youth loved Jesus, and in the second fragment that Jesus loved the youth.

Although Smith notes the possible connection between Mark and John in connection with Secret Mark, he does not suggest any connection to the disciple Jesus loved.[29] In our discussion of the identity of the disciple Jesus loved, we found that Lazarus and Andrew had the strongest claims to being identified with this figure. Certainly if we give significant weight to Clementine Mark as a parallel to the Gospel of John, the disciple Jesus loved would appear to be Lazarus since the youth Jesus loved in Clementine Mark is raised as was Lazarus in John.

How then to relate the episode of the nude youth in Secret Mark to the Johannine tradition of the disciple Jesus loved? Two alternatives are available. The nude youth is either to be identified with the figure we know in the Gospel of John as the disciple Jesus loved, or he is, in Bentham's phrase, a "rival or candidate for the situation of rival to the Apostle" (that is, the Johannine disciple Jesus loved).[30]

If we accept the former view, then the Markan youth would seem to be identified with Lazarus (who was also raised), who then becomes "the disciple Jesus loved." That is, Mark and John have decidedly different versions of narratives concerning the same person: a resurrected youth with whom Jesus inaugurates an erotic relationship shortly before his death (Mark) and Lazarus whom Jesus loved (John 11:3) and who figures prominently also in the narrative concerning Jesus' last days. Indeed the seizure of the youth in Gethsemane accords rather well with the notice in John 12:10–11 that "the chief priests planned to put Lazarus to death as well since it was on account of him that many of the Judeans were deserting and believing in Jesus."

The alternative — that we are to think of two distinct figures, and Jesus enters into an erotic relationship with each of them — seems less likely. This is not because we must attribute something like monogamy to Jesus' affectional life but because the relationships appear at approximately the same point in the respective narratives.

Thus, canonical Mark (the nude youth in Gethsemane), Clementine Mark with its account of the youth as raised and then appearing nude (under his linen covering) to be instructed in the mystery of the reign

---

29. Smith, *Secret Gospel*, 45–62.
30. Crompton, *Byron*, 281.

of God, and Carpocratian Mark with its apparent indication of sexual consummation all probably bear traces of the sort of relationship that is presented in John as existing between Jesus and the disciple he loved. All three versions of the Gospel of Mark testify indirectly to the memory of Jesus as the lover of another man.

The possible connection between the homoerotic relationship depicted in Clementine and Carpocratian Mark and the traditions concerning the disciple Jesus loved has been recently developed in a suggestive way by Robert Williams.[31] Although Williams does not attempt to produce a critical investigation of these materials nor argue extensively for the appropriateness of a homoerotic interpretation, he does, nevertheless, intuit the connection among these materials.

Williams's procedure here is simply to link together all the episodes in the Markan and Johannine materials that we have considered to make the portrait of a homoerotic romance beginning with the encounter with the "rich young ruler" and continuing though his resurrection, which is harmonized with the resurrection of Lazarus who thus becomes the "disciple Jesus loved." This person is then the one who flees the garden naked, is present at the cross, and so on.

Williams's procedure of simply lumping together and harmonizing these various elements will not commend itself to scholars who recognize the difficulty of comparing material from distinct traditions as well as the hazards of combining elements from disparate traditions. However, Williams's method is suited for the task he had apparently set himself: that of recasting the whole story in the form of novel, which will enable the reader to enter into the story with a degree of identificatory intuition not possible for scholarly reconstruction.[32]

More in keeping with scholarly method, however, would be using material in John and in the Markan tradition as independent confirmation that the traditions concerning Jesus had at a very early stage to contend with the dangerous memory that Jesus was himself homoerotically attached to another man. The differences, not only the similarities, in these narratives tend to confirm the place of homoerotic attachment in the memories concerning Jesus.

---

31. Williams, *Just As I Am*, 122–23.

32. Williams's intention is indicated by Robert Goss in *Jesus Acted Up* (San Francisco: HarperSanFrancisco, 1993), 214, n. 59. Robert Goss informs me that Williams had completed a manuscript of the novel before his death.

Dangerous Memory

Now this memory would be a "dangerous memory"[33] indeed as Christian leaders moved toward an ascetic, erotophobic, and antipederastic (or, as we would now say, homophobic) perspective under the influence of prestigious hellenistic intellectual traditions. Just as the antisexist and antipatriarchal elements of the Jesus tradition had to be increasingly erased, marginalized, or interpreted away, and the economic and political radicalism of the Jesus tradition had to be similarly subjected to hermeneutical legerdemain, so also the dangerous memory of Jesus' relationship with another man (or youth).

Clementine Mark may give us a clue to the way this was done; not only does Clementine Mark expurgate what appeared to be too susceptible to pederastic interpretation but it also reserves the remaining material for purposes of instruction into philosophic gnosis by way of secret and allegorical interpretation. This allegorical interpretation then diverts attention away from the homoerotic character of the relationship between Jesus and the youth and toward notions of assimilation to Jesus' moral perfection, which were to characterize the true Christian gnostic or sage. At the same time, Clement introduces into the commandments a prohibition against what he calls the corruption or seduction of youths, further diverting attention from the homoerotic aspects of the Jesus tradition.

This veiling of homoerotic elements of Secret Mark is facilitated by the public distribution of a version of Mark in which the homoerotic content is reduced to the fragments (look of love, nude youth in the garden) that we have in our New Testament.

Matthew and Luke recognize the puzzling homoerotic fragments in canonical Mark and expurgate them in their own retellings of Mark's story, though not without betraying possible knowledge of Secret Mark (the references to *neaniskos*).

This veil of secrecy is momentarily torn away by the appearance of the Gospel of John, which had been produced by a small community isolated from these developments and revealing from a different angle of vision homoerotic elements at the base of the traditions concerning Jesus.

The labor of homophobic tradition has been to hide this dangerous memory of Jesus as the lover of a man. The work of counterhomophobic interpretation is to once again tear away the veil.

---

33. In the sense of Johann Baptist Metz in *Faith in History and Society: Toward a Practical Fundamental Theology*, trans. David Smith (New York: Seabury Press, 1980).

The material that canonical, Clementine, and Carpocratian Mark provide for an interpretation of the episode(s) concerning the nude youth is rather slender, certainly in comparison to the material from John with respect to the disciple Jesus loved or even with respect to the other material to which we turn shortly. In the nature of the case, all that can be required of an interpretation is that it account for the textual evidence without doing violence to it. In proposing a "gay" reading of the nude youth, I am not supposing that this interpretation is the only possible one, but instead that it fits the textual evidence as we have it.

Chapter 8

The Centurion's "Lad"

We have seen that Matthew and Luke eliminate from their revisions of Mark's material all references to a homoerotic relationship between Jesus and an unnamed youth. Both eliminate the phrase "looking intently at him, Jesus loved him..." from the story known to tradition as that of the "rich young ruler." Moreover, both eliminate the episode of the nude youth in Gethsemane and eliminate the presence of an anonymous youth in the tomb of Jesus that may have been the sequel to the youth-in-the-garden episode. But we have also seen that this editorial work seems to betray some knowledge of the material in Secret Mark concerning the youth. The result of this editorial work is to eliminate from their versions of the Markan tradition the suggestion of a homoerotic relationship between Jesus and a youth.

However, the Gospels of Matthew and Luke are not devoid of homoerotically charged content. Although they seem to eliminate homoerotic themes from the depiction of Jesus himself, both bear traces of another homoerotic relationship that elicits an apparently positive response from Jesus. This episode may be termed the "centurion's boyfriend."

In his book *Jonathan Loved David*, Tom Horner suggests that the story from Matthew's Gospel concerning the healing of the centurion's "lad" may be understood as referring to a relationship between the centurion and the lad which would have been understood by at least some parts of the early Christian community as a relationship inclusive of sexual practice. Horner supposes that the Gospels include hints that Jesus would not "have been hostile" to "homosexual relationships." He continues:

> The first evidence is the possible homosexual motif in the story of the healing of the Centurion's servant (Matt. 8:5–13 and Luke 7:1–10). It has always seemed to me that it was more than an ordinary concern that this Roman official displayed in this case for a mere slave. Luke uses here the word *doulos*, which is the ordinary Greek

131

word for slave, but Matthew uses the word *pais,* "boy" or, in this particular context, "servant boy." *Pais* is the same word, however, that any older man in Greek culture would use to refer to a younger friend — or lover.[1]

What are we to make of this suggestion?[2]

One of the odd features of this story is precisely that it is a healing/ exorcism episode common to Matthew and Luke but not found in Mark. In general, the material common to Matthew and Luke but not found in Mark is designated by scholars as deriving from a hypothetical source referred to as Q, which both writers used in ways comparable to their use of Mark.

Virtually all the material in this hypothetical source consists of sayings, parables, or teachings of Jesus.[3] The episode concerning the healing of the centurion's lad (or slave) is the only significant healing narrative that appears in the reconstruction of Q.[4] In both Matthew and Luke, this episode is placed at the conclusion of their respective versions of Jesus' first extended discourse, best known from its Matthean version as the Sermon on the Mount. In both Gospels, this episode is the first time that one who is clearly marked as a Gentile is the object of Jesus' healing powers.

Even apart from a consideration of its content, this episode is quite remarkable. When to these more formal features we add the potentially explosive homoerotic features of its content, the story becomes all the more important for our purposes.

We consider each version of the story, beginning with Matthew and also noting a distant parallel in the Gospel of John, and then consider what it may have to tell us about homoerotic themes in the Jesus tradition.

Matthew

It may be useful first to remind ourselves of the story as it is found in Matthew:

---

1. Tom Horner, *Jonathan Loved David: Homosexuality in Biblical Times* (Philadelphia: Westminster Press, 1978), 122.

2. The suggestion, while not appearing in most earlier discussions, does occur in John J. McNeill, *Freedom, Glorious Freedom* (Boston: Beacon Press, 1995), 132–36, and in Robert Williams, *Just As I Am: A Practical Guide to Being Out, Proud, and Christian* (New York: Crown Publishers, 1992), 60–63.

3. For a reconstruction of Q, see Robert J. Miller, ed., *The Complete Gospels* (Sonoma, Calif.: Polebridge Press, 1992).

4. One-verse healing reference (Matt. 12:22 and Luke 11:14) in both cases is used as an introduction to the controversy (from Mark) concerning Jesus being in league with Beelzebub.

When he returned to Capernaum, a Centurion came to him, appealing to him and saying, "Lord my [*pais*] is lying at home paralyzed, in terrible distress." And he said to him, "I will come and cure him." The Centurion answered, "Lord, I am unworthy to have you come under my roof; but only speak the word, and my [*pais*] will be healed. For I am a man under authority, with soldiers under me; and I say to one, 'Go,' and he goes, and to another, 'Come,' and he comes, and to my [*doulos*], 'Do this,' and he does it." When Jesus heard him, he was amazed and said to those who followed him, "Truly I tell you, in no one in Israel have I found such faith. I tell you, many will come from east and west and will eat with Abraham and Isaac and Jacob in the kingdom (reign) of heaven, while the sons of the kingdom will be thrown into outer darkness, where there will be weeping and gnashing of teeth." And to the Centurion Jesus said, "Go; let it be done unto you according to your faith." And the [*pais*] was healed in that hour. (Matt. 8:5–13)

In the story I have placed in brackets the transliterated words that appear in Greek since the NRSV uses "servant," which is an attempt to harmonize Matthew's version with the similar story we find in Luke.

What about Horner's suggestion concerning Matthew's word *pais* for the object of the centurion's concern? Is it true that the word *pais* would be understood as suggestive of a pederastic relationship?

The term is one of two roots that together form the word "pederasty." The other root is *erastes* (from *eros*) which means "lover." The term "pederasty" means "love of youths" and was the technical term for male homosexual relationships in the hellenistic world. These relationships were regarded as a typical "vice" of the gentile world in Jewish as well as pagan propaganda.[5] Within the Greek-speaking world the term *pais* was regularly used of the male beloved in a same-sex relationship.[6] The

---

5. See David F. Greenberg, *The Construction of Homosexuality* (Chicago: University of Chicago Press, 1988), 199–202; Robin Scroggs, *The New Testament and Homosexuality* (Philadelphia: Fortress Press, 1983), 81–98.

6. Thus, in his groundbreaking discussion of Greek homosexuality, K. J. Dover discusses the problem of translating terms from Greek to English as follows: "Since the reciprocal desire of partners belonging to the same age-category is virtually unknown in Greek homosexuality, the distinction between the bodily activity of the one who has fallen in love and the bodily passivity of the one with whom he has fallen in love is of the highest importance. In many contexts, and almost invariably in poetry, the passive partner is called *pais*, 'boy' (plural *paides*), a word also used for 'child', 'girl', 'son', 'daughter', and 'slave'. The *pais* in a homosexual relationship was often a youth who had attained full height (the vase-paintings leave no doubt about that)." K. J. Dover, *Greek Homosexuality* (New York: Vintage, 1978), 16. In a note, Dover makes

conventional ideal beloved for a man was a younger male, but this convention was not always honored. The situation is somewhat similar to the way in which it was customary, until recently, to refer to even older women as "girl"; or to refer to the female object of affection as "girlfriend" and the male object of affection as "boyfriend," no matter the age of the beloved. Thus in the hellenistic world, despite the literal connotation of "boy," the "beloved" referred to in this way would not normally have been a minor. That is, the beloved would be called "boy" even if the beloved were fully adult.[7] So the best translation for the term *pais* in Matthew's version of this story seems to be "boyfriend."

Possibly, too, the construction used in Matthew, *ho pais mou,* further stresses, and so draws attention to, the relation between the centurion and the object of his concern, further justifying the translation of "boyfriend."

But how could such a story find its way into the Gospel of Matthew with its emphasis upon the fulfillment of the law? Would Matthew let pass unnoticed a pederastic relationship? Although this consideration at first seems to rule out the possibility of a pederastic interpretation of the relationship, matters are not quite so simple as they may seem.

In fact, Matthew at several points has a version of events that to conservative sensibilities is more shocking than other Gospels. The story of the so-called wise men, and the Matthean version of the story about the Syrophoenecian woman, offer two striking illustrations.

The story of the magi that occupies all of Matthew 2 is a staple of Christmas tradition. But in Matthew, they are not called kings, we are not told that there were three of them, nor are we given the names and races legend has added. In fact what the text deals with is the appearance of sorcerers from the east. The word *magi* is the word for sorcerers: a class of powerful Eastern magicians with whom Israel was forbidden to have dealings. They appear in the time of Persian influence (after the Babylonian captivity) and the prophets regard them with dread and revulsion. They represent all that is loathsome to Israel. The rabbis taught, "He who learns

---

clear that the use of *pais* to designate a girl or daughter is archaic and rare, disappearing after the fifth century B.C. Ibid., 7, n. 31.

7. John Boswell writes: "In terms of sexual adulthood persons were still classed as 'boys' by Roman writers when they were serving in the Roman army. What 'boy' in such cases probably intends is a suggestion of youthful beauty rather than chronological minority. Writers of other nationalities specifically criticize Roman men for limiting their eroticism to older youths" (John Boswell, *Christianity, Social Tolerance, and Homosexuality: Gay People in Western Europe from the Beginning of the Christian Era to the Fourteenth Century* [Chicago: University of Chicago Press, 1980], 81). See also the reference by K. J. Dover in the note above to vase paintings in Greece.

from a magus is worthy of death."[8] For Matthew to represent them as the ones who first give tribute to Jesus is thus an exercise of considerable daring. Matthew is obviously not afraid to outrage traditional religious sensibilities.

The story of the Syrophoenecian woman makes a similar point (Matt. 15:21–28; compare Mark 7:24–30). In Mark, this woman is said to be Greek, but in Matthew she is made to be a Canaanite, a worshiper therefore of Baal. Again nothing could be more offensive to the sensibilities of those who have learned from the law and the prophets the urgency of avoiding contact with these practitioners of heathen rites. Moreover, the Canaanites are regarded in the law as the practitioners of sexual deviance (possibly fertility rites) and the source of male and female cultic prostitution. Indeed the word dog (*kunariois*) that is used here of the woman is a word otherwise used of cultic prostitutes (Deut. 23:18; Rev. 22:15)![9]

The story plays with the hint of sexual and ritual irregularity while making the woman (rather than Jesus) the source of insight regarding the mission to the Gentiles.

Thus the suggestion of a pederastic relationship does in fact suit Matthew's purpose very well. Hellenistic Jewish propaganda identified Gentiles as peoples given to sorcery, idolatry, and pederasty. In the story of the magi, Matthew has introduced sorcerers into the account. In the case of the Canaanite woman, Matthew has more clearly introduced an "idolater." The suggestion of the pederastic relationship of the centurion serves to underscore in a parallel way the gentile-ness of the centurion. Precisely this gentile-ness of the centurion is necessary for the contrast with the "sons of the kingdom" who think that they — rather than those "from the east and west" — will dine with Abraham and the ancestors of faith.

As thus formulated, the story may be regarded as a gentile version of the saying of Jesus to the chief priests and elders in the temple that "the tax collectors and the prostitutes are going into the kingdom of God ahead of you" (Matt. 21:31, see also verse 32). This saying concerning prostitutes is unique to the Gospel of Matthew, and the repetition of the terms "tax-collectors and prostitutes" (*pornai*) in verses 31 and 32 draws even greater attention to it. In this saying, what is at stake is the disreputable of Israel going into the reign of God on account of their readiness to respond

---

8. Gerhard Kittel, ed., *Theological Dictionary of the New Testament,* trans. Geoffrey W. Bromily (Grand Rapids: Wm. B. Eerdmans, 1964), 5:358.

9. In the bad old days, the references in Deuteronomy and Revelation were mistranslated to refer to "sodomites." See Derrick Sherwin Bailey, *Homosexuality in the Western Christian Tradition* (London: Longmans, Green, 1955), 41–45.

to John the Baptist. In the case of the centurion, what is at stake is the entering of one who is a disreputable Gentile. As centurion and pederast, he combines the features of the tax collector (servant of the oppressor) and the prostitute (sexually disreputable). This combination would tend to confirm that Matthew's version of the centurion story is a parallel to the saying concerning prostitutes and tax collectors. The evidence mounts that Matthew wants us to read the relationship of the centurion and the lad as pederastic.[10]

Another illustration of Matthew's penchant for disturbing traditional sensibilities is found in his genealogy of Jesus. Here Matthew specifically mentions four women in the list of ancestors: Tamar, Rahab, Ruth, and "the wife of Uriah" (Bathsheba). At least three of the four may be regarded as shady characters at best. Tamar posed as a (temple) prostitute to seduce Judah, her father-in-law, who had promised to give another son in marriage to her after the death of her first husband (Gen. 38:6–30). The ancestry of Jesus then emphasizes the place of a relationship that is triply illicit: it is incestuous (father-in-law with daughter-in-law); it is a relationship with a prostitute; and it is a relationship that involves cultic prostitution and thus idolatry. Her twin sons then are born of this completely illicit union.

Although the reference to Rahab is anachronistic, she is known both in the Hebrew Scriptures and in the New Testament simply as Rahab the prostitute (Josh. 2:1–21, 6:22–25; Heb. 11:31; James 2:25). To the image of prostitution already anticipated in the reference to Tamar is added the identity of a Gentile, indeed a Canaanite (thus anticipating the Canaanite woman).

The wife of Uriah who becomes the mother of Solomon is, of course, Bathsheba. She is the victim of a royal rape/seduction that David seeks to cover up by securing the death of her husband Uriah.

This accounting leaves Ruth. Certainly the fact that she is a Moabite may be regarded as sufficiently scandalous since this is enough to exclude her from the people of Israel. According to Deuteronomy 23:3, all descendants of a Moabite are cut off "even to the tenth generation," which would obviously include David, who was the third generation after Ruth and Boaz. But does this mean that, unlike the others, she is not sexually

---

10. We must also place in this same set of passages the saying of Jesus regarding eunuchs (Matt. 19:11–12), which manages to overturn the proscription of Deuteronomy 23:1: "He whose testicles are crushed or whose male member is cut off shall not enter the assembly of the Lord." Jesus' saying concerning eunuchs again places Jesus squarely on the side of the sexually marginalized. See the discussion of this text in the next chapter.

suspect? Or does Matthew hear the erotic overtones in the story of her relationship to Naomi?

Whatever we may suppose about this last, the very Matthew who is regarded as "strait-laced" is consistently making space in the narrative for the sexually stigmatized as well as for Gentiles.

When we place the story of the centurion's "lad" in this context, we may more readily see how Matthew could have either transmitted or even have created a story suggestive of a pederastic relationship.[11] From the genealogy onwards, the Gospel of Matthew manifests the intention to emphasize the inclusion of the Gentiles and the inclusion of the sexually marginalized within the narrative of the accomplishment of God's purposes in Jesus the Messiah. Thus at the beginning of the narrative of Jesus' activity as messiah, Matthew places the story of Jesus' encounter with the centurion. It is precisely as centurion, as Gentile, and as pederast that he serves the purpose of demonstrating the hope for healing that makes him respond to the one that the "insiders" of God's people reject. He is then a dramatic sign of the way in which God's purposes will come to fruition even in the situation in which the upholders of the traditions of God's people are scandalized. As pederast, the centurion represents the point of Matthew's narrative of the gospel.

Luke

In the Lukan version of the story, we never meet the centurion. He sends Judean elders to Jesus to make his case. They claim that he has built their synagogue for them and so is a worthy man. Jesus responds and goes to the house where "friends" of the centurion tell him to come no closer and then they repeat the words about authority. In Luke, the reference to Abraham and so on is missing, but we do hear that when the intermediaries of the centurion return to the house, they find the slave (*doulos*) in good health (Luke 7:1–10).[12] Here the word "slave" (*doulos*) is applied four times to the object of the healing.[13]

---

11. In the earlier discussion of the disciple Jesus loved, I suggested that Matthew might have eliminated such a figure in the interest of not unnecessarily raising questions about Jesus' fulfillment of the law among Jewish readers, or readers acquainted with the Old Testament. We have now seen that Matthew does not blindly apply the norms of the law to (his) narrative. However, Matthew possibly either did not know of the story of the beloved or chose not to report this relationship in order not to unduly prejudice the anticipated readers. But then he gives greater place to the sexually marginalized generally and by retaining or even emphasizing the pederastic features of the relationship between the centurion and his "boyfriend."

12. The business about Abraham's descendants and especially the fire and brimstone are characteristic additions that Matthew makes to many stories.

13. Not three as Horner, *Jonathan Loved David,* 122, says.

What more can be made of the story? Luke may be using the account to locate within his narrative a "mirror" of the ideal reader. Luke writes the narrative to a certain Friend of God (Theophilus). The centurion is portrayed as a "god-fearer" — that is, as a Gentile who had attached himself to the synagogue, who was not yet exactly a convert to Judaism but was a strong supporter of it. If Luke is indeed writing to an audience constituted in this way, then he might find it important to substitute *doulos* for the more ambiguous *pais* if indeed the latter term lent itself too obviously to a "homosexual" interpretation. The "god-fearer" would be a Gentile who accepted the Jewish characterization of gentile vice as the practice of pederasty. God-fearers would then have been among the Gentiles who rejected this practice, either for their own reasons or because of Jewish teaching. Luke thus has clear motives for not wanting to emphasize the pederastic character of the relationship in an account that mirrors the situation of the "god-fearer" reader. Moreover a person engaged in a relationship that might be construed as pederastic would scarcely have been recommended by Jewish elders.

We may also note that Luke's terminology here (*doulos*) does not eliminate the suggestion of a sexual relationship. It only makes this possibility recede somewhat from the forefront. In Roman times, one of the primary permitted outlets for male sexuality was the male slave (again, generally younger).[14] Thus Luke's terminology here does not rule out a sexual relationship, but Matthew's terminology seems to bring this possibility into somewhat sharper focus.

We may note that although the object of the centurion's concern is referred to four times as *doulos* (slave) in Luke, he is once referred to as *pais*. This term appears when the "friends" of the centurion (not Judeans) quote the centurion directly (7:7). Since Luke has provided a context in which the person is identified as a slave, an appropriate translation of *pais* here might be "servant-boy." Luke might also have simply left intact the reference to *pais* that had been earlier modified by the mediation of the Judeans who intercede for the centurion. Thus the Judeans in the story regard the relationship as one between a slave and his master, while the Gentiles use the term that more readily connotes the problematic "boyfriend."

The type of relation that the centurion had to the slave is hinted at in Luke at the beginning of the story where the slave is said to be "dear" to

---

14. Note Boswell, *Christianity, Homosexuality, and Social Tolerance,* 78, and Greenberg, *The Construction of Homosexuality,* 120.

the centurion. The word here is *entimos*. Although some have suggested "costly" or "valuable" as the meaning here, no warrant whatever exists for this translation. As far as I can tell, the only meanings for *entimos* in the New Testament are "honored" or "esteemed" (as in persons of high rank) or "dear," as in especially close or intimate friends. No uses permit the sense of "valuable" or "costly" in either the New Testament or the Septuagint.[15]

Why does Luke play down the homoerotic elements in this story?

We should note that, like Matthew, Luke is concerned to portray Jesus as the fulfillment of the hopes of Israel. Now Matthew is concerned to argue that the Jewish community loyal to Jesus represents the correct reinterpretation of the law and the prophets over against the synagogues of the late first century that were excluding these same Jewish-Christians. Matthew does not agree with the sort of literal application of legality that this Gospel portrays as characteristic of the synagogue. Rather Matthew suggests that the law and the prophets focus properly upon justice and mercy. Matthew thus consistently opposes attempts to restrict the identity of the people of God and represents a policy of openness as consistent with the prophetic reinterpretation of the law.

Luke on the other hand represents Jesus and his followers as more attentive to the traditions of Judaism, including temple worship and synagogue participation. To this we may add Luke's depiction of Paul's policy in Acts of demonstrating his own pharisaic orthodoxy and orthopraxis (even to the point of circumcising Timothy). The mission to the Gentiles, while a theme of absolute importance to Luke, is still represented as compelled by the nonresponse of Jewish authorities to the proclamation concerning Jesus.

Thus Luke wishes to portray the opening to the Gentiles as in continuity with a respect for the traditions of Judaism rather than as representing the rupture that is more apparent in other accounts. This perspective explains Luke's tendency to play down the more divisive aspects of the Jesus tradition. Consistent with this approach, Luke represents gentile converts as being as closely tied to Judaism as possible — hence the tendency to make the centurion as Jewish as possible (playing down the pederastic character of his relationship to his slave/youth). Luke therefore does not eliminate the story of an outreach to a Gentile but chooses to make it conform to the pattern of the Gentile-Jew by downplaying the homoerotic content of the relationship of the centurion to his dear youth.

---

15. The only other uses in the New Testament are Luke 14:8; Phil. 2:29; and 1 Peter 2:4, 6.

The episode that immediately follows this one in Luke is that of the resurrection of the widow's son at Nain. We have seen that this story may be a revision of a tradition known to us from Secret Mark in which homoerotic themes were apparent. In both cases, then, Luke has attempted, without complete success, to eliminate homoerotic themes from the memory concerning Jesus.

John

Horner seems unaware that we have what appears to be a third version of this story in the Gospel of John. This episode occurs upon Jesus' return to Cana where, we are reminded, he had earlier performed the transformation of water into wine. Instead of a centurion we have a "royal official" (*basilikos*), and instead of Capernaum we are in Cana. Where Matthew uses *pais* and Luke uses *doulos,* John uses *uios* generally but also uses *paidion,* which is a diminutive variation of *pais.* Unlike Matthew and Luke, no great stress is laid on the non-Jewishness of the petitioner. If John was aware of the same story that we have in Matthew or Luke, then he chose to play down this aspect and turns the story into one about a family member rather than a "boy" or a slave. All three stories emphasize the theme of healing at a distance as well as a theme common to many other healing stories: the role of faith. All three place the story at an early stage of their narrative and give it a certain prominence.[16]

John's version of the story appears to rule out a pederastic relationship since the lad is specifically identified as the son (*uios*) of the official (*basilikos*). Are we to suppose that John has expurgated a relationship that Matthew may be suggesting? This seems unlikely in view of the scandalous character of many episodes in John's narrative, even if we don't take into account the figure of the disciple Jesus loved. Two other explanations seem more likely here. First, John may not have known the version of the story told by Matthew. As we have seen, Matthew may have had reasons for making the story more suggestive or scandalous than it was in the tradition that he knew. John's Gospel also has a strong tendency to recount episodes in such a way as to conflate aspects of stories that we have in other traditions. In this case the conflation might be with the story of the ruler who sends to Jesus concerning his daughter who is dying

---

16. It is prominent in Matthew not only because of its foreshadowing of the mission to the Gentiles but also because it is the second miracle of Jesus. In John the healing is identified as the "second sign" that Jesus performed. In Luke it is the beginning of a series that culminates in the question of John the Baptist's emissaries, "Are you the one who is to come?"

(Mark 5:21–43; Luke 8:40–56; Matt. 9:18–26). The conflation results in a *basilikos* (neither Jewish *archon* nor pagan centurion) and the healing (from the centurion narrative) rather than a resurrection (from the Jairus narrative) of a son (not daughter or slave/*pais*). Thus it may simply be that John has found a way to put several stories into one without telegraphing themes related to the end (the resurrection of Lazarus, or the appearance of the beloved).

Interpretation

From this analysis, we may say first that Matthew's version of the healing of the centurion's lad is suggestive of a pederastic relationship between the centurion and the lad. Determining whether Matthew's version is more "historical" than either Luke's or John's is difficult.[17] As we have seen, we can account for peculiarities of each version on the basis of each text's own theological perspective. My own inclination, on this as on all questions about what really happened, is to acknowledge that I simply don't know.

However, Matthew's version should be read as deliberately suggestive of a pederastic relationship between the centurion and the lad. What does this mean for a gay-affirmative reading? Or for an understanding of the gospel, whether or not one is "gay"?

It seems to me that it does no violence to the text to suppose or even assert that Jesus responds to the call for help of a centurion for his beloved (or, as we would say, his lover). In this case as in others, Jesus does not inquire about the lifestyle or the background of those people who ask his help. People need not demonstrate worthiness; the need is itself the claim upon Jesus' response.

Moreover, Jesus nowhere demonstrates squeamishness about sexual "irregularity." The supposition that he would have found a homosexual or, rather, a pederastic relationship especially difficult is absurd on the face of it.

Now a reader steeped in traditional Christian readings of the text may presume that since the centurion is represented as a model of faith, he could not be regarded as a pederast. Let us see what the text can tell us about this conclusion.

In the first place, the faith of the centurion is like the faith of others who come to Jesus for healing in the early part of the Gospel. The character of their faith is not determined by a particular doctrinal content, but

---

17. Horner, *Jonathan Loved David*, 122, suggests the priority of Matthew's account.

rather an audacious desire for health and wholeness. The impertinence, the impatience, the risking of everything for the sake of this desire is what Jesus everywhere calls "faith."

In the case of the centurion, his concern for his boy/lover motivates the faith, driving him to seek out an itinerant Jewish healer. His concern overcomes whatever may have been his own reluctance to be seen with such disreputable company or his reluctance to be chastised by a Jew for his love life.

The centurion displays his confidence that the one he cares for can be healed, that his paralysis is not the "will of God" but can and must be overcome. In this, his faith corresponds to Jesus' announcement and demonstration of the coming of the reign of God, for from Jesus' point of view this does entail the overcoming of sickness and madness.

Now the centurion expresses his confidence in a characteristically gentile way, in terms of the hierarchy of command and obedience. But Jesus will be sharply critical of this entire worldview. "You know that the rulers of the Gentiles lord it over them, and that their great ones are tyrants over them. It will not be so among you" (Matt. 20:25–26). Jesus excludes in principle the very notion of authority that is the basis of the centurion's worldview.

We may go even further, for the centurion supposes that Jesus is a commander of demons. The words used in the Greek to describe the torment of the boyfriend suggest that the youth is being tortured by evil spirits. The term is also used in connection with the account of the Gerasene demoniac (Matt. 8:29; Mark 5:7; Luke 8:28; see also Matt. 18:34). The centurion thus supposes that Jesus can command his underlings, the demons, to leave the youth and so deliver him from torment. As we know, others supposed the same thing about Jesus. The scribes and Pharisees accused Jesus of being in league with Beelzebub (Matt. 9:34; 12:24). They supposed that this connection was how Jesus had his power over demons and illness. The centurion seems to share this view. So one could scarcely suppose that the faith of the centurion has to do with his beliefs about Jesus or the character of Jesus' authority.

What then is the faith of the centurion? Although he may have had the same idea as Jesus' enemies about whence Jesus received his power, the centurion had a very different attitude toward this power. The scribes used this view to discredit Jesus' work of healing minds and bodies. The centurion didn't care where the power came from so much as he wanted it used for the healing of his boyfriend. The scribes didn't care about healing. They could even imagine that sickness was God's will. But the centurion didn't care whose will it was; he wanted, he yearned, for healing and wholeness for his beloved. And he would do anything, risk everything, to get it.

On this desire he acts. He knows that religious Jews revile the whole idea of pederasty, having no understanding of, or sympathy for, the sort of love he knows; yet he goes out into the street to find a Jewish healer and, risking rejection and ridicule, asks for help for the boyfriend he loves.

The centurion has heard of this man, perhaps hearing that he is a powerful sorcerer. One does not lightly approach such people; they are dangerous. If this Jesus is in command of demons, as the centurion seems to think, then he is a very dangerous man indeed. But impelled by undaunted love and unquenchable hope, the centurion is willing to risk this encounter for the sake of the one he loves.

The faith of the centurion then does not refer to the ideas in his head but the desire in his heart for healing and wholeness for his beloved. Jesus responds to this faith unconditionally. The centurion's care for another and his audacious expectation, however either of these are expressed, draw Jesus into action.

The variations that we have found in this story help to make this central point. Whether the concern is for a slave, a son, or a young lover, the important aspect of the story is the concern that draws one to take risks, to become vulnerable in hope, to reach out in yearning for well-being, to refuse to give disease or madness or paralysis the last word, to suppose that divine power is not on the side of calamity but on the side of wholeness: Jesus calls this outlook faith. This faith — rather than the legal compliance, or the ritual cleanness, or the doctrinal orthodoxy, or the moral rectitude of the petitioner — calls forth Jesus' astonishment and wonder. For this miracle demonstrates that the reign of God has indeed drawn near.

Conclusion

The story of the healing of the centurion's boyfriend in the Gospel of Matthew may be fairly read as Jesus' acceptance of, and even collaboration in, a pederastic relationship. Indeed not only does this reading not do violence to Matthew's Gospel, it serves to bring into focus dimensions of that narrative that are often ignored, especially the role of the sexually marginalized. By bringing this dimension of Matthew into focus, we are able to rescue this Gospel from the one-sided distortion that produces the image of this narrative as moralistic and legalistic. Indeed, Matthew's depiction of Jesus as in fundamental sympathy with the sexually marginalized has implications not only for gay readers but for straight readers as well. The "good news" of this reading is not restricted to gay and lesbian readers.

And the challenge of this reading is not only to "conservative" upholders of traditional sexual morality. Even "liberal" readers, including those within or sympathetic to the gay community, may be troubled by the place given in this narrative to a specifically pederastic relationship. In our own era, the style of homosexual relationship that has become both culturally and morally paradigmatic is one between "consenting adults" — that is, between equals in age and status. This is certainly not the sort of relationship signaled by the terminology either of Matthew or Luke. What both versions do indicate, however, is that neither the status nor the age of the "partners" to this relationship is important (still less, of course, the gender), but rather the depth of concern of the one for the other. On the basis of Matthew at least, developing a sexual ethic that remarginalizes either prostitutes or sexual relationships between putative unequals is not possible.

Here I am especially thinking of those who, following Scroggs's interpretation of terms in hellenistic vice lists, want to claim that those terms refer to pederastic or prostitutional relationships rather than to the more paradigmatic relationships between "consenting adults."[18] This approach all too easily becomes a way of stigmatizing and remarginalizing certain relationships in order to exempt others from moral condemnation. This process only replicates the scapegoating tendencies of homophobic and heterosexist hermeneutics. As Gayle Rubin has noted in another connection, the erotic practices of any one of us will be regarded with loathing by a substantial number of other people.[19] The matter is not one of saying that "anything goes," but rather of basing ethical judgments on ethical criteria: solidarity with the marginalized and concern for the quality of the relationship rather than the status of the lovers.

---

18. Scroggs, *The New Testament and Homosexuality,* 126–29, 138–39.

19. Gayle S. Rubin, "Thinking Sex: Notes for a Radical Theory of the Politics of Sexuality," in *The Lesbian and Gay Studies Reader,* ed. Henry Abelove, Michele Aina Barale, and David M. Halperin (New York: Routledge, 1993), 15.

Chapter 9

Troubling Gender

One element of same-sex relationships that is often troubling to hetero-sexist structures is the perceived tendency of same-sex eroticism to scramble the gender roles that support heterosexist and masculinist institutions. Of course, same-sex relationships may be so patterned as to reflect, and indeed buttress, gender identities. This patterning appears to be true of the ideological justifications for institutionalized pederasty in classical Athens, the military-style associations of Sparta or the Theban bands, or the initiatory rites of some New Guinea tribesmen. However, a more common outlook is to regard same-sex eroticism as subverting or troubling the gender categories of a society or even as constituting a "third sex."[1]

In this chapter, we turn to aspects of the Jesus tradition which appear to subvert the gender categories of the hellenistic world, Roman as well as Palestinian. The presence of these elements in the Jesus tradition tends to support the impression of a dangerous memory of same-sex eroticism in the traditions concerning Jesus.

We limit ourselves in this chapter to two kinds of material. The first is the material concerning eunuchs, which has often been taken by gay-friendly exegesis to indicate the presence of a group of persons who are cognates of modern "homosexuals." The second kind of material is composed of sayings and dramatic episodes that appear to invert gender categories.

We shall also note a marked tendency, perhaps beginning with Paul, and finding clear expression in the Pastoral Epistles, to reinscribe rigorous gender role expectations into Christianity, a move later connected with the emergence of a Christian homophobia. The association of this homophobia with gender role enforcement only serves to underline the probable

---

1. See the collection of essays in Gilbert Herdt, ed., *Third Sex, Third Gender: Beyond Sexual Dimorphism in Culture and History* (New York: Zone Press, 1994).

connection between gender role subversion and the dangerous memory of same-sex eroticism in the Jesus tradition.

Eunuchs

An aspect of the Jesus tradition that has drawn increasing attention from antihomophobic interpreters of the Bible is the attitude toward eunuchs taken by Jesus in a saying from Matthew and by the author of Acts in the episode concerning an African (Ethiopian) eunuch.

This material is often interpreted as suggesting a positive attitude toward the sexually disenfranchised and stigmatized and thus as providing a precedent for the inclusion of gay males and lesbians as similarly stigmatized and marginalized.[2]

In order to see how this material may be understood, a helpful approach would be to first see to what extent or in what way the eunuch was stigmatized. We may also see to what extent the eunuch was associated in antiquity with homosexual practices. We then look at the saying of Jesus in Matthew's Gospel and then at the narrative concerning the Ethiopian eunuch in Acts.

Exclusion and Inclusion

The New Testament attitude toward eunuchs is often contrasted with that of the Old Testament. But in fact the Old Testament manifests a variety of perspectives. Some traditions in Judaism exclude eunuchs. Thus Deuteronomy 23:1 asserts, "No one whose testicles are crushed or whose penis is cut off shall be admitted to the assembly of the Lord." This view seems to coincide with the later rabbinic view that "it is the duty of every Israelite to have children."[3] On this view, one who was incapable of having children would then be excluded from the house of Israel.

However, the view of Deuteronomy and of the leaders of the synagogues at the beginning of the Christian era was by no means the only view of the matter to be held in the traditions of Israel. In the prophetic tradition

---

2. See, for example, John J. McNeill, *The Church and the Homosexual* (Kansas City, Mo.: Sheed, Andrews, and McMeel, 1976), 65; Tom Horner, *Jonathan Loved David: Homosexuality in Biblical Times* (Philadelphia: Westminster Press, 1978), 124; and Robert Williams, *Just As I Am* (New York: HarperCollins, 1992), 59–60. The most extensive use of this material is to be found in Nancy Wilson, *Our Tribe: Queer Folks, God, Jesus, and the Bible* (San Francisco: HarperSanFrancisco, 1995), 120–31. The book also includes a helpful appendix that deals with all biblical texts referring to eunuchs. Ibid., 281–85.

3. Gerhard Kittel, ed., *Theological Dictionary of the New Testament,* trans. Geoffrey W. Bromily (Grand Rapids: Wm. B. Eerdmans, 1964), 2:767.

we discover an Ethiopian eunuch (Ebedmelech) who is instrumental in delivering Jeremiah from imprisonment in a dry cistern (Jer. 38:7–13).

Moreover, in a poem written during the Babylonian exile, we even hear of a "gospel to the eunuchs":

> ...do not let the eunuch say "I am just a dry tree"
> For thus says the LORD,
> To the eunuchs who keep my sabbaths,
> who choose the things that please me and hold fast my covenant
> I will give in my house and within my walls,
> a monument and a name better than sons and daughters
> I will give them an everlasting name that shall not be cut off.
>
> (Isa. 56:3–5)

And in the Wisdom of Solomon, a text written just before the time of Jesus, we hear a similar announcement:

> Blessed also is the eunuch whose hands have done no lawless deed,
> and who has not devised wicked things against the LORD;
> For special favor will be shown him for his faithfulness,
> and a place of great delight in the temple of the LORD.
>
> (Wisd. 3:14)

The fate of the just eunuch is here contrasted with that of the unjust who, though biologically fruitful, is ethically sterile.

We clearly see that we have contrary tendencies at work within the literature of ancient Israel. On the one hand we have the concern with procreation and with purity (understood as the lack of blemish) that tends toward the exclusion of the eunuch. On the other hand, and perhaps intending to overthrow this tradition, we have the insistence that the eunuch is not cut off but instead is incorporated into the people of God through deeds of justice. The presence of these contrary tendencies should give us pause when we try to characterize the "biblical view" or the "Jewish view" of matters that are in fact differently viewed in different parts of the tradition.

The Jesus tradition certainly sides with Isaiah and with Wisdom (otherwise two very different kinds of tradition) against the Deuteronomic exclusion of eunuchs. Jesus is not simply opposing himself to "Jewish law," as some exegetes carelessly formulate it. Rather Jesus and early Christianity are choosing among traditions of Israel — approving some and rejecting others.

Nor does the story end there. Later developments in early Christianity return to the Deuteronomic legislation in excluding eunuchs from the priesthood.[4] Rather than a contrast between Judaism and Christianity, we have a contrast between Jesus, Isaiah, and Wisdom on the one hand, and the legal traditions of Deuteronomy and the *Apostolic Constitutions* on the other.

This should serve as a warning that in discussing the gay-positive features of the Jesus tradition we are discussing a tradition that has roots in Ancient Israel just as it also has opposition there. Subsequent opposition will come again not from Judaism, but from within Christianity itself.

The Eunuch in Antiquity

In order to understand the context of New Testament statements concerning eunuchs, one needs to consider not only the traditions of Israel but also the place of eunuchs in the wider hellenistic culture of antiquity that was the context for the formation both of normative Judaism and of "catholic" Christianity.

In both negative and positive sayings about eunuchs that we have considered in the traditions of Israel, the main point seems to be their incapacity to have progeny. This condition makes them unfit (and disfigured) for participation in the life of the people of God. But their condition also makes them apt recipients of divine favor, which is represented as surprising and as putting to shame those people who thought that their progeny signaled divine favor. In both cases, what is at stake is the inability to produce progeny.

This inability was indeed the distinguishing factor for the eunuch in the hellenistic world as a whole. They were trusted administrators of royal or imperial business for they could not set up a rival dynasty to that of the king or emperor. For this reason, eunuchs often held considerable power in antiquity (see Gen. 39; Dan. 1:3ff; Jer. 38:7; Jth. 12:11).

Castration served another purpose than that of making one eligible for certain responsibilities within the court. It was also a means of ensuring the prolongation of the androgynous beauty of youth. Just as in early modern times young boys were castrated to preserve the purity of their voices — thus producing operatic stars who, like the great Faranelli of the eighteenth century, remain legendary — so other features of "beardless youth" could be preserved by means of castration. Castrated youths then would retain into adulthood the appearance that made them the object

4. *Apostolic Constitutions*, 47, 21–24.

of pederastic attention. Some of antiquity's most famous courtesans were eunuchs. Alexander the Great, for example, was known to develop a life-long attachment to the young Persian eunuch Bagoas. Nero fell in love with one of his slaves, Sporus, who was then castrated to preserve his beauty. Nero then publicly married this beloved, whose beauty had thus been enhanced and prolonged.[5]

Hence also eunuchs gained fame in antiquity as male prostitutes. Indeed the castration of abandoned boy children and slaves was one of the chief means of filling the male brothels that were an important part of Greek and Roman culture. The practice of castrating slaves for sexual purposes was criminalized by the (pederastic) emperor Hadrian in the early second century C.E.

The eunuch whose testicles were crushed prior to adolescence would, as I indicated, not develop secondary masculine characteristics. While this act could be seen as prolonging the ideal of youthful beauty, it could also be seen as the "feminization" of the male and thus as a "transgendering" of the male. In the highly gender-conscious atmosphere of much of late antiquity, persons could be described as eunuchs who preferred the passive (or "feminine") role in sexual intercourse with other males. In this case, being a eunuch could be as much symbolic as literal.

We should also make mention of the *galli* who were male devotees of the goddess Cybele. These men castrated themselves in ritual ecstasy. Greenberg notes concerning them: "bands of *galli* roamed the country-side dressed as women, scourging themselves, dancing and begging. In the *Metamorphoses,* also known as *The Golden Ass,* Apuleius portrays the *galli* as passive homosexuals who seek out virile young peasant lads to satisfy their cravings; Lucian paints a similar picture in *Lucius, or the Ass.*"[6]

Contrary to popular imagining, the incapacity to produce progeny by no means excludes the eunuch from sexual practices. The crushing of the testicles may prevent the production of sperm, but it does not otherwise impair genital sexuality. Indeed we are told that Potiphar was a eunuch, yet it was his wife who tried to seduce Joseph (Gen. 39:1, 6–20)!

Aline Rouselle remarks concerning the *galli* that they "were still able to feel desire and to achieve erection and ejaculation of seminal fluid from the

---

5. While the literature often assures us that these eunuchs were "passive" sexual partners, this was by no means necessarily the case. Eunuchs, after all, often remained capable of active sexual roles, including anal penetration. This result could not be guaranteed, and the more extreme cutting off of the penis would, of course, restrict the sexual role of the eunuch.

6. David F. Greenberg, *The Construction of Homosexuality* (Chicago: University of Chicago Press, 1988), 98.

prostate and the seminal vesicles after they had removed their testicles."[7] Rouselle also refers to the "reputation which the Galli had of leading a very active sexual life."[8]

Greenberg also gives considerable attention to the place of castrated "temple prostitutes" in the general area of Asia Minor.[9] Greenberg's contention seems to be that these functionaries of fertility worship may have served as sperm receptacles for the goddess to whom they were devoted.

This brief review of the roles of eunuchs in antiquity suggests a wide array of meanings associated with the practice of castration. Court officials, male prostitutes, courtesans, and "temple prostitutes" were among the most notable roles which they played in antiquity. Against this background, as well as that provided by a consideration of Prime Testament texts, we must understand the New Testament passages that deal with eunuchs.

Matthew

With this background in mind we can turn to a discussion of the specific references to eunuchs in the New Testament. And here we turn first of all to the saying of Jesus concerning eunuchs in the reign of heaven reported only in the Gospel of Matthew 19:10–12. This saying is unique to Matthew, just as are the references to Tamar or Rahab in Matthew's genealogy of Jesus, or the reference to prostitutes entering the reign of God ahead of the respectable. Thus the saying concerning eunuchs appears to be of a piece with Matthew's concern for the sexually marginalized, which played an important role in the interpretation of the centurion's "boyfriend" in the preceding chapter.

The saying concerning eunuchs is appended to Matthew's version of the prohibition of divorce, a prohibition common to the first three Gospels (Mark 10:1–12; Matt. 19:3–9; Luke 16:16–18).[10] That remarriage constitutes adultery is the saying which sparks the following exchange:

> His disciples said to him, "If such is the case with a man and his wife, it is better not to marry." But he said to them, "Not everyone can accept this teaching, but only those to whom it is given. For there are eunuchs who have been so from birth, and there are eunuchs who have been made eunuchs by others, and there are eunuchs who have made themselves eunuchs for the sake of the reign of heaven. Let anyone accept this who can."

7. Aline Rouselle, *Porneia: On Desire and the Body in Late Antiquity*, trans. Felicia Pheasant (Oxford: Blackwell, 1988), 122.

8. Ibid., 123.

9. Greenberg, *The Construction of Homosexuality*, 101–6.

10. See further discussion in part 3 on "Marriage."

We have already noted that the saying is unique to Matthew. But even here the comments are carefully protected as if they were too obviously scandalous in character to be openly disseminated.

We may notice first that the encounter with the disciples provides a rather clumsy link to the saying concerning divorce. Although we should presume a connection between the adulterous character of remarriage and being or becoming a eunuch, this link is odd on several grounds. First, the natural extension of Jesus' saying concerning remarriage would be either don't divorce or, if you do, don't remarry. The "moral" of the story is left this way in Mark's version. Matthew's version of the saying concerning divorce and remarriage is by no means so severe that it would seem to elicit the disciples' view that it would be better not to marry. In fact, Matthew's version of this saying is significantly less severe than that of Mark since Matthew has explicitly allowed an exception "except for unchastity."

This exemption corresponds to the legal situation in Rome in that, in Roman law, the divorce of a wife who had been unfaithful was not optional but obligatory for citizens, since otherwise the man would be guilty of pimping his wife.[11]

Thus the saying concerning divorce does not of itself seem sufficiently severe as to motivate the saying of the disciples concerning not marrying. This concern is indeed a separate matter since apparently not marrying was something that characterized both Jesus and Paul and, presumably, at least some of their followers in the late first century. That is, the "not marrying" seems to follow not from the saying about divorce and remarriage at all but from wishing to emulate Jesus.

But if the connection between the observation of the disciples and the prior saying of Jesus appears tenuous then so too does the connection between what they say and what Jesus then says about eunuchs, for no necessary connection exists between not marrying and being a eunuch. As the case of Potiphar and Joseph shows, eunuchs could marry; other examples are well known from the hellenistic world.

The issue raised by the disciples then seems to make an awkward bridge between the saying concerning divorce and the saying concerning eunuchs.

Moreover Matthew has the saying concerning eunuchs carefully marked out as both odd and possibly scandalous. Jesus introduces the saying with the words, "Not everyone can accept this teaching but only those to whom it is given," and concludes with "let anyone accept this who can."

---

11. Rouselle, *Porneia*, 87–92.

These cautionary words serve to bracket the saying concerning eunuchs. This is an extraordinary sort of bracketing, even more so in the Greek. "Not all grasp [*xorousin*] this saying" and "the one who grasps, grasp it." Matthew appears well aware of handling dynamite here and so takes extraordinary precautions.

The saying itself speaks of three kinds of eunuchs: those born that way, those made so by others, those who make themselves so "for the sake of the reign of heaven." Of the three categories, only the second is more or less self-explanatory in accordance with our earlier discussion of eunuchs. As we have seen, the custom of castrating prepubescent male slaves for purposes of prostitution or of castrating postpubescent males for cultic purposes was well established in the hellenistic world. In neither case, did castration mean the end of sexuality. Nor did it lead necessarily to celibacy in the sense of refraining from marriage.

The third category corresponds in the hellenistic world to the *galli* and perhaps to other participants in mystery cults. The self-castration was a kind of offering or sacrifice of reproductive capacity (Rouselle, 125–26). Again the act did not necessarily entail the end of sexual activity, and indeed the sexual appetite of the *galli* was apparently legendary.

The first category is the most surprising. Literally it refers to those who "are born so from a mother's womb." In this case something other than castration is referred to, but what? Are we to think here of hermaphrodites who were unable to reproduce? Are we to think of less spectacular forms of congenital reproductive incapacity? Only the first would correspond to a category known to the hellenistic world. Some have suggested that this category may be taken to refer to the equivalent of the modern category of homosexual, defined in terms of exclusive same-sex orientation. In this case, the exclusive orientation to sexual fulfillment with a person of the same sex would make one reproductively a eunuch.

There continues to be debate about whether this category of persons was known or suspected in hellenistic discourse. To be sure the standard view of same-sex practice was that it did not preclude cross-sex practice. What we today call bisexuality was far more the expected pattern of behavior. But this should not be taken to mean that antiquity was wholly unfamiliar with the more or less exclusive orientation toward finding sexual fulfillment only in a person of the same sex.[12]

---

12. See John Boswell's discussion of this in "Revolutions, Universals, and Sexual Categories," *Hidden from History: Reclaiming the Gay and Lesbian Past*, ed. Martin Duberman, Martha Vicinus, and George Chauncey, Jr. (New York: Meridian, 1989), 17–36.

For congenital eunuchs then we are left, it would appear, with either hermaphrodites who blended the biological attributes of the sexes or (perhaps less likely) with that minority of persons who engaged in same-sex practice whose practice was known to be exclusive.

The saying of Jesus is scandalous, linking together hermaphrodites or persons who engaged exclusively in same-sex practices, men castrated for purposes of prostitution, and persons who castrated themselves in religious frenzy. Like many of Jesus' sayings, this one is shocking in daring to link the reign of God with apparently absurd or outrageous behavior.[13]

In terms of the saying's apparent incursion into the sphere of sexual impropriety, it is entirely consistent with Matthew's policy elsewhere in the Gospel, as we have already seen.

Jesus' saying is often sanitized by making it speak directly of celibacy. Commending celibacy in the hellenistic world, even in Judaism, is by no means impossible.[14] But if celibacy were the focus, the connection would more naturally be made to sayings not about remarriage but about forsaking the family (see, for example, Matt. 10:37 or texts discussed in chapters 10 and 11). Indeed, L. William Countryman infers this meaning of the saying: "Jesus was acknowledging then, that his prohibition of divorce effectively dissolved the family and made eunuchs of all men, for it deprived them of the authority requisite to maintain their patriarchal position."[15] In Countryman's view, then, this saying does not refer to a special class of followers of Jesus but to all in the sense that all give up their role in the patriarchal family structure.

The saying in Matthew's Gospel more likely simply associates followers of Jesus who have renounced family structures with stigmatized or marginalized groups in the hellenistic world: exclusive "homosexuals," hermaphrodites, *kinaedi* (male same-sex prostitutes), or the *galli,* who were dedicated to the goddess Cybele and infamous for their sexual appetite.

In the course of centuries, this marginal or liminal status would come to be moralized in such a way that, instead of identification with the marginal and disreputable, it would become a badge of spiritual superiority and finally become the passport to the exercise of spiritual dominion over the

---

13. For a discussion of a number of examples of forceful and dramatic language in the sayings and parables of Jesus, see Robert C. Tannehill, *The Sword of His Mouth* (Philadelphia: Fortress Press, 1975).

14. See Peter Brown, *The Body and Society: Men, Women, and Sexual Renunciation in Early Christianity* (New York: Columbia University Press, 1988).

15. L. William Countryman, *Dirt, Greed, and Sex* (Philadelphia: Fortress Press, 1988), 176.

laity. But this development will require several centuries and must not be read back into the setting of either early first-century Palestine or of Matthew's late first-century readership.

Jesus' words associate his followers with often-ridiculed sexual minorities. This solidarity with the most marginal is the hallmark of the authentic Jesus tradition, and abandonment of this solidarity is the measure of the church's betrayal of the one it calls "Lord, Lord" (Matt. 7:21).

Acts

Luke, who has an even more explicit opposition to the institution of marriage and family than Matthew, does not have the saying concerning eunuchs that we find in Matthew. This fact is consistent with what we have learned to expect of Luke from our discussion of the centurion's boyfriend: no gratuitous marginalization of Christians. Instead, Luke has a eunuch in Acts who is, like Luke's centurion, as respectable from a Jewish point of view as possible.

Although Acts is largely devoted to the activities of Peter and Paul, the initial mission activity outside Jerusalem is attributed to Philip (8:4–13). The first individual conversion of which we are told is that of the Ethiopian eunuch (8:26–39) to whom Philip is directed first by an "angel" and then by "the Spirit" in a way that anticipates and parallels the conversion of the Roman centurion by Peter (10:1–11:18). These two conversions, of an Ethiopian official and of an "Italian" official, anticipate the extension of the gospel "to the ends of the earth" (respectively, to Africa and Europe).

Both of these officials are presented as god-fearers, a category of persons met with only in Lukan narrative — Gentiles strongly attracted to Judaism. In the case of the Ethiopian eunuch, we are told that "he had come to Jerusalem to worship...[and] was reading the prophet Isaiah." The eunuch is perplexed about what he is reading, a further indication that he is not being depicted as a Jew. That he has been to Jerusalem "to worship" [*proskunason*] does not necessarily suggest regular temple worship but something more like homage (the action of the centurion toward Peter in Acts 10:25 is described with the same term).

In the Gospel of Luke there was, as we saw, a previous episode concerning an encounter with a centurion (7:1–10). As we noted, Luke's version of this episode veils, without entirely obscuring, the pederastic character of the relationship between the centurion and his "dear slave" (or "dear youth"). In the subsequent centurion story in Acts there is no hint of a pederastic relationship or of sexual marginality of any kind. But the Ethiopian convert (who anticipates the centurion in Acts) is, in a different way, sexually marginal. As we have come to expect from Luke, however, nothing here is overtly disreputable.

The Isaiah being read by the eunuch is the same prophet who specifically includes the eunuch in the divine dispensation. Moreover, the passage the eunuch was pondering is one that may well have connected to his situation as a eunuch:

> In his humiliation justice was denied him
> who can describe his generation?

As a "court official of Candace, queen of the Ethiopians, in charge of the entire treasury" (8:27), he was a man of considerable responsibility. But he would also have been entrusted with responsibility precisely because of reproductive incapacity and thus have experienced the humiliation that was too often the lot of those who were first enslaved and then castrated to serve the whims of their masters.

In his lifelong humiliation and marginalization (for which his responsibilities as court treasurer could not entirely compensate), he was in a position to receive the "good news about Jesus," who was himself humiliated and marginalized by the respectable and powerful. Through some such recognition, the African eunuch is moved to join himself more intimately with Jesus and his Way and so requests baptism. Being thus joined with Jesus he, though separated from Philip, "went on his way rejoicing" (8:39).

The result of homophobic exegesis has been that sexual minorities have not only been marginalized and humiliated, but have also been prevented from this rejoicing by which the spread of the gospel to "all the earth" is here signified.

Yet the preservation of this story in Acts has had the result that those who identify with this Ethiopian eunuch, whether as African, under conditions of colonialism or racism, or as sexually marginalized, under conditions of heterosexism and homophobia, have been enabled to recognize their own significance in the history of God's dealings with humanity.

Crossing Gender

We have noted that the status of the eunuch is a threat to the stabilization of gender roles, especially of male gender roles, so important to the masculinist society of the Roman hellenistic world. Prepubescent boys castrated for sexual purposes would not develop secondary traits of masculinity. This would both prolong their boyish beauty and tend to feminize them in the estimation of others. Similarly the castration of persons for cultic purposes could also be understood as feminization since the male, like the female cultic "prostitute," may become a receptacle for the collection of sperm. In the highly gendered world of late antiquity, the transgendering produced by castration was one of its most troubling aspects. Thus the positive reference to eunuchs in the traditions concerning Jesus and his followers suggests an undermining of the gender expectations of this cultural world.

These positive references to eunuchs are not the only way in which gender roles are destabilized in the traditions concerning Jesus and his disciples, however. Indeed in a number of ways the Jesus tradition serves as an assault upon the gender identities of the Jewish and Roman hellenistic world.

One of the ways in which gender roles are destabilized and indeed subverted has been the subject of much feminist biblical hermeneutics. Scholars now generally recognize that the Jesus traditions show evidence of, at least partial, liberation of women from the conventional expectations of female roles in both Jewish and Roman society of the first century. Certainly the indication that women as well as men followed Jesus on his vagabond ways (Luke 8:1–3), that they were encouraged to leave behind the familiar routines of domesticity (Luke 10:38–42), that one was singled out as exemplary in her recognition of the way of the cross (Mark 14:3–9), that women are always singled out as witnesses to the execution of Jesus, to his death and burial, and that they are the primary witnesses to and messengers of his resurrection signifies a fundamental rupture with the gender role expectations of the first century.

In part 3 of this study, we have occasion to examine another body of material that undermines gender roles: the way in which the traditions concerning Jesus undermine the institutions of marriage and family which the gender roles served.

A third general dimension of the Jesus tradition that subverts gender categories is the renunciation of the ways of violence and domination so often associated with hypermasculinity in ancient and modern cultures. The Matthean advice concerning nonviolent response to threats to one's honor such as the advice to "turn the other cheek" (Matt. 5:39) is even further radicalized in the renunciation of masculinist striving for domination most clearly expressed in the teaching of Jesus common to Mark and Matthew:

You know that among the nations those whom they recognize as their rulers lord it over them, and their great ones are tyrants over them. But it is not so among you; but whoever wishes to become great among you must be your servant, and whoever wishes to be first among you must be the slave of all. (Mark 10:42–44; Matt. 20:25–27)

These characteristics of the early Jesus movement clearly move in the direction of undermining the relatively rigid gender categories and expectations of first-century society, whether Jewish or pagan.

Other texts represent an even more direct or pointed assault upon these gender roles. We begin by looking at sayings attributed to Jesus in the Gospel of Thomas that appear to summarize in a programmatic way the gender destabilization of the Jesus tradition. We then look at two episodes, one from the Gospel of Mark (and Luke), the other from the Gospel of John, which exhibit some of these features dramatically and which return us to the narrative documents most suggestive of a dangerous memory of same-sex eroticism in the Jesus tradition. This study brings our discussion of that tradition full circle.

The Gospel of Thomas

We turn first to the Gospel of Thomas, a document previously known to have existed but actually discovered in Coptic translation only in 1945 as part of a library of scrolls discovered in Egypt at Nag Hammadi. This document is composed of sayings of Jesus and is attributed to a Didymos Judas Thomas or Judas the twin (of Jesus?), who may be the same Thomas or Didymos (both names mean "twin") known to us from the Gospel of John. Subsequent documents, especially an *Acts of Thomas,* are also attributed to or concerned with this figure who is credited in early Christian tradition with the evangelization of Ethiopia and India.

The current assessment of the value of this document is fairly represented by Stevan Davies when he writes:

A consensus is emerging in American scholarship that the *Gospel of Thomas* is a text independent of the Synoptics and that it was compiled in the mid to late first century. It appears to be roughly as valuable a primary source for the teachings of Jesus as Q, and perhaps more so than the Gospels of Mark and John. Today many of those seriously concerned with the historical Jesus, with determining the most original forms of the sayings of Jesus, or with the study of Jesus' parables turn to the *Gospel of Thomas* for information as readily as to the Synoptics.[16]

This view is in part dependent on the fact noted by Helmut Koestler that of the many sayings in the Gospel of Thomas which are paralleled by sayings of Jesus in the canonical Gospels, "the Gospel of Thomas almost always appears to have preserved a more original form of the traditional saying."[17]

Thus, although not canonical and so not binding on the traditional church as a source of teaching, the document is nevertheless an invaluable aid in clarifying or amplifying aspects of the primitive Jesus tradition. To that purpose we put it here.

Much in the Gospel of Thomas would reward close scrutiny in terms of developing an erotics of the gospel as a general context for placing the elements of homoeroticism that we have focused on in this study. Here, however, we limit ourselves to sayings that clearly undermine the gender categories of late antiquity.

The first of the sayings we consider comes from the end of the document and is one of the few actual dialogues in the text:

> Simon Peter said to them, "Let Mary [Magdalene] leave us, for women are not worthy of life."
>
> Jesus said, "I myself shall lead her in order to make her male, so that she too may become a living spirit resembling you males. For every woman who will make herself male will enter the kingdom of heaven." (Saying no. 114)[18]

The attitude of Peter in this brief dialogue is quite similar to that reported in another text from this "Library" of Nag Hammadi, namely, the so-called Gospel of Mary in which Peter is reproved by Levi for his churlish attitude toward Mary, to whom Jesus had entrusted important teaching.[19]

In some ways this saying is the clearest in the Gospel of Thomas since it is provided with a context. It has to do with Mary Magdalene being

---

16. Stevan Davies, "The Christology and Protology of the Gospel of Thomas," *Journal of Biblical Literature* 111, no. 4 (Winter 1992): 663–64.

17. In the "Introduction" to the Gospel in *The Nag Hammadi Library*, ed. James M. Robinson (New York: Harper & Row, 1988), 125.

18. *Nag Hammadi Library*, 138.

19. For the "Gospel of Mary," see Robert J. Miller, ed., *The Complete Gospels* (Sonoma, Calif.: Polebridge Press, 1992), 351–60; or *The Nag Hammadi Library*, 523–27. The text is Gospel of Mary 10:1–10.

entrusted with the male work of proclaiming the gospel after the resurrection. Although other Gospels minimize the role of the women around Jesus, the consequence of feminist hermeneutics is to bring this exchange into the light. This saying then corresponds with what is supposed by many to have been the attitude of Jesus.

To say in this connection that Mary may be masculinized and that women in general should become male may at first seem to valorize the position of the male in society. But we know that Jesus was critical of all forms of patriarchy and hierarchy. What the text means then is that Mary becomes male in the sense that she acquires the freedom of discipleship and is not restricted to woman's work. In this sense the saying is quite in keeping with other aspects of the Jesus tradition — for example, the encounter with Mary and Martha reported in Luke 10:38–42. But circumstances here go further, for this is now after the resurrection and Mary of Magdala is commissioned to be an apostle, to the dismay of the males who guard their own privilege.

Of course, the age-old attack upon lesbians is precisely that they do what Jesus here commends: they make themselves male, engaging in gender nonconformity. Consequently, when we look for a hidden history of lesbianism we look precisely for evidence of this sort of gender nonconformity. We recall, too, that in Christian Europe this activity was punishable in extreme ways.[20]

In any case the making oneself male that Jesus seems to commend for all women who seek to be related to him is, at the least, a clear subversion of gender roles so important to patriarchy both then and now. But Jesus does not content himself with one way of subverting these roles. This saying concerning Mary (and, by extension, all other women followers) is set within an even more radical context by another saying of Jesus, which comes much earlier in the document:

> When you make the two one ... and when you make the male and the female one and the same, so that the male will not be male nor the female female ... then you will enter [the kingdom]. (Saying no. 22)[21]

Here Jesus counsels the subversion of gender roles for both males and females. This subversion runs directly counter to the view of normative Judaism concerning gender roles as expressed in the following saying from Deuteronomy: "A woman shall not wear a man's clothing, nor shall a man

---

20. See the essay by Judith C. Brown, "Lesbian Sexuality in Medieval and Early Modern Europe," in *Hidden from History*, 67–75.

21. Translation from the *Nag Hammadi Library*.

put on a woman's garment, for whoever does such things is abhorrent to the LORD your God" (22:5).

This same legal code excludes eunuchs from the assembly of the people of Israel before God (23:1) and stigmatizes those born "of an illicit union" (23:2) and temple prostitutes of both sexes (23:11). Thus the same normative tradition that excludes eunuchs also excludes gender role nonconformity.[22]

Gender role nonconformity was by no means less troublesome for Gentiles of the Roman hellenistic world. Thus the attitude of Jesus stands in contrast to the position of Gentile as well as emerging Jewish ideologies of patriarchy.

Water Jars in Mark and Luke

In order to see how gender role subversion is embedded in narratives concerning Jesus, we may first look at an intriguing episode in the Gospel of Mark. In preparation for the celebration of the Passover on the last evening of Jesus' mission with his disciples, he sends two of them on ahead, telling them "a man carrying a jar of water will meet you; follow him"(Mark 14:13; see Luke 22:10). In this way the two anonymous disciples or understudies will discover the appropriate place where the group may gather safely in the midst of the city whose leaders are plotting Jesus' demise.

The one detail upon which we focus our attention is that of the man carrying the jar of water. Morton Smith notes: "Carrying water was women's work, so this was like saying, 'Look for a man wearing lipstick.'"[23] If Smith's observation is correct, and it appears quite plausible,[24] then how should we interpret the significance of this startling image?

---

22. Just as we discovered that Deuteronomy's attitude toward eunuchs is not the whole story of the attitude taken toward them by important traditions in Israel, so also we should not imagine that all strands of Jewish tradition were as negative toward the possibility of gender role nonconformity as this one. Indeed the narratives concerning the female judges of Israel suggest an altogether different attitude, at least where women were concerned.

In the story of David from 1 Samuel we discover a somewhat different attitude. There David curses Joab for having killed Abner: "may the house of Joab never be without one who has a discharge, or who is leprous, or who holds a spindle, or who falls by the sword, or who lacks food" (2 Sam. 3:29). The curse lists misfortunes that occur within a family and among these is "one who holds a spindle." This appears to mean a male who adopts the female social and gender role. There is nothing either rare or reprehensible about being in some way or other transgendered, but simply one of life's all too common misfortunes. For a warrior, the loss of one of his sons in this way appears to weaken the house just as if one had fallen by a sword or been afflicted with disease.

23. Morton Smith, *The Secret Gospel: The Discovery and Interpretation of the Secret Gospel According to Mark* (New York: Harper & Row, 1973), 80.

24. See the confirming note in the Oxford Annotated edition of the RSV to Luke 20:10.

We begin by noting that this is yet another of those elements of Markan narrative that is not repeated by Matthew (though it is by Luke). In its disappearance from Matthew's retelling of Mark's story, it is like other narrative episodes that we have examined earlier: the "look of love" in the story concerning the "rich young ruler" and the naked youth in the garden of Gethsemane.

In order to clarify its significance, recall that this story is a doublet to the instructions that Jesus gives in Mark 11:1ff concerning the acquisition of a horse (*polos*) with which to ride to the walls of Jerusalem. In both cases, two anonymous disciples are sent (in Luke it is Peter and John) on a mysterious errand. They are given signs to watch for and words to say that sound like instructions for a mysterious quest. In both cases, we are told that the disciples did as instructed and that things worked out exactly as Jesus had said. On one level, these stories of strange instructions given and followed assure the reader that Jesus knows what he is doing, that he is reliable even when his instructions seem bizarre or outlandish. In the narrative as a whole, this seems to underscore the reliability of Jesus' strategy for taking on the centers of power even when his methods result in his own execution or in the persecution of the disciples.

In Mark, doublets in the narrative often have the function of demonstrating both a gentile and a Jewish ambience for the mission and ministry of Jesus. Thus the two feedings of the multitudes in Mark appear to signal alternatively Jewish territory (6:30–44) and gentile territory (8:14–21) for the constitution of community. In this case, the Jewish and gentile elements are not completely segregated from each other, but the emphasis does indicate this bicultural reality of the early community.

In the case of the acquisition of a horse, the dramatic event that is being prepared is Jesus' kingly ride to Jerusalem in which his followers hail him as the Davidic heir. In the case of the acquisition of a room, what is at stake is the securing of a space in hostile territory for the remembrance of the liberation of slaves from Pharaoh's Egypt (Passover) under conditions that are appropriate to those who must anticipate this deliverance amid the threat of persecution and death. In the first case, the horse may represent the passing of the rule of Judah to another (Jesus), who therefore acquires the horse of Judah (Gen. 49:10–12). In the case of the man with a water jar, we have what may be (from the standpoint of some sensibilities) a distinctly pagan subversion of gender that then anticipates and echoes the subversion of the religiously respectable Passover celebration by the distinctly unorthodox meal of Jesus with his disciples accompanied by its symbolism of body and blood.

In any case the man who is here flouting the conventions of gender is incorporated into the subversive practices of the community itself. He becomes a guide to a place of refuge for those who themselves transgress religious and ideological customs of respectability.

The subversion of gender roles in the case of the man carrying water is fully consonant with what Mark, and especially Luke, do elsewhere in the narrative: giving prominent place to women, displacing family values, and renouncing the masculinist system of rule.

This transgendered figure so fleetingly glimpsed serves as an emblem of the way that the community follows. It is no small irony then that, as Christianity makes itself respectable, it turns its back on this figure and on all those who, like him, subvert the gender role expectations of heterosexist social order.

Foot Washing in John

The brief glimpse of the man carrying water in the Gospel of Mark (and Luke) is like the episode of the intent look of love, or the naked youth in the garden — fleeting and easily overlooked, as if the writer winked surreptitiously at the knowing reader without unduly alarming those innocent of these elements of the dangerous memory concerning Jesus.

The Gospel of John, however, is characterized by a more open depiction of an erotic relationship between Jesus and an unnamed adherent. The greater openness of the Fourth Gospel in this regard is nevertheless covered over by a tradition that refuses to see what is before its eyes (Groddeck).

The same is true for Jesus' flouting of gender role expectations. In the Gospel of John, this subversion of gender roles occurs in the dramatic episode that replaces the scene of the other Gospels concerning Jesus' "Last Supper" with his disciples: the account of Jesus' washing the feet of his disciples.

> Now before the festival of the Passover, Jesus knew that his hour had come to depart from this world and go to his Father. Having loved his own who were in the world he loved them to the end. . . . And during supper Jesus, knowing that the Father had given all things into his hands, and that he had come from God and was going to God, got up from the table, took off his clothes,[25] and tied a towel around himself. Then he poured water into a basin and began to wash the disciples' feet and to wipe them with the towel that was tied around him.

---

25. The NRSV prudishly, and incorrectly, translates the term as "outer robe."

He came to Simon Peter, who said to him, "Lord, are you going to wash my feet?" Jesus answered, "You do not know now what I am doing, but later you will understand." Peter said to him, "You will never wash my feet." Jesus answered, "Unless I wash you, you will have no share with me." Simon Peter said to him, "Lord, not my feet only but also my hands and my head!" Jesus said to him, "One who has bathed does not need to wash,[26] but is entirely clean. And you are clean, though not all of you...."

After he had washed their feet, had put on his robe, and had returned to the table, he said to them, "Do you know what I have done to you? You call me Teacher and Lord — and you are right, for that is what I am. So if I, your Lord and Teacher, have washed your feet, you also ought to wash one another's feet. For I have set you an example, that you should also do as I have done to you." (John 13:1–15)

Before attending to the gender subversion that occurs in this text, we should remind ourselves of certain of its general features.

First, while the text precedes the supper of Jesus with his disciples, it replaces the significance attributed to that supper in the Synoptic Gospels with the action of foot washing. In the other Gospels, the supper is the action that is to be repeated by the disciples and which thus becomes the ground of the characteristic celebration of Christian ritual as the Eucharist. But the Gospel of John includes no instructions to perpetuate the supper. Rather the action of washing one another's feet is specifically enjoined upon the followers.

We should also note that this scene of washing feet immediately precedes the introduction of the disciple Jesus loved (13:23ff). Linking these two elements is the anticipation of Judas's betrayal (13:2, 11, 18–19, 21, 27), which is to be the occasion for the introduction of the disciple Jesus loved. The general theme of the entire section that stretches through to the end of chapter 17 is the love of Jesus for his disciples — a love that is dramatically enacted through this washing of their feet and which is counterpoised with the special love of Jesus for just one of the disciples.

Now precisely in this context so fraught with significance do we have the scene of Jesus washing the disciples' feet. But what is perhaps most surprising about this scene is that tradition has generally overlooked its most characteristic feature. When the radicality of Jesus' action is noted,

---

26. Some manuscripts insert "except for the feet."

it is generally interpreted as an act of self-humiliation in that Jesus is said to act here as a slave. No textual basis exists for this supposition. Instead what Jesus does here is to act as a woman. In order to see this point, consider those texts where a person is said to wash another's feet. In every case in biblical literature, the person who washes the feet of another is a woman.

1. The first example is from the narratives concerning David. Virtually the entirety of chapter 25 of 1 Samuel is concerned with David's wooing of Abigail, the wife of Nabal. The culmination of the story comes after Nabal's death when David sends his servants to propose to Abigail. Her response is as follows: "She rose and bowed down with her face to the ground, and said, 'Your servant is a slave to wash the feet of the servants of my lord' " (1 Sam. 25:41). In the Septuagint (the Greek translation of the Old Testament), all other occurrences of the verb to wash (*niptein*) that concern feet (*podas*) indicate that the person washes his or her own feet (Gen. 18:4; 19:2; 24:32; 43:24; Judg. 19:21; 2 Sam. 11:8; Song 5:3). The act of hospitality consists in offering to provide water for this purpose.

2. The second example is from the story of the woman in Luke 7: "She stood behind him at his feet, weeping, and began to wash his feet with her tears and to dry them with her hair. Then she continued kissing his feet and anointing them with the ointment" (7:38).

3. A third example is from the Gospel of John itself in a version of a story found in other Gospels (Mark 14:3–9; Matt. 26:6–13). In John's Gospel this concerns Lazarus's sister: "Mary took a pound of costly perfume made of pure nard, anointed Jesus' feet, and wiped them with her hair" (John 12:3).

4. Finally in 1 Timothy, we meet with the description of an official widow: "she must be well attested for her good works, as one who has brought up children, shown hospitality, *washed the saints' feet,* helped the afflicted, and devoted herself to doing good in every way" (1 Tim. 5:10). Despite the command for the men to wash one another's feet in John, 1 Timothy reverts to the old ways of a woman being the one who washes the feet of the saints.

Where the agent of washing is other than the person whose feet are to be washed, in every case (listed above) the agent is a woman. The only case of a male washing the feet of others is in the case of Jesus, who washes his disciples' feet and requires them to do the same for one another.

Now what are we to make of the gender role subversion at this central point in John's narrative?

We first note that the location of this episode corresponds quite well with the glimpse of the man carrying water in Mark and Luke. It occurs, that is, as the preparatory event to Jesus' last meeting with his disciples. In all three of these Gospels, the transgression of male gender roles is connected with the narrative of the distinctive meal-ritual of the Christian community!

In Mark and Luke the emphasis falls on the meal itself as the event that the subsequent community of faith will commemorate through its distinctive cult meal. But in John the meal is completely overshadowed by the act of foot washing (and the subsequent appearance of the disciple Jesus loved). Jesus' washing of the feet, his performance of women's work, is to be imitated in his memory and in obedience to his command. In this way, through an act that transgresses gender categories, the community is to acknowledge him as teacher and Lord.

That Jesus is teacher (master) and Lord is connected in this narrative with his knowledge of where he had come from and whither he was going. That is, his transcendence of worldly structures comes to expression in his subversion of gender categories. Jesus' "divine" identity thus is expressed in his disregard for the most intimately enforced institutions of worldly society: gender role expectations.

The subversion of gender roles is often regarded as sacred in character. Perhaps the most famous illustration is the custom of the "berdache" (males who adopt typically female tasks and garb) among many of the indigenous peoples of North America.[27] Something similar appears to occur among the "hijras" of India[28] and, of course, the *galli,* to whom we referred earlier in this chapter.[29] The logic of berdache-type institutions appears to be that the mixing of gender categories suggests the transcendence of these and thus of the human social world that the categories govern.

The action of Jesus in this regard is by no means restricted to him as the divine "Son." On the contrary, the pattern is set for all of his disciples. They are commanded to imitate precisely this disregard for gender identity. In this way, they too become those who are like the wind/spirit: born from above, concerning whom the world knows neither from whence they come nor whither they go (John 3:8, compare with 13:3).

---

27. Walter L. Williams, *The Spirit and the Flesh: Sexual Diversity in American Indian Culture* (Boston: Beacon Press, 1986).

28. Serena Nanda, "Hijras: An Alternative Sex and Gender Role in India," in Herdt, *Third Sex, Third Gender,* 373–417.

29. Other examples are cited in Greenberg, *The Construction of Homosexuality,* 56–65.

The action of Jesus and its imitation by those who seek to belong to him is the obverse of the saying we considered earlier from the Gospel of Thomas. There Jesus spoke of Mary (and of other women who sought to enter the reign of heaven) as becoming "male" (Thomas no. 114). Here Jesus and his (male) followers become "female." In this way, the saying of the Gospel of Thomas about male not being male, nor female being female (no. 22), is concretely expressed for all of Jesus' followers.

Precisely in this context, so strongly marked by gender subversion, do we meet the disciple Jesus loved. We have already seen that this relationship is an erotic relationship clearly characterized by emotional and bodily intimacy. Such same-sex relationships are often stigmatized through the suspicion that they undermine male gender privilege. One way to deflect this charge or suspicion is to link same-sex practices with initiation into male privilege, as in classical Athenian ideology or the practices of some New Guinea tribesmen. Alternatively, same-sex behavior may be linked with values of hypermasculinity as in the military associations of Thebes or Sparta, or the Samurai codes of Japan. But in the Gospel of John, a far more radical way is followed. Rather than trying to link the suggested same-sex relationship between Jesus and the beloved with the enforcement of masculinity, John first decisively subverts this role. Only then are we introduced to the same-sex erotic relationship between Jesus and the man he loved. In consequence, the subversion of male gender privilege and the intimacy of same-sex eroticism become the concrete signs of the realization of the value of love, which is the core of the Gospel.

Gender Trouble

The subversion of gender categories that appears to characterize elements of the Jesus tradition is not characteristic of the early Christian community as a whole. Indeed a counter tradition can be discerned already in Pauline literature and comes to predominate in the later Christian community: a tradition that conforms Christianity more and more to the gender role expectations characteristic both of normative Judaism and of pagan Rome.

Some ambivalence surrounds this approach in the letters of Paul. The baptismal theology of Galatians 3:28 in which Paul affirms (or agrees with a tradition independently extant) that "There is no longer...male and female; for all of you are one in Christ Jesus" seems quite consistent with the gender subversion that appears, for example, in the saying of the Gospel of Thomas:

Saying no. 22: "When you make the two one . . . and when you make the male and the female one and the same, so that the male will not be male nor the female female . . . then you will enter [the kingdom]." (*Nag Hammadi Library*)

The Galatians passage, whether it reflects Paul's views or those of the community, is consistent with elements we have encountered in the Jesus tradition.

But the matter does not end here. In an obscure passage in 1 Corinthians, Paul seems to endorse a certain degree of gender role discrimination. He explicitly affirms that women must have their heads covered when they pray in public while men must not and that men should have short hair while women should have long hair (1 Cor. 11:2–16). Here Paul's argument appears to depend both on the fittingness of fundamental distinctions between the sexes and on the grounding of these differences in "nature" (v. 14) or universal custom.

What is perhaps even more surprising is that later in the same letter Paul appears to endorse the silencing of women in the life of the community (1 Cor. 14:34–35). In spite of the fact that the passage from 1 Corinthians 11 seems to presuppose that women do in fact speak in the congregation (even though they should observe gender markers in doing so), here Paul seems to maintain that women are not to be permitted to speak at all in the life of the congregation. The gender role distinction becomes gender oppression.

Because of the apparent contradiction between 1 Corinthians 14 and the baptismal formula of Galatians 3:28 or even the situation presupposed in 1 Corinthians 11, the silencing of women from 1 Corinthians 14 has often been presumed as a later insertion deriving from post-Pauline community traditions in which the conformity to the ethos of normative Judaism and Roman paganism is rather far advanced.[30]

An illustration of the advance of this conformist tradition is available from a letter attributed to Paul but which was almost certainly produced after his death:

I desire then, that in every place the men should pray, lifting up holy hands without anger or argument; also that the women should dress themselves modestly and decently in suitable clothing. . . .

---

30. On this, see Neil Elliott, *Liberating Paul: The Justice of God and the Politics of the Apostle* (Maryknoll, N.Y.: Orbis Books, 1994), 52–54.

Let a woman learn in silence with full submission. I permit no woman to teach or to have authority over a man; she is to keep silent. For Adam was formed first, then Eve; and Adam was not deceived but the woman was deceived and became a transgressor. Yet she will be saved through child bearing, provided they continue in faith and love and holiness, with modesty. (1 Tim. 2:8–15)

Here we can see the way in which the insistence on gender role conformity (1 Tim. 2:8–9) easily becomes a justification for the subordination of women and for the defense of male gender privilege (vv. 11–12).

It is unquestionably the Pauline and pseudo-Pauline tradition, rather than the Jesus tradition, that has had the upper hand in the development of classical Christianity. (In part 3, we find a similar tension between these two traditions with respect to what may be termed marriage and family values.) As is so often the case, the more radical elements of the Jesus tradition are simply overwhelmed and finally silenced in favor of the attempt to bring Christianity into conformity with respectable cultural and social values of the late hellenistic world. The result is that Christianity will eventually pass itself off as the bulwark of respectable gender conformity, allowing the Jesus tradition itself to be marginalized within the community that pretends to derive from Jesus and claims to honor him.

Conclusion

What are we to make of the subversion of gender roles in the Jesus tradition, both in respect of the material concerning eunuchs and the sayings and deeds that invert gender categories? Of course, very important differences exist between our own situation and that of late antiquity. Gender roles are differently patterned today, and the relations of these roles to same-sex practices are also differently constructed. Certainly to say either for antiquity or for the contemporary situation that eunuchs are/were homosexuals or that gender role subversion is/was invariably related to same-sex eroticism is too simple. But then as now, same-sex eroticism could bring into question the male privilege defended by gender role conformity, and the necessity of this conformity could be used as a way of casting aspersions upon same-sex erotic practices.

From our consideration of the Jesus tradition, the sanctity of gender roles cannot be urged as an argument against same-sex erotic practices without utterly surrendering connection to the traditions concerning Jesus. Indeed the Jesus tradition is far more consistent in subverting these roles, and especially the masculine privilege defended by these roles, than "homosexuality" was then or is now.

Certainly those persons who find conventional gender roles to be oppressive may find that the Jesus tradition speaks an astonishingly strengthening word to them. Persons who are, in the modern parlance, "transgendered" may find that they have a place of honor in the Jesus traditions whatever may be the opprobrium heaped upon them by those who pretend to defend Christian culture and civilization against the very existence of persons who call into question social conventions regarding gender.

An important word of warning applies as well to those within the gay and lesbian community itself who seek to adopt the mantle of respectability by marginalizing transgendered persons. Modern "gay liberation" dates from the Stonewall riots, in which drag queens — often despised as much within as outside the gay community — finally resolved to take no more police harassment. Ironically, many gay people continue to marginalize those who were the vanguard of their own liberation. Yet this is scarcely more ironic than the way in which Christianity has itself become a dependable ally of gender role conformity.

The significance of this gender role subversion in the Jesus tradition is not restricted, however, to issues confronting gay and lesbian and transgendered people. One of the most powerful movements for change in our world is that women are discovering the possibility of escaping from the gender role straitjackets in which they have for too long been confined with the collusion of Christianity itself. In response, many men are discovering that the presumed male privilege defended by gender role conformity has been in fact also a kind of prison from which it is now becoming possible to imagine escaping.

The texts we have been considering not only make it more plausible that the Jesus tradition, because it was so little concerned with upholding gender role conformity, could retain for so long the dangerous memory of Jesus' relationship with another male; they also demonstrate the liberative potential for all people that has for too long lay buried beneath the rubble of heterosexist and homophobic official interpretation.

Part Three

MARRIAGE AND FAMILY VALUES

ONE OF THE WAYS in which the openness of the Jesus tradition to same-sex eroticism has been hidden from view is through the appropriation of the Christian tradition in general, and the Jesus tradition in particular, to buttress the marriage and family values that have come to be perceived as inimical to same-sex eroticism.

In the world of classical antiquity, same-sex eroticism was not generally regarded as entailing contradiction to the prevailing institutions of marriage and family. The male citizens of Athens, for example, were expected to fulfill the roles of husband and father whether or not they engaged in socially approved forms of same-sex eroticism (pederasty, use of male prostitutes, and so on). Much the same could be said of Roman culture.

However, in the case of Rome, in certain quarters a critique emerged of same-sex eroticism as standing in some tension with the austere self-control of the Roman paterfamilias, a self-control deemed necessary to the effective control of household and empire. The awareness of potential conflict between homoeroticism and the enforcement of familial and imperial values that begins to emerge in the Roman world has become a widespread point of view in the modern period.

One of the ways that the "issue of homosexuality" is dealt with in society and the churches is to claim that an approbation of homosexual acts, relationships, or persons would result in the subversion of family values. In recent U.S. presidential campaigns, we have seen how the religious right seeks to use the rallying cry of family values to buttress their attack on what they view as unacceptable lifestyle choices. This stance serves to stigmatize women who seek full equality, gay and lesbian persons who struggle for dignity and integrity, and so on.

One could, of course, attempt a defensive strategy in support of gay and lesbian people by claiming that "homosexuals" are good sons and daughters, can be good parents, and can constitute family units scarcely distinguishable from the Ozzie and Harriet (either Ozzie and Steve, or Harriet and Janet) model of cultural iconography.

But I believe that something more is at stake here and that a more radical strategy must be pursued, for the "traditional family" is the bulwark not only of patriarchy but also of heterosexism. A gay-affirmative theology and ethics has the responsibility of challenging the hegemony of a system of values and structures that produce and reproduce heterosexism and homophobia.

More is involved here than the question of gay-affirmative theology and the overcoming of homophobia. We are increasingly aware of ways in which the family is a scene of violence and abuse, of the violation of persons and the distortion of persons' lives. The emergence of psychotherapy disclosed for many persons the coercive and distorting function of family life. Growing sociological knowledge of child and spouse abuse demonstrates that the family is dangerous to the well-being of vast numbers of human beings, old and young, male and female, gay and straight.

Inhibiting us from a radical critique of this institution, however, is the supposition that the family is somehow at the core of biblical ethics. Certainly churches in the modern period have universally portrayed themselves as the mainstay of marriage and family values. To attack these values from within the church or from within Christian theology then seems virtually impossible.

An essential aid, however, can come from a "gay-affirmative" hermeneutic that is unafraid to challenge the hegemony of heterosexism and thus the hegemony of what are called "marriage and family values." In the following discussion, I want to demonstrate the ways in which the Jesus tradition, as we have it in the Gospels, transmits a fundamental critique of marriage and family values.[1]

In the following consideration of family values, I first address the way in which the Gospels represent Jesus as fundamentally opposed to the institution of the family (chapter 10). This opposition appears to stem from Jesus' profound critique of all structures that mediate and enforce

---

1. Rosemary Ruether has written an important study of the way in which Christianity has come to ally itself with "marriage and family values" in spite of the positions on these matters discernible not only in the Jesus traditions but also, to some extent, in Paul. See Rosemary Radford Ruether, *Christianity and the Making of the Modern Family: Ruling Ideologies, Diverse Realities* (Boston: Beacon Press, 2000), esp. 25–28 on Jesus and 28–31 on Paul.

the social status quo, a social world that is passing away as the divine reign of justice, generosity, and joy takes shape in the world.

In chapter 11, I turn to Jesus' attitude toward marriage itself and show the presence of a contrast between Jesus' attitude toward marriage understood as the initiation of the family and the wedding feast as suggestive of the celebration of human happiness. This topic leads, in chapter 12, to a consideration of the question of procreation as the goal of sexual activity, a view absent not only from the Jesus traditions but also from the perspective of authentic Pauline documents as well.

That the Jesus tradition is fundamentally critical of marriage and family values places it in tension with other developments in early Christianity as represented by Paul and later letter writers of the New Testament. But Pauline acceptance and post-Pauline valorization of some of the family values of antiquity should not be allowed to obscure for us the radicality of the narrative traditions about Jesus that consistently subvert these values. Noting the parallel between the valorization of certain family values and acquiescence in the institution of slavery in later New Testament documents helps to indicate how the Gospel tradition's critique of family structures may have wider relevance (chapter 13).

This review of "marriage and family values" demonstrates that appeal to the self-evidence of these institutions cannot be used either to obscure the elements of same-sex eroticism in the Jesus tradition or to bring contemporary same-sex eroticism into disrepute. To the extent that same-sex eroticism undermines the self-evidence of these institutions or the absoluteness of their claims, such eroticism is consistent with the traditions concerning Jesus contained in the Gospels. If anything then, these reflections further substantiate the gay-affirmative rereading of the Gospels that I have been proposing.

Chapter 10

The Critique of the Family

We turn first to the critique of the institution of the family in the Jesus tradition. In all the Gospels, Jesus is represented as adamant in his critique of this institution and its values.

In order to make Jesus' position clear, I begin with the Gospel of Mark and the appropriation of that material in Matthew and Luke. Then we turn to material common to Matthew and Luke (commonly referred by scholars to an early sayings source designated as "Q"), as well as material unique to each of these Gospels. We also attend to texts that are used to create the impression of Jesus' support for the family, texts on children and on corban. Finally we consider texts from the Gospel of John that parallel the perspective of the first three Gospels.

Even if a contradiction were present between homoeroticism and family values, we shall see that the Jesus tradition sets its face resolutely against the latter. A study of the text finds no ground in the Jesus tradition's attitude toward the biological family for devaluing same-sex erotic relationships.

Mark

The Gospel of Mark offers four passages that bear upon our theme and which are taken over and developed in different ways by Matthew and Luke.

The New Family (Mark 3:21, 31–35; Matt. 12:46–50; Luke 8:19–21)

In the Gospel of Mark, the theme of family is explicitly broached in the third chapter when Jesus' family come to extract him from the crowds of sinners and the needy who have gathered about him. As often happens in Mark, the narrative is a kind of sandwich in which a story about Jesus and his family serves as the "bread" or frame for another narrative about the

174

scribes from Jerusalem who suppose that Jesus is in league with Beelzebul. The sandwich technique serves to emphasize the links between Jesus' birth family and the leaders of Jesus' religious and social culture. Both groups believe that Jesus is, in their own terms, crazy. This pair of confrontations brings to a close the initial phase of Jesus' ministry in Galilee. Here we concentrate on the encounter with the family.

Jesus has just appointed the twelve to be sent out, and the list concludes with the name of Judas Iscariot "who will betray him."

> Then he went home; and the crowd came together again so that they could not even eat. When his family heard it, they went out to restrain him, for they were saying, "He has gone out of his mind." (Mark 3:19b–21)

> Then his mother and his brothers came; and standing outside, they sent to him and called him. A crowd was sitting around him; and they said to him, "Your mother and your brothers and your sisters are outside asking for you." And he replied, "Who are my mother and my brothers?" And looking at those who sat around him, he said, "Here are my mother and my brothers! Whoever does the will of God is my brother and sister and mother." (Mark 3:31–35)

The reply of Jesus to his family's summons does not seem calculated to allay the suspicion that he has "gone out of his mind."[1] But his reply does serve to establish a clear distinction between what we may call "family of origin" and the new "family" of those who are committed to the will of God, which is the establishment of the reign of justice and generosity and joy.

As it turns out, this distinction has already been prefigured in the text by the call of the first disciples who, in order to follow Jesus, abandon the ties of work and family (Mark 1:16–20). Thus of James and John we are told that they "left their father Zebedee in the boat, with the hired men, and followed him" (1:20). The alternative — either the will of God or family of origin — is being established within the narrative.

The only kinship tie that Jesus will acknowledge is that of shared mission in performing that which God wills or purposes. All other ties are abolished. Whoever stands with Jesus is his mother. The one who does as

---

1. Both Matthew and Luke omit the supposition that Jesus was "out of his mind." The NRSV deflects this supposition from Jesus' family to "people," but the Greek has only "they." The introduction of a different subject (people rather than family) is not warranted. That Jesus is out of his mind is the motivation for the family coming out to restrain Jesus. The view of the family (his own) is similar to the view of the religious authorities: he is in league with Beelzebul.

Jesus does is his sister. The one who does what God desires, and no other, is brother to Jesus.

And what is God's will? Nothing is claimed here of special religious duties. Instead Jesus has concretely demonstrated the divine will: that outcasts are befriended, that the maimed are healed, that the demon possessed return to sanity. And *whoever* does this is Jesus' brother, mother, and sister.

Blood ties are irrelevant. The woman who bore him and the siblings who shared the same womb have the same access to fellowship with Jesus as any other and on the same condition: join with those around him who are learning to do what God wants, which is making creation whole again.

Hometown: Mark 6:1–6; Matthew 13:53–58 (see Luke 4:16–30)

A second episode common to Mark and Matthew concerns Jesus' return to his "hometown."

> He left that place and came to his hometown, and his disciples followed him. On the sabbath he began to teach in the synagogue, and many who heard him were astounded. They said, "Where did this man get all this? What is this wisdom that has been given to him! What deeds of power are being done by his hands!
>
> "Is not this the carpenter, the son of Mary and brother of James and Joses and Judas and Simon? And are not his sisters here with us?"
>
> And they were scandalized by him. Then Jesus said to them, "Prophets are not without honor, except in their hometown, and among their own kin, and in their own house." And he could do no deed of power there, except that he laid his hands on a few sick people and cured them. And he was amazed at their unbelief.

Jesus is known "at home" as an ordinary tradesman and as a member of a rather large family. Nothing extraordinary is to be expected of that which is familiar. Indeed from the standpoint of this settled community, Jesus may be a "dropout," having left home, work, and family to live as a vagabond. His own family regards him as crazy (3:21), and he has in turn repudiated them in favor of his vagabond and dropout friends — a group that includes untouchables, certified lunatics, and assorted persons of ill repute. As one would expect of God-fearing hometown folk, "they were scandalized by him" (Mark 6:3).

The response of Jesus is an ironic commonplace that agrees well with experience in all ages. Characteristically Jesus claims for himself no other role than that of teacher and prophet. In this context, "prophet" only means one who speaks audaciously inverting hallowed traditions (like Amos or Hosea), and who performs deeds of power (like Elijah and Elisha). The vocation of Jesus is in these ways identical to that of his predecessors and is, moreover, fully shared with his followers (3:14–15).

The link between the family and the familiar — between the family of origin and the resistance of the status quo to radical transformation — is becoming clear. Yet this radical transformation is precisely what the mission and message of Jesus is enacting and announcing.

Luke's version of Jesus' return to his hometown is best known for Jesus' inaugural sermon and for the initial approving response of the hearers (Luke 4:14–30). But the reaction to Jesus' words about the work of Elijah and Elisha far exceeds the "disbelief" of the hometown folks as recorded in Mark and Matthew. In Luke, they actually seek to kill Jesus on the spot.

> When they heard this, all in the synagogue were filled with rage. They got up, drove him out of the town, and led him to the brow of the hill on which their town was built, so that they might hurl him off the cliff. (Luke 4:28–29)

It is not only that the hometown people cannot recognize the new in what they suppose to be familiar. Here the reaction is also sparked by ethnocentrism, which previews the reaction of the Jerusalem authorities later in the story, the reaction that leads to Jesus' being delivered over to the Roman occupation forces who then execute him

Leaving Family: Mark 10:29–31; Luke 18:28–30; Matthew 19:27–30

The contrast between the mission of Jesus and the kinship ties of this age has been played out first in the contrast between Jesus' own family of origin and the new family he is gathering about him, and then in the impotence of his mission within the familiar structure of the hometown where he is seen in terms of his family of origin. Now is the time to make evident the same contrast for the understudies or disciples of Jesus.

> Peter began to say to him, "Look, we left everything and have followed you." Jesus said, "Truly I say to you, there is no one who left house or mother or father or brothers or sisters or children or fields for my sake and for the sake of the gospel, who does not receive, now in this time, a hundredfold houses and brothers and sisters and mothers and children and lands, with persecutions, and in the coming age, life everlasting.

"And many that are first will be last and the last first."

In spite of the disciples' very limited understanding of Jesus and his mission, they have at least understood something of the requirements of discipleship. The words of Peter, "See, *we* have left everything and are following you," include all those who are following Jesus, a group that is by no means restricted to the twelve. Those people who are with Jesus are exclusively those who have left everything, who have divested themselves of both possessions and family ties. Note that family ties here are "sandwiched" between material goods: House introduces the series and "fields" ends the series. The intervening list of family terms — brothers or sisters or mothers or fathers or children — is thus set squarely within the economic sphere of possession, of security within the world.[2] The question here is not of abolishing ties of affection but of abolishing the family as an economic and social reality that secures one's life in the world.[3]

The promise of Jesus is made to those who have renounced ties to possessions and family. The promise is that those people who have renounced these possessions will receive "a hundredfold." That is, those who have left brothers and sisters will receive hundreds of brothers and sisters. Those who have left mothers and children will receive hundreds of mothers and children.

How are we to understand the content of this promise? From the episode concerning the family of Jesus, we know what both renouncing family and receiving a new family mean. Jesus has renounced the special claim of his own mother and brothers and sisters and in this way has found in the multitude who are with him a "hundredfold" mothers and brothers and sisters. Thus, the sisters and brothers the disciples receive are those they find in their shared mission, just as Jesus has done. In view here are the adopted relatives of the community of mission. They leave behind the blood ties of the old era and receive the companionship of the new era. Jesus obviously is not talking about receiving a hundred times the number of biological relatives he or his followers have left behind. What would it mean to have a hundred such "mothers," for example? The renunciation of physical kinship is tied to the reception of "adopted" kin, which conforms exactly to the experience of mission: that those who enter into

---

2. The definitive treatment of this relation of family to economic possession is L. William Countryman, *Dirt, Greed, and Sex: Sexual Ethics in the New Testament and Their Implications for Today* (Philadelphia: Fortress Press, 1988), 168–89.

3. To the list common to Matthew and Mark, Luke adds "wife." This corresponds to Luke's even more insistent opposition to marriage as an institution. See chapter 11 in this volume.

solidarity with the poor and afflicted find that they have hundreds of sisters and brothers and mothers.[4]

We may note that while the disciples are said to leave fathers, they are not said to receive fathers, still less "a hundredfold." The only parents they get are mothers, which is consistent with the tendency of the Jesus tradition to abolish the structures of patriarchy.[5] The rights and claims of "paternity" that are the basis of patriarchy are abolished.

Enmity: Mark 13:12; Matthew 24:21; Luke 21:16

The final saying concerning family in the Gospel of Mark is found in the "apocalyptic discourse" of chapter 13. The discourse announces the theme of final conflict and warns the followers of Jesus that this conflict will concern them. They will face opposition from religious and political authorities. This conflict is, moreover, "brought home" to them in the following way:

> And brother will deliver up brother to death, and the father his child, and children will rise up against parents and have them put to death; and you will be hated by all for my name's sake. But that which endures to the end [goal] will be saved. (Mark 13:12–13)

The crisis introduced by loyalty to the gospel not only brings into the open the enmity of the public institutions of religion and government to the reign of God. The institution of the family shatters as well. A scene of domestic tranquility explodes into conflict and betrayal.

The Gospel of Mark sets out a very clear line of opposition between the Jesus movement and the claims of family of origin. This opposition appears first as the leaving of home to follow Jesus. It then becomes the theme of explicit teaching when Jesus not only renounces the claims of his own family of origin but points to the establishment of a new family constituted by all who identify themselves with the coming of the divine reign. This old family that "domesticates" life is represented as making impossible the enactment of the transformation of reality indicated by the coming of the divine reign. Thus the need to break with family ties for all of Jesus' followers is indicated in Mark 10:29–31 together with the

---

4. The followers will also receive children a "hundredfold." Again, they obviously will not receive hundreds of biological progeny. Instead their mission will be fruitful; the mission of those sent two by two will be "fruitful and multiply." We consider this issue of fruitfulness under the heading of procreation in chapter 12. The promise of multitudes of children is also related to the teaching concerning children discussed later in this chapter.

5. This tendency is highlighted in Matthew with the injunction to "call no one your father"; see below, pp. 183–84.

promise that this means not only loss but also the reception of a new family with multitudes of mothers and sisters and brothers and children. Finally we are warned that loyalty to the reign of God means the outright hostility of the family of origin, whose prerogatives have been shattered by loyalty to the cause of the new humanity (son of man) and the divine reign of justice and generosity and joy.

Matthew and Luke bring over from Mark this unrelenting opposition between the way of Jesus and the institution of the family. And to it the later Gospel writers add new elements from the remembered materials concerning Jesus.

Source Q

In addition to the material in Mark that is common to Matthew and Luke, we have three sayings common to Matthew and Luke that are not found in Mark. Traditional scholarship now holds that material common to Matthew and Luke comes from a source known to them but not to Mark. Many scholars regard this material as having an especially strong claim to represent the earliest memory of the community concerning Jesus.

The Dead

In each Gospel, someone who is about to follow Jesus says, "First let me go and bury my father," to which Jesus responds, "Leave the dead to bury their own dead" (Matt. 8:21–22; Luke 9:59–60). Here following Jesus is contrasted with fulfilling the most simple and natural of family responsibilities. In both Gospels, the saying is preceded by "foxes have holes and birds of the air have nests but the son of man has nowhere to lie his head." This saying concerning the son of man or the "human" clearly designates all who would follow Jesus. They are to be, as it were, without a home — specifically, without a family.

The topic here is not celibacy but rather the family ties of a father or of those at home who must first be bid farewell. In this regard we should recall that a den or a nest is not a bachelor pad, but is a place associated with security — the security involved in the raising of a family, with family ties, responsibilities, and obligations.

In the Gospel of Luke, the saying that follows the one about the dead makes this point all the more clear: "I will follow you, Lord, but first let me say farewell to those at home." Jesus' reply is uncompromising: "No one who puts his hand to the plow and then looks back is fit for the reign of God." The concern for family here is the looking back that disqualifies one for the reign of God.

People who raise objections here seem quite willing to follow Jesus, to substantially compromise their relationships and responsibilities with their families. Jesus objects, though, to any attempt to balance these desires at all. They are viewed as incompatible.

Following Jesus then, or responding to the announcement of the in-breaking of the divine reign, does not produce better family relations. Instead responding to Jesus appears to mean opposing family ties in principle and absolutely.

In the sayings from "Q" and the setting given them by Luke, the disciples' leaving of homes and family is not incidental but essential. Thus, Peter's report in Mark 10:29 that the disciples have indeed left home and family is even more plausible. Furthermore, the opposition between Jesus and his own family cannot be understood as a simple misunderstanding, but rather as an example that sets the pattern for all who follow.

Conflict

The next saying, which is substantially the same in Matthew and Luke, concerns conflict in the family. "Do not think that I have come to bring peace to the earth; I have not come to bring peace but a sword. For I have come to set a man against his father, and a daughter against her mother and a daughter-in-law against her mother-in-law; and one's foes will be members of one's own household" (Matt. 10:34–36; see Luke 12:51–53).

This text most closely corresponds to what we encountered in Mark concerning the times of persecution (Mark 13). But here a general principle is highlighted, rather than the special situation of persecution. The setting of son against father also generalizes the situation of potential conflict in the previous saying concerning the dead.

This saying also more strongly emphasizes the situation of the woman; two clauses are directed to her and only one to the man. Moreover the reference to daughter-in-law and mother-in-law suggests a troubling of the marriage relationship as well. In any case we have here situations involving both the unmarried woman (mother and daughter) and the married woman (mother-in-law and daughter-in-law).

The saying makes clear in no uncertain terms that Jesus does not intend to promote domestic harmony, nor to improve family relations. Rather his deliberate intention ("I have come") is to provoke discord in this domestic sphere.

Intensified Conflict

Matthew continues the above statement with a saying that further highlights the situation of conflict. Luke has a similar saying but places it in a different context. Because these sayings are significantly different, however, we begin with Matthew first. "Whoever loves father or mother more than me is not worthy of me; and whoever loves son or daughter more than me is not worthy of me; and whoever does not take up the cross and follow me is not worthy of me. Those who find their life will lose it and those who lose their life for my sake will find it" (Matt. 10:37–39).

The saying concerning the cross (which, of course, is also in Mark) does at least propose something of a basis for the sayings about the overthrow of domestic harmony.

Unfortunately the first part of the statement is often interpreted in such a way as to permit the view that loving parent and child is readily compatible with loving Jesus and, indeed, is a way of demonstrating one's adherence to the way and the work of Jesus. Of course, such an interpretation must ignore all that the previous verses have said and indeed all that Matthew's Gospel has to say concerning family relations. This interpretation has only bolstered a determined heterosexist and indeed patriarchal hermeneutic. Within the context of Matthew's Gospel, this saying makes clear that the "loving more" of Jesus means coming into conflict with fundamental structures of the self and of the domestic institution that shapes the self.

The saying in the Gospel of Luke, however, makes an accommodationist misunderstanding of the Jesus tradition far more difficult.

If anyone comes to me and does not hate his own father and mother and wife and children and brothers and sisters and even his own life, that one cannot be my disciple. Whoever does not bear the cross and come after me cannot be my disciple. (Luke 14:26–27)

We also have a similar saying in the Gospel of Thomas:

Jesus said, "Whoever does not hate father and mother cannot be a follower of me, and whoever does not hate brothers and sisters and bear the cross as I do will not be worthy of me." (Logion no. 55)

If this saying from Thomas is more "primitive" as some suppose, then Matthew and Luke have added the reference to children and Luke has added the saying concerning the wife. As we shall see, Luke is more critical than other Gospels of the marriage relationship.

The main point, however, is the radical character of the opposition to family members. Family members are not becoming irrational enemies on account of some misunderstanding. Rather the follower of Jesus actively turns against the family, creating a relationship that has more in common with hate than with love.

What really seems at stake here is the way in which families and family members define their own interest. It is against this interest that the follower turns. In this sense, the follower hates the family and is opposed to what seems to be in the best interest of the family as family — just as persons may be said to hate themselves in the sense of turning against their own self-interest, their own desire for self-preservation. Precisely this concern for self-preservation must be opposed if one is to take up the dangerous business of following one who deliberately courts the outrage of the authorities, to the extent of daring them to crucify him.

The hating of mother and father then — to take this position as the starting point — is not an animus toward them as human beings, but precisely as mother and father; in their role as family members with special rights and expectations and demands. This special position of the family is radically and fundamentally opposed, and the same holds true for brothers and sisters. As family members, they claim a special loyalty that must be resolutely and ruthlessly opposed. Perhaps this approach is most obvious with respect to one's own children. Clearly Jesus places a high value on children as children, but what is opposed here is the special relationship to "my child" as opposed to any child whatever. The special claim of this one as opposed to all the others is to be opposed.

The supposition that a child is "my child" is fundamentally the source of a great deal of destructiveness in the family. First, such an outlook allows a person to ignore the needs of all other children in the name of caring for one's own. In this way, if I have the means I can lavish all upon this one and suppose that others have no claim upon me. But far more is going on here as well. The notion that a certain child is mine leads me to make unreasonable demands upon the child. That this person is a child is not enough. The child must also be an instrument of my ambition as a mother or a father. The child must bear the burden of being my future, an extension of me. For that reason, families are so often the most dangerous places on earth for children.

Matthew and Fathers

We have noticed that in the saying about giving up family and possessions (Mark 10:29–31), the followers are said to leave fathers but are not said to receive them back "a hundredfold." This omission may be regarded as deliberate. In Matthew, we have further clarification of this deliberate omission in a saying distinctive to that Gospel:

> But you are not to be called rabbi, for you have one teacher, and you are all students. And call no one your father on earth, for you have one Father — the one in heaven. Nor are you to be called instructors, for you have one instructor, the Messiah. The greatest among you will be your servant. All who exalt themselves will be humbled, and all who humble themselves will be exalted. (Matt. 23:8–12)

Jesus' program for his disciples clearly entails the abolition of distinctions among them and thus the abolition of hierarchical relationships. In this connection, Jesus prohibits calling anyone "father" and thus prohibits the recognition of the claims of paternity and so of authority on the part of any human being, including biological fathers.

A frequent claim is that the "fatherhood of God" serves to buttress patriarchy. Certainly this has happened regularly in the course of Christendom. But the Jesus tradition uses the appellation of God as Father (or Father in heaven) precisely to overthrow the rule of patriarchy. Jesus' saying is quite radical in this regard since, on the face of it, it seems to fly in the face of the command to "honor your father."

The saying attributed to Jesus in Matthew's Gospel clearly undermines human fatherhood, and so patriarchy, in the context of abolishing all hierarchical relationships. This aspect of the familial structure at least is considered to be completely antithetical to the values of the divine reign whose coming Jesus is concerned to announce and enact.

Luke and Mothers

The Gospel of Luke also has an episode peculiar to itself that undermines the importance of biological motherhood, including, by implication, the role of Mary. "As he said this, a woman in the crowd raised her voice and said, 'Blessed is the womb that bore you and the breasts that you sucked!' But he said, 'Blessed rather are those who hear the word of God and keep it' " (11:27–28).

In spite of the fact that Luke gives greater attention to Mary than the other Gospels, making her the center of the birth narrative that serves as a prologue to the Gospel, Luke nevertheless undermines her role insofar as it is based on biological grounds. In this saying, Mary as birth mother has no particular place of honor, but rather anyone who hears and keeps the divine word. In the Gospel of Luke, these categories are not exclusive. Mary is precisely represented as one who hears the word and keeps it (1:38, 46–55; 2:19, 34–35, 51). Her place in the narrative as one who is honored is not as "mother" but as believer, which corresponds precisely with the intention of Jesus' saying concerning his family in Luke 8:19–21. His only "mother and brothers and sisters" are "those who hear the word of God and do it."

In this way Luke, manages to make attention to Mary consistent with the undermining of family relationships generally and thus of the institution of the family as a whole.

Summation of the Synoptics

How are we to account for this radical suspicion of, and outright hostility to, the ties of the institution of the family? Here we may find initial help from the Lukan passage considered earlier.

> If anyone comes to me and does not hate his own father and mother and wife and children and brothers and sisters and even his own life, that one cannot be my disciple. Whoever does not bear the cross and come after me cannot be my disciple. Whoever does not carry the cross and follow me cannot be my disciple. For which of you, intending to build a tower, does not first sit down and estimate the cost, to see whether he has enough to complete it? Otherwise when he has laid a foundation and is not able to finish, all who see it will begin to ridicule him, saying, "This fellow began to build and was not able to finish." Or what king, going out to wage war against another king, will not sit down first and consider whether he is able with ten thousand to oppose the one who comes against him with twenty thousand? If he cannot, then, while the other is still far away, he sends a delegation and asks the terms of peace. So therefore, none of you can become my disciple if you do not give up all your possessions. (Luke 14:26–35)

Renunciation of family ties is clearly understood from the standpoint of the turn from the old to the new. Such renouncing is specifically at stake here in the commitment to the new order that Jesus is inaugurating and to the service of which order the disciples are summoned as understudies in Jesus' mission. Leaving family and possessions behind is in no way incidental or peripheral to Jesus' message. The renunciation of self-interest, of family, of possessions, and of life itself in taking up the cross is an integral part of the cost of discipleship as portrayed in the Gospels.

But we may still be perplexed about how this demand comes into being. How does the family institution prevent one from following Jesus? We may gain some help in understanding this if we return to the initial passage from the Gospel of Mark with which we began our discussion of the synoptic tradition concerning Jesus' subversion of family values. That passage dealt with the true family and the contrast between the blood ties of the old family and the ties of solidarity of the new.

Crucial for our purposes now is the context of the passage. Immediately after the family comes out to restrain Jesus, believing that he had "gone out of his mind," we have the following: "And the scribes who came down from Jerusalem said, 'He has Beelzebul, and by the ruler of the demons he casts out demons'" (Mark 3:22).

Jesus' response seeks to demonstrate that even if the scribes are right to think that Jesus were in league with demonic powers, his actions of healing and exorcism still demonstrate the end of the rule of these powers and the in-breaking of the divine rule.

The incident with Jesus' relatives is interrupted by the incident with the "scribes from Jerusalem." The stories are told as a sandwich, which is Mark's way of calling our attention to the relation between the incidents. Here Jesus' relatives and the scribes from Jerusalem both have the same general diagnosis of Jesus: He is crazy. Jesus' craziness is precisely the way in which he stands outside the conventional order of meaningfulness — an order that is represented on the one hand by the family and on the other by the religious authorities from Jerusalem.

The stability of familial institutions is directly linked to the stability of religious and social institutions. Indeed we may say that the family is the base, and religion the superstructure and ideology of the basic social structures of life: cultural, social, political, and economic. The family is the place where these values are inculcated, and religion is the manner of validating and sanctioning them. Jesus' enactment of a new social order of open friendship, of solidarity and generosity, shatters the social world that both family and religion serve and protect. From the standpoint of both, Jesus is impious; Jesus is "crazy."

The creation of a new world necessarily brings one into contradiction with the most elemental social structure of the old world — the seedbed of the old order — the family.

Countertendencies

In addition to the material we have considered, which clearly sets up opposition between Jesus and the institution of the family, two kinds of passages are often cited as suggesting a more accepting attitude toward these same institutions: sayings concerning children and the saying concerning the obligation to parents in relation to the dispute concerning "corban." We consider these passages to see if any reason exists for supposing that the Jesus tradition in some way supports the institution of family.

Children

We turn first to sayings concerning children that are common to the first three Gospels. As before, we take the Markan form of the sayings as the basis for discussion. The saying concerning the leaving of children or the renunciation of one's own children in Mark 10:30 may be misunderstood as suggesting a callous attitude toward children as such. This interpretation is already countered in the same passage in the promise concerning the reception of children a hundredfold. The situation is further clarified when considering specific texts concerning children. "And taking a child he set it in the midst of them, and embracing it he said to them, 'Whoever welcomes one of these in my name, receives me, and whoever welcomes me welcomes not me but that which sends me' " (Mark 9:36–37; see also Matt. 18:2–5; Luke 9:47–48).

In all three Gospels, this story is placed within the discussion of the disciples concerning "greatness" in the reign of God. Jesus is here emphasizing the importance of a concern for the most vulnerable as the sign of relationship with him. In this case what is at stake is the attitude toward children as those who are vulnerable. Thus, the abandonment of one's own children as suggested by other sayings should by no means imply encouraging a hostile relationship to children as such. Rather the difference is between children as the object of possession and the means of assuring security within the world (my children) and children as the vulnerable ones whose protection and embrace is an indispensable expression of the values of the reign of God.

The difference then is that between children as children (vulnerable) and children as possession (which make parents secure in the world). The crux of this distinction bears upon the difference between "my" children and other children. The question is whether a concern for my children produces an indifference to other children. Where this distinction is abolished, any child whatever, regardless of parentage, is the proper object of concern for the follower of Jesus, for in welcoming and embracing any child whatever, one welcomes that which sends Jesus; one embraces, that is to say, God.

This proclamation is further clarified by another saying concerning children common to the first three Gospels:

And they were bringing children to him, that he might touch them; and the disciples rebuked them. But Jesus saw it and was furious, and said to them, "Let the children come to me, don't stop them, for the reign of God belongs to those like them. Truly I say to you, whoever does not receive the reign of God as a child does will not enter it at all." And folding them in his arms, he blesses them, laying his hands upon them. (Mark 10:13–16; see Matt. 19:13–15; Luke 18:15–17)

The coming of the reign of God is here identified with the need of children. For to them, the reign of justice and generosity and joy is especially directed.

The rage of Jesus in the Gospel of Mark is directed against his own followers who have concluded that the reign of God is for adults and who therefore seek to separate children from him. Jesus wants none of this sentiment. Again we are told that the reign of God especially concerns these most vulnerable of human beings.

Jesus' apparent repudiation of family ties by no means entails a repudiation of children as children. Indeed the attitude of Jesus toward children is dramatically underscored in these texts by his exceptional tenderness toward them, which contrasts with his rage directed not only against his opponents but, even more noticeably, against his adult followers. However, the extraordinary concern for children that Jesus demonstrates in no way contradicts the radical opposition of the Jesus tradition to the institution of the family, including the way in which children represent the perpetuation of this institution.

Corban

The last text to consider in relation to the attitude toward the family in the Jesus tradition is one that concerns parents. The text occurs in the midst of a dispute occasioned by the disciples' disregard of religious tradition and social (ethnic) custom.

And he said to them, "Well did Isaiah prophesy of you hypocrites, as it is written,

'This people honors me with their lips but their heart is far from me.

In vain do they worship me, teaching as doctrines the precepts of men.'

You leave the commandment of God and hold fast the tradition of men."

And he said to them, "You have a fine way of rejecting the commandment of God, in order to keep your tradition! For Moses said, 'Honor your father and mother' and 'He who speaks evil of father or mother let him surely die.' But you say, 'If a man tells his father or his mother, 'What you would have gained from me is corban' (That is, given to God) — then you no longer permit him to do anything for his father or his mother, thus making void the word of God through your tradition which you received. And many such things you do." (Mark 7:6–13; see Matt. 15:3–6. There is no parallel in Luke.)

In order to see what is at stake here, we must notice that what Jesus opposes is a religious practice (corban) that interferes with a response to human need. Careful attention is required here because of the reversal of terms. We begin with the opposition "of God" and "of man." We are to honor the first (divine command) instead of the second (human tradition). What looks like a sacred/secular distinction is then reversed. What is of God is regard for — attention to — human need. What is "of man" is attention to and regard for "religion" (corban). The divine command points to a humanistic obligation while the human tradition points to a religious obligation. What is "of God" is secular humanism. What is "of man" is religious piety.

Thus Mark has Jesus maintain that "religion" is a human invention (Feuerbach) and that it functions to prevent us from seeing and responding to the need and suffering of the other (Marx). Jesus' comments come within the radical context of the prophetic view that God requires not religion but justice.

The context of this saying means that we cannot use it to justify the legitimacy of family structures. Jesus in no way urges his followers to honor their (own) parents. Rather he notices how the upholders of tradition themselves find a way to ignore their responsibility for elders. The point of Jesus' response then is that they have no ground to stand on in criticizing the disciples for not obeying tradition, for their tradition is a violation of what God really requires: a concern for human need.

Thus we are in a situation similar to that which we found in regard to children. Jesus summons people to a concern for vulnerable human beings in need. The renunciation of parents, like the renunciation of children, is not to be understood as a legitimation of callous disregard for the vulnerability of others or as an escape from responsibility. Rather Jesus widens the circle of responsibility to include all children and all parents (or elders). Precisely because of widening the circle of care and responsibility in this way, Jesus' instruction comes into basic conflict with the institution of family, which seeks to enforce the distinction between one's own (children, mothers, siblings) and the others.

The Gospel of John

In contrast to the first three Gospels, the Gospel of John maintains a conspicuous silence with respect to the institution of family. It is, for the most part, simply ignored. This Gospel could not be construed, though, as somehow supportive of this institution or as taking it for granted. Rather, for the community of the beloved disciple, it appears that the old institution of the family was irrelevant. This outlook becomes clear in passages concerning birth and in passages concerning Jesus and his mother, the only passages that have any relation to our theme.

On two occasions, the Gospel of John mentions birth as a process that may be connected to family. In both cases this birth is contrasted with the birth that is of interest to the writer(s) and to Jesus. In the prologue to the narrative we are told: "But to all who received him, who believed in his name, he gave power to become the children of God, who were born, not of blood, or of the will of the flesh or of the will of man, but of God" (1:12–13).

This passage, which we will consider again in relation to the issue of procreation and sexuality, clearly contrasts the divine generation of the believer with the "natural generation" that is so often regarded as the purpose of the institution of marriage and family.

The second passage is the lengthy discussion between Jesus and Nicodemus concerning contrasting births in 3:1–14. Here again the contrast is made between womb birth and the divine birth that Jesus maintains is necessary to "see the reign of God." Again this passage cannot in any way be taken to legitimate the institution of marriage and family understood as the context for the womb birth, which according to Jesus, is superseded.

We also have a parallel to the "hometown" episode in the Synoptics. Here the question concerns not a literal return to Jesus' birthplace but rather nonbelief based upon an acquaintance with Jesus' family of origin: "They were saying, is not this Jesus, the son of Joseph, whose father and mother we know? How can he now say, 'I have come down from heaven'?" (6:42).

The knowledge of Jesus' family of origin has the same function here as in the other Gospels, namely, to make faith impossible. The familiarity of family serves to make impossible an expectation of radical transformation.

The Gospel of John also narrates an episode concerning the brothers of Jesus that emphasizes the distance between them. In a dispute concerning a visit to Jerusalem to attend the "festival of Booths," the brothers of Jesus urge him to go in order to make a public declaration of his mission. Jesus declines (his "hour is not yet come"). And the narrator notes, "for not even his brothers believed in him" (7:6). When the brothers appear again it is as those who misunderstand the saying of Jesus concerning the disciple that he loved (21:23).

We come then to the place that this narrative gives to Mary, the mother of Jesus. We should note that Mary is the subject of narrative only in Luke and John.[6] In Luke, Mary is a principal subject of the prologue concerning the conception, birth, and childhood of Jesus. Yet in that Gospel her son explicitly relativizes her biological role in keeping with what we have seen in the Gospels generally.

The relation depicted between Jesus and his mother in the Gospel of John corresponds with what we find elsewhere. We have already had occasion to look at this in connection with the scene at the cross, but recalling it again in connection with the issue of family may be useful.

Mary is present for and instigates Jesus' first "sign" at Cana. This fact is sometimes cited as indicating a special relationship between Jesus and his mother, but a closer inspection of the text quickly dispels such an impression. "When the wine gave out, the mother of Jesus said to him, 'They have no wine.' And Jesus said to her, 'Woman, what concern is that to you and me? My hour is not yet come'" (2:3–4).

The saying of Jesus to Mary is more abrupt than the translation (NRSV) indicates. The phrase is one of pure dismissal, closer to "what are you to me?" Moreover his reply to her is like that which he uses to rebuke what the narrator has characterized as the unbelief of the brothers: "my hour is not yet come."

But equally telling is the fact that Jesus does not refer to her as his mother but rather as "woman" — the same form of address as the one he uses to the Samaritan woman and to the woman taken in adultery. Mary is here treated by Jesus precisely as any woman whatever. She has no special claim on him by virtue of being his mother.

Jesus nonetheless accedes to her request, which is also characteristic of Jesus' response to other requests made of him. He heals those who come

---

6. The birth narrative in the Gospel of Matthew places the emphasis on Joseph rather than Mary.

to him for healing; he teaches those who come to him for enlightenment. Mary is in this respect in the same situation as others.[7]

This same situation is represented at the scene of Jesus' execution when Mary and the disciple Jesus loved are found together at the foot of the cross. Mary is again addressed by Jesus not as Mary nor as "mother" but as "woman." And, as we have seen, the emphasis in the text is on these two figures' mutual adoption of one another. The scene then gives an especially dramatic representation to the constitution not of the old family of origin but of the new family of solidarity in the ministry and mission of Jesus.

The texts we have considered from John serve to confirm the thesis that the Jesus tradition repudiates the structure of the family in order to point to the new reality he is announcing and enacting. This repudiation is not a rejection of individuals but of roles, structures, and institutions — of values, if you will. The individuals concerned, whether parents or children or siblings, are invited to take their place in the new community not as having any special claim, but as members like any others of the new society of love and justice.

Conclusion

Our review of Gospel texts concerning the family shows that the subversion of this institution is a consistent characteristic of the Jesus tradition. This institution is rejected because it is the basic unit of society as presently constituted, the basic form of the old world. As such, the family is characterized by division (between "my own" relatives and the others) and by the domination that follows from possession.

This attitude toward the institution of the family is not like the one generated in ascetic traditions. The Jesus tradition is consistent in its celebrative rather than ascetic attitude toward life, a perspective that is well represented in the episode concerning the wine at Cana. Nothing here smacks of a suspicion directed against enjoying life. Rather, we find a critique of that which limits this enjoyment to those who "belong" to one's own family or group.

---

7. My point here is not to debate the issues of Mariology, which concern the implications of Christology for a veneration of Mary. Typically, Mariological claims derive from a consideration of the divinity of Jesus, something that is not here in dispute. For my initial sketch of the foundations of Christology, see my *Loyalty to God: The Apostles Creed in Life and Liturgy* (Nashville: Abingdon, 1992).

The repudiation of "family values" characteristic of the Jesus tradition may be heard as good news by those who are regularly denigrated because their very existence is regarded as a threat to these values. Gay and lesbian Christians may have particular reason to be glad of the attitude taken toward this system of exclusion and "compulsory heterosexuality" on the part of the Jesus tradition.

But this word also speaks to others as well who find themselves the victims of the institution of the family. We are increasingly aware that sentimental portraits of family life all too often disguise the way in which the family is the scene of violence and violation. By way of its "Babylonian captivity" to the institution of the family, the church has too often been silent about, and complicitous in, the violence against women and children that this institution perpetrates.

A reconsideration of the Jesus tradition in this regard would also allow recognition of the importance of nontraditional families and the value, so often emphasized among gays and lesbians, of "families we choose."

Chapter 11

Marriage and Wedding Feasts

One of the ways of disqualifying same-gender relationships is to regard them as undermining the institution of cross-gender or heterosexual marriage. In reaction to this disqualification and stigmatization, some people have argued (for example, Norman Pittenger in *Time for Consent*) that same-gender relationships should approximate as nearly as possible heterosexual monogamous marriage. Before the existing institution of heterosexual marriage is taken to be normative by either opponents or proponents of same-sex relationships, however, we should address the deep ambivalence with which this relationship is regarded in the Jesus tradition.

One of the characteristics of Protestantism is that the institution of marriage and the concomitant institution of family are regarded as a given mandate, order, or institution ordained "of God." This view leads us to suppose that the Bible, and especially the New Testament, is unambiguous in its affirmation of this "holy estate of matrimony." But this view rests upon an ignorance of the deep ambiguity of the Jesus tradition as it comes to expression in the Gospels. Accordingly I want to focus attention on this tradition in order to uncover this ambiguity and ambivalence.

The Critique of Marriage

In the Gospel of Mark, three texts should be taken into account in a discussion of marriage in the Jesus tradition. Two of these texts concern the question of divorce, and the third has to do with the question of the resurrection. We deal with the first two texts later in connection with the general view of divorce. First we address the question about the resurrection.

Mark on Resurrection

The episode with which we are concerned occurs in a series of confrontations with the Jerusalem authorities in the days preceding Jesus'

194

arrest. These confrontations begin with questions. The first concerns Jesus' authority for his extraordinary behavior (the march on Jerusalem and blockade of the temple); the second concerns the payment of imperial taxes and hence the authority of the empire. In the two previous questions, Jesus has confronted the priests, scribes, and elders (11:27–12:12) and the Pharisees and Herodians (12:13–17). In these confrontations, Jesus has abolished the basis of religious and "secular" authority. Now he turns to the Sadducees.

> And the Sadducees come to him, who say that there is no resurrection; and questioned him saying, "Teacher, Moses wrote for us that if a man's brother dies and leaves a wife, but leaves no child, the man must take the wife, and raise up children for his brother.
>
> "There were seven brothers; the first took a wife, and when he died left no children; and the second took her, and died, leaving no children; and the third likewise; and the seven left no children. Last of all the woman died. In the resurrection whose wife will she be? For the seven had her as wife."
>
> Jesus said to them, "You fall into error because you do not know the written nor do you know the power of God. For when they rise from the dead, they neither marry nor are given in marriage, but are like the angels in heaven.
>
> And as for the dead being raised, have you not read in the book of Moses, in the passage about the bush, how God said to him, 'I am the God of Abraham, the God of Isaac and the God of Jacob'? He is not the God of the living but of the dead; great is your error." (Mark 12:18–27)

The Sadducees are the party of the aristocracy. For this class, the question of inheritance is of fundamental importance. By means of the principle of inheritance, the family maintains its position through the passing of generations. One way of maintaining the prestige and power of the family is the custom of levirate marriage; that is the basis of the question that they bring to Jesus. Marriage to the widow of the elder brother serves to maintain the property, influence, and offspring of the dead brother(s) within the family circle.

The Sadducees were also traditionalists. They held to the authority of the Torah, but not the prophets, in matters of doctrine. For this reason they opposed the notion of a resurrection of the dead, which for them was viewed as the importation of strange Hellenistic ideas. In fact, the idea of a resurrection of the dead does not seem to enter the faith of Israel until after the time of Alexander the Great, and we encounter it for the first time in unambiguous form in the book of Daniel — a book whose authority the conservative aristocracy denied. The Sadducees were also opposed to the gentile mission of the Pharisees. They naturally regarded Judaism as a matter of racial and cultural identity rather than a matter of belief. This outlook is the typical predisposition of the aristocracy in all nations.

The question of the Sadducees serves to demonstrate the absurdity of the resurrection hope. If resurrection were to occur, then impossible problems would follow, one of which concerns the indissoluble contract of marriage. If marriage is a divine institution, then it too must be "raised." But then the woman would be the wife of all seven brothers. The whole thing is a problem. Before we too quickly dismiss the question, we should ask whether we share similar conceptions regarding life after death. Whose wife *would* she be?

The answer of Jesus is, again, quite radical. Jesus maintains that the institution of marriage and family has no future in the reign of God but is instead abolished by the resurrection of the dead. God thus abolished the most fundamental institution of society.

We may gain a clearer view of what is at stake here if we recall that the question of the Sadducees views marriage as a question of ownership. The woman serves as the vessel or means of securing ownership. Through her, sons are acquired who will inherit and so perpetuate the family. But not only is she the vehicle of ownership, she is also herself "owned." She belongs to the husband. The question is a question about to whom she will belong. The answer is that the resurrection abolishes this ownership altogether. No marriage nor giving of marriage will exist when they rise. They become like the messengers of God, freed of the shackles of human institutions. The domination or ownership of one by another is abolished.[1]

Exegetes are usually hasty to assure us that this aspect of resurrection means the abolition of sexuality as well, but nothing in the text of Mark warrants such a conclusion. What Jesus critiques in this narrative is not sexuality but the institutions that bond it to the structures of social and economic self-preservation.

The conclusion of Jesus' reply is one that the Pharisees themselves would have used in their discussion with the Sadducees. The Sadducees used the claim that God is God of the living and not the dead to oppose the doctrine

---

1. This conclusion is consistent with the interpretation offered by Countryman, *Dirt, Greed, and Sex,* 182–83.

of the resurrection of the dead. God has nothing to do with the dead, for he is God of the living. But if God self-identifies as the God of those who are now dead (Abraham, Isaac, and Jacob), then does not this God have to do with the dead as well as the living? Jesus here adopts this rejoinder of the Pharisees as his own.

Far more is at stake here, however, than settling a doctrinal dispute between the Pharisees and the Sadducees (a dispute that the Pharisees won once the home base of the Sadducees was destroyed by the Romans in the devastating wars that lay ahead). The assertion of the resurrection of the dead means that those people who are committed to the in-breaking of God's reign have a future even as they are slain. The religious establishment has no future — it is the establishment of those who murder the representatives of God. The empire has no future — its claim to dominion over humanity is exposed as falsehood. Even the most basic social institution, marriage and family, has no future. The in-breaking of the reign of God means the abolition of every structure of domination, whether temple, throne, or family. All of these semidivine surrogates are exposed and abolished in the advent of the new humanity.

Luke

The critique of marriage undertaken in the synoptic account of the confrontation between Jesus and the Sadducees is developed somewhat further in the Q saying concerning division in the family. In Matthew 10:35 we noted (in the discussion of family relations) that this division extends to that between "a daughter-in-law against her mother-in-law." This division is stressed in the Lukan form: "mother-in-law against daughter-in-law and daughter-in-law against mother-in-law" (Luke 12:53). We notice that both forms of the saying emphasize the relational disruption from the standpoint of women. Their perspective is adopted here, but of more immediate concern to us is that the great disruption applies not simply to blood ties but to relationships constituted by marriage.

While Matthew and Luke differ little concerning this particular saying, Luke has an especially negative attitude toward the marriage relationship.

In our discussion of the division in the family, we noted Luke's especially strong language: "hate father and mother...." But to this list he adds, "wife and children" (Luke 14:26). And to the saying of Jesus in Mark and Matthew in which Jesus speaks of his followers having left "house, brothers, sisters, mother or father or children," Luke pointedly adds "wife" (Luke 18:29; see Mark 10:29; Matt. 19:29).

For Luke, at least, the turning against wife and children and even leaving them is seen as necessary to committing to Jesus' mission. Finding in the Jesus tradition any solace for those who regard marriage and family values as central to Christian faith and practice is increasingly difficult.

In this connection we may recall Luke's allusion to the women who followed Jesus (8:1–3), including Joanna, wife of Chuza, an official of Herod's court. The impression that a woman had left her husband behind in order to follow Jesus seems verified by Luke's view of the appropriateness of dissolving or ignoring the marriage bond when it comes to following Jesus.

We should also address the parable of the great feast that is found in quite different versions in Matthew 22 and Luke 14. In Matthew, the feast is said to be occasioned by a wedding, but this setting plays no role until the incident peculiar to Matthew concerning the wedding garment (22:11–14). In Luke, we have simply a great feast held by a king who invites persons to attend, but many invitees send excuses. Both Matthew and Luke use this motif of invitations refused. In Luke (not in Matthew), one of the excuses given is, "I have married a wife, and therefore cannot come" (14:20). The set of excuses — acquisition of a field, of oxen, and of a wife — make clear that we are in the "register" of economic security and possession. The acquisition of a wife is not here a matter of romance or even of sexuality, but of economic security. Like the field and the oxen, the woman is a possession that secures the owner's place in the world.

This passage should assist us in understanding why Luke can take such a negative view of marriage while at the same time giving a significant role to women in the narrative. Luke's opposition to marriage is not set within the framework of misogyny or gynophobia. An important aspect of Luke's narrative is that women accompany Jesus and are his most faithful followers. The suspicion, then, is not of women but of marriage, of marriage as an institution of ownership, of worldly security, and of economics. Luke exposes these as opposed to the welcoming of the reign of God.

Neither does the Gospel of Luke frame its suspicion of marriage within an ascetic perspective. Jesus appears here as in other Gospels as one who celebrates life in food and drink (7:34) and who is not at all scandalized by apparent sexual impropriety (7:36ff). The motivation for opposition to marriage must be sought elsewhere. It appears to be found in the area of marriage as pertaining to the world of possession and economic security — a sphere that is radically opposed to welcoming the in-breaking of God's rule.

In order to understand Luke's perspective, we can return to the story with which we began this reflection on the critique of marriage: the Sadducees' question concerning the resurrection. All three versions of this encounter demonstrate that what Jesus opposes here is marriage as possession. Remember that the Sadducees wanted to know to whom the woman would belong in the resurrection, and Jesus' reply suggests an end to the structure of ownership in the reign of God. People then will not own or possess one another.

Now in Mark's and Matthew's versions of this encounter, marriage and kinship structures are relativized by Jesus' perspective. In this connection, the Lukan version is either more radical or more explicit. "And Jesus said to them, 'The sons of this age marry and are given in marriage; but those who are accounted worthy to attain to that age and to the resurrection from the dead neither marry nor are given in marriage, for they cannot die anymore, because they are equal to the angels and are sons of God being sons of the resurrection'" (Luke 20:35–36).

Before discussing the relation to marriage, we should clarify the meaning of the term "sons" in this passage. The term here functions as an Aramaicism referring to that which belongs to or pertains to the reality of which one is a "son." Thus "son of this age" is one who belongs to or is of this age, and the same holds true of resurrection or the divine. Thus "sons of God" are those who belong to or are "divine" in character; "son of the resurrection" is one who belongs to or is characterized by the reality of the resurrection. Moreover, the term "sons" is explicitly "unisex" or bisexual, which is clear from the "marry or are given in marriage" that is repeated. The male is traditionally the one who marries (takes a wife), while the female is the one who is given in marriage (is taken as a wife). A son in this case therefore explicitly includes male and female. This is of interest not only for this text but also for others that refer to "sons" in the Gospels, because this passage warrants our understanding this term as referring to both male and female.

This text contrasts therefore two classes of persons: those men and women who belong to this age and those men and women who belong to God or the resurrection. "This age" is the foundation for the life of the first group, while God — and especially the divine act of resurrection — is the foundation for, and characterizes the life of, the other group.

People who are accounted worthy to attain to the resurrection from the dead are at the same time those who are "sons" of the resurrection — that is, those who are already characterized by the resurrection reality. Here we have the tension between "already" and "not yet" that is characteristic of much New Testament discussion of the life of the follower who belongs to a reality that is both already here and still to come.

In this passage, all those who belong to or participate in the reality that Jesus is announcing and enacting are to be classed not within the group that belongs to this age but within the group that belongs to the resurrection reality. Thus the reality of the resurrection is already characterizing all of the followers of Jesus.

The characteristic difference here between those who are followers of Jesus and those who are not is that the former are those males who do not marry and those females who are not given in marriage, while those who belong to this age are the males who marry and the females who are given in marriage. From the standpoint of this passage, rejecting marriage appears obligatory for those who belong to the new reality that is breaking into the world in the message and ministry of Jesus.

"Obligation" may not, however, be the correct term here, for this is no admonition or exhortation. Instead it is simply the recognition of a reality. The absence of marriage here signals a renunciation of a way of belonging to this world. To be married is to give hostages to this world, to be engaged in seeking security within the reality that "is passing away."

Luke, at least, understands Jesus' saying to the Sadducees concerning the resurrection ("they neither marry nor are given in marriage") to apply not simply to the end time but to the present as well.

This interpretation then makes clear how Luke could suppose that the follower of Jesus not only does not marry or permit herself to be given in marriage but also renounces the institution of marriage into which he or she may already have entered (12:53; 14:26; 18:29). We would expect this to be reflected in a different interpretation of the tradition of Jesus' sayings concerning divorce. This expectation will be verified in our discussion of that theme in the next section.

Before turning to the discussion of divorce, however, we should pause to see the basis of the Jesus tradition's critique of the institution of marriage. Many church theologians regard heterosexual marriage as the appropriate model of Christian life. This view is certainly not warranted by what we find in the Jesus tradition. But why the suspicion directed against marriage? We have already seen that this suspicion has in large part to do with the assimilation of marriage to the sphere of economic security and stability within this world. The call of Jesus is to forsake the attempt to secure one's life in this world in order to rely entirely on the divine reality, a reality as uncontrollable as resurrection from the dead.

Divorce

The critique of the institution of marriage may strike the reader as odd, given the better-known sayings of Jesus concerning the possibility of divorce. These sayings have regularly been interpreted as absolutizing marriage and thus as legitimating and sanctifying this institution. Is this what is really going on in the texts?

Mark on Divorce

Again we begin with a text from Mark.

> And he left there and went to the region of Judea and beyond the Jordan, and the crowds gathered to him again; and again, as his custom was, he taught them. And Pharisees came up and asked him, "Is it lawful for a man to divorce his wife?" He answered them, "What did Moses command you?" They said, "Moses allowed a man to write a certificate of divorce, and to put her away." But Jesus said to them, "For your hardness of heart he wrote you this commandment. But from the beginning of creation, 'God made them male and female.' 'For this reason a man shall leave his father and mother and the two shall be one flesh so that they are no longer two but one.' What therefore God has yoked together let not humanity separate."
>
> And in the house again the disciples asked about this. And he said to them, "Whoever dismisses his woman and marries another commits adultery with her; and whoever dismisses her man and marries another she commits adultery." (10:1–12)

The setting of the teaching as well as the structure of its presentation recalls the earlier encounter with the Pharisees in 7:9–13 concerning "corban." There Jesus was surrounded by the crowds (6:55–56); there the Pharisees question him (7:1); and there the response of Jesus turns on the distinction between religious custom and the divine command. Here the answer depends on the distinction between the command of Moses (Deut. 24:1–6) and the creative intention of God. The Mosaic command was of course understood as the word of God, the command of God. But Jesus lumps it with the religious traditions. Both are human. (For that reason, the reference here is to Moses rather than God as the author of the command.)

The command here is taken to be simply a concession to willful or stubborn blindness (*sclerosis*). The permission of Moses (expressed here as order and command) is contrasted with creation. Thus what is appealed to here is not that which is peculiar to Judaism but common to humanity as such. The response of Jesus combines two texts: Genesis 1:27 and Genesis 2:24. The first is understood as pointing to the divine intention that male and female belong together. The second points to the way this happens in a sexual union that yokes two to one another on the basis of delight and desire. What Jesus adds is that this union of delight and desire should be understood as the work of God and therefore not compromised by human tradition (religious command).

Both the question of the Pharisees and the response of Jesus deal with something rather broader and less "formal" than what we think of today as marriage. The passage has in view simply the determination to live together as male and female. No distinct terminology appears for legal spouse (husband and wife) but only the universal "man" and "woman." The teaching then applies to any such relationship and not just to those legitimated in a religious or legal way. In this sense, nothing here relates to the "holy estate" of matrimony but instead the universal context of "conjugal relations." We are not to think exclusively of the institution of marriage but of the joining together, the coupling of man and woman. The distinction between "living in sin" and marriage has nothing whatever to do with this text.

What Jesus opposes is the concession to realism that leads Moses to set up forms for the dissolution of this tie, which is in some way to be seen as the act of God. Concessions to "reality" here, however they may be legitimated by appeal to God or Moses, amount to human rebellion against God.[2]

That God has yoked two persons seems to mean that their natural desire to be together, to start a new life together, is itself the divine act. No reference to further legal or religious acts or institutions is made. We are so constituted (created) that this yoking is natural to us and appropriate to us. We want to live together, and this is truly the divine yoking. We should notice the absence of suspicion directed against sexual desire and delight, which are instead taken to be expressions of the divine creative intent. This approach further substantiates our view that the saying concerning the abolition of marriage in the reign of God by no means should be understood as abolishing sexual desire and delight.

According to Mark, this argument is carried a step further "in the house," where they leave behind the situation of Jewish law and enter the

---

2. However, this rebellion is not attributed to the woman and man but to the religious authorities, who make these concessions and so separate what God has yoked.

sphere of Roman or hellenistic custom. The aim at mutuality and equality of this "yoking" then becomes even more obvious, and the same rule applies equally to male and female. The woman is not to send her man away; the man is not to send his woman away, especially not for the purpose of contracting a different alliance. In good times and bad, loyalty to one another should continue.

A narrow interpretation of this teaching in terms of marriage and family seems to oppose the attitude that Jesus takes toward his own family in 3:33–35. There he repudiates his "natural" family in favor of the relationship of sisters and brothers constituted by "doing the will of God." That is, he allies himself with the adoptive family of shared loyalty rather than the natural family of blood ties, and he does precisely that here as well. As the saying from Genesis 2 indicates, the new relationship of the man and the woman entails a rupture with the familial relationship of parent and child. The man leaves his parents and adheres to this woman (Gen. 2:24). In both cases, a new loyalty takes the place of the family tie of kinship. In both cases, the kinship tie is repudiated in favor of a relationship that is chosen in love and loyalty.

This freely chosen loyalty — the exact point of both sayings — thus takes priority over the nest of familial security. "Adultery" is the abandonment of such a freely chosen loyalty for another, making nonsense of the very idea of loyalty itself. For that reason, the prophets can describe the hedging of Israel's loyalty to Yahweh as adultery. In that case, the Israelites sought an alliance with a foreign imperial power in order to achieve a level of "national security." Israel was not prepared to depend wholly on Yahweh for its security and thus compromised its loyalty to Yahweh. The effect of this compromise was that the imperial gods were admitted into the temple alongside Yahweh.

The same concept is also the basis for the teaching about adultery here. By using the metaphor of fidelity and adultery in sexual relationships, what comes to the fore is the importance of a loyalty that is not vacillating, that does not seek to protect its own self-interest, but which commits itself unreservedly.

What is really at stake then is not a teaching about marriage, but a teaching about loyalty. The loyalty that is in view is especially the freely chosen loyalty to Jesus and his cause and his way, for the sake of which the followers have "left father and mother." The alternative to this loyalty is betrayal, the abandonment of commitment and so adultery/idolatry.

What if, in spite of this analysis, one wishes to use this text to develop a sexual or relational ethic? One would have to say that the relationship of love and loyalty between two persons drawn to one another by desire and delight is here offered as a sign or parable of the relationship between the disciples and the one to whom they are most basically committed as those who desire to follow the way of Jesus.

Matthew and Luke on Divorce

How do Matthew and Luke modify the teaching of Jesus as represented in Mark?

The teaching we have found in Mark 10:1–12 is modified by Matthew 19:1–12 in two ways. First, the saying in Matthew is directed only to the male. The saying about the woman remarrying is omitted. This difference may correspond to the differing situation of the texts; that is, divorce was a possibility also for women among Mark's (gentile) readers but not for Matthew's (Jewish Christian) readers.

The other difference is that Matthew makes an exception to the absolute prohibition of divorce and remarriage: "except for unchastity." Thus, for Matthew a man can divorce and remarry if the woman is found to be promiscuous. This exception is not otherwise found in the New Testament. This modification changes the "center of gravity" of the saying, making it appear now not as a teaching concerning loyalty but as a moral instruction concerning divorce narrowly viewed.[3]

Although Luke does not develop a version of this saying in the same context as Matthew and Mark, the third Gospel nevertheless has a similar teaching: "Everyone who divorces his wife and marries another commits adultery, and he who marries a woman divorced from her husband commits adultery" (Luke 16:16–18). This statement corresponds to Matthew in that it focuses only on the male, but it lacks Matthew's caveat, "except for unchastity."

All of these versions have in common that they do not argue against divorce but against remarriage.

The effect of Luke's version is also to eliminate the saying concerning the attraction of male and female based on Genesis 2:24 (Mark 10:6–9; Matt. 19:11–16). This elimination makes it easier to understand Luke's tendency to eliminate marriage as such.

We should also note here that Matthew appends to this teaching the saying concerning eunuchs (Matt. 19:10–12). In chapter 9 we discussed

---

3. This change may be related to the portrayal of Joseph as a just man who nevertheless resolves to end his betrothal to Mary when he discovers that she is pregnant. That is, it may be dictated by concerns about narrative coherence rather than serving as an independent teaching about divorce.

the first two kinds of eunuchs, eunuchs by birth and those made eunuchs by others. The third category of men who make themselves eunuchs for the sake of the reign of God is, in its present setting, indicative of those who refrain from marriage or remarriage. They make themselves without progeny and so without security in the world or a hold on the worldly future.

The sayings concerning divorce and remarriage then are entirely consistent with a negative view of the institution of marriage. Divorce remains a possibility since loyalty to the reign of God may entail separation from a marriage. But remarriage is an excluded possibility, not because marriage is itself valued but because remarriage entails a change of loyalties.

Yet marriage is not entirely opposed (save in Luke) because it does represent the freely chosen loyalty that embodies the ethos of the reign of God. In this way, marriage is different from the relationship to family of origin or even to one's own children. Marriage is not a "blood tie" but one freely chosen that indeed entails a separation from family of origin (Gen. 2:24 as cited by both Mark and Matthew). In this way, marriage can serve to symbolize the new society constituted by loyalty and solidarity. But when viewed (as in Luke) as a way of consolidating one's security in the world and as perpetuating the family institution, then marriage must be resolutely opposed.

The Wedding Feast

The possibility of positively valuing at least some aspect of the sexual relationship represented by male/female relations is suggested by the reference to Genesis 2:24 in Mark and Matthew (but not Luke) to the joining of male and female in desire and delight. This possibility is also represented in the place of the wedding feast in the teaching of Jesus concerning the reign of God and in the image of the bridegroom in the Jesus tradition.

Matthew (and Luke)

In Matthew we have two parables that take a wedding feast as their point of departure. The first is the parable of the invitations that is also found in Luke but without reference to the wedding as the occasion for the feast. The setting of the wedding feast serves no particular purpose for the parable of the invitations in Matthew, in which the emphasis falls on mistreatment of the king's messengers and his subsequent retaliation. In this way, Matthew's version of the parable of the invitations is a close parallel to the parable of the unjust stewards of the vineyard that immediately precedes it (Matt. 21:33–43). That Luke eliminates this setting is not surprising given Luke's strongly negative view of marriage.

The point of the feast being a wedding feast in Matthew is to set up the parable of the wedding garment that immediately follows the parable of the invitations (22:11–14). In the parable of the wedding garment, the allegory of a wedding feast that earlier helped to interpret the destruction of Jerusalem and the launching of the gentile mission now turns to the situation within the community of faith constituted by those who have been brought in, "both good and bad" (22:10). The man who is found without the proper party clothes for a wedding is then thrown out into "the outer darkness." The tag line — "for many are called but few are chosen" — makes clear that what is involved is a separation of the bad from the good in the community at the end time. This question of the judgment to be passed upon the members of the community who do not correspond to the values of the divine reign is of particular concern to Matthew.[4] This concern, and so the parables that Matthew uses to articulate it (like that of the wedding garment), is absent from Luke. Thus the absence of the setting of the wedding feast as the occasion for the invitations (which sets up Matthew's parable of the wedding garment) may owe not only to Luke's suspicion of weddings but to the absence in Luke of the theological point about the separation of the good and the bad within the community of faith.

The second Matthean parable concerning a wedding feast is found in Matthew's version of the extended discourse of Jesus concerning the end time. Here Matthew uses the story of the ten maidens who go out to meet the bridegroom in order to light the way into his wedding feast. Only half are prepared for a long wait (having brought sufficient oil). When the bridegroom is delayed, they sleep for a while but nevertheless have oil prepared to accompany him when he arrives. Thus they enter into the feast while the others are shut out. Obviously this parable is being used as well to indicate a division between those people who are prepared and those who are not and thus the importance of being ready for the coming of God's reign.

Although this parable is missing from Luke (who is, again, not concerned with the issue of judgment that preoccupies Matthew), the image of the wedding feast does make an appearance. The first occasion is in many respects similar to Matthew's story of the maidens since it emphasizes the importance of being alert: " . . . and be like those who are waiting

---

4. See also Matthew's parables of the wheat and weeds (13:24–30, 36–43) and the parable of the fish in the net (13:47–48).

for their master to come home from the wedding banquet, so that they may open the door for him as soon as he comes and knocks" (Luke 12:36). The parable includes the promise that the master will not only feed the slaves but also serve them if they are ready at whatever hour. The emphasis falls then not on judgment but on promise, as is characteristic of Luke.

The second use of the wedding feast motif is found in Luke 14 as the beginning of a series of parables and teachings on "party etiquette." The specific parable set in this way is as follows: "When you are invited by someone to a wedding banquet, do not sit down at the place of honor in case someone more intimate than you has been invited by your host..." (14:8).[5] The parable presupposes that everyone goes to wedding feasts and warns only against "exalting oneself" and encourages one to "humble oneself" as appropriate conduct both at a party and in life.

Luke's uses of the image of the wedding feast are similar to Matthew's (waiting for a bridegroom, accepting an invitation) but are developed in ways that do not emphasize Matthew's point about judgment.

John

None of these uses of the image of the wedding are as dramatic, however, as the episode in the Gospel of John concerning the wedding feast in Cana of Galilee. Here, instead of a story told by Jesus about wedding feasts, we have Jesus himself present as a guest at a wedding feast. When his mother brings him the alarming news that the wine has run out, Jesus turns the barrels of water which the guests had used to wash themselves into barrels of wine of astonishingly good quality. The narrator tells us that this "sign" was the first that Jesus performed in his mission and ministry. Thus, the setting of the wedding feast has a prominence here in the Gospel of John that exceeds that in the other Gospels.

Although used regularly to indicate Jesus' positive attitude toward "the holy estate of matrimony," this story involves no such thing. In the first place, Jesus is not present for any ritual or cultic act, but for the party. In our terms, he doesn't show up for the ceremony but for the fiesta. Nor does he seem to have any role with respect to the bride and groom. Instead he is acting as Jesus characteristically acts in other Gospels: showing up at parties and banquets. His action then is not related to "solemnization" but, on the contrary, to transforming bath water into good wine so that the party can continue through the night.

---

5. This is the same term (*entimos*) used to designate the centurion's slave that we considered in part 2. Here it cannot mean "costly," and there it cannot mean "distinguished"; in both cases, the term means "intimate."

Bridegroom

In addition to the image of the wedding feast, the canonical Jesus tradition presents apparent references to Jesus as "bridegroom."

In a saying common to all of the Synoptic Gospels Jesus explains that his disciples, unlike those of John the Baptizer or the Pharisees, do not fast. "Jesus said to them, 'The wedding guests cannot fast while the bridegroom is with them, can they? As long as they have the bridegroom with them, they cannot fast. The days will come when the bridegroom is taken away from them, and then they will fast on that day'" (Mark 2:19–20; see Matt. 9:15; Luke 5:34–35).

The reference to the bridegroom being taken away enables the saying to point forward obliquely to the passion of Jesus and thus marks Jesus as, in some sense, "the bridegroom."

This saying has a counterpart in the Gospel of John where the designation of Jesus as bridegroom is placed on the lips of John the Baptizer. "He who has the bride is the bridegroom; the friend of the bridegroom, who stands and hears him, rejoices greatly at the bridegroom's voice; therefore this joy of mine is now full. He must increase but I must decrease," (3:29–30).

John here rejoices at the union of Jesus with the people of Israel, as signified by their following him. Again Jesus is indicated the bridegroom, as the one who is consummating his desire.[6]

Thus, alongside the distinctly negative view of the institution of marriage in the Gospels, we have a distinctly positive use of metaphors from the wedding: the feast and the bridegroom. These positive symbols suggest that the consummation of desire and delight aptly characterizes the coming of the divine reign, the accomplishment of the mission of Jesus. How is this to be related to the negative attitude toward the institution of marriage?

Conclusion

The references to marriage in the Jesus tradition have produced a somewhat ambiguous picture. On the one hand, marriage, when assimilated to the institution of the family, is renounced and rejected. On the other hand, when viewed as the coming together of two persons in desire and delight,

---

6. This image of Jesus as the bridegroom also figures prominently in the Apocalypse of John. See 3:29; 18:23–29; 22:17.

marriage is accepted and approved. This ambiguity is by no means the product of confusion or contradiction. Nor is it, in itself, paradoxical.

The ambiguity does, however, produce paradox when one assumes that the point of uniting in desire and delight is to produce the estate or status of matrimony in which two people collaborate in the mechanism for the reproduction of the institution of the family. So self-evident has this connection been made to seem that weddings and marriage have been indissolubly linked in Christian imagination and ideology. Under these circumstances, celebrating one (wedding) and critiquing or rejecting the other (marriage) appears arbitrary or, at best, paradoxical.

But in fact the situation is clear, and the position (of the Jesus tradition) radical. What is approved and, indeed, regarded as fundamental to human nature is being drawn to one another in desire, enjoyment of one another in delight, commitment to one another in gladness, the two becoming one — in short, the whole sphere of sexuality and the erotic. This activity is not simply tolerated but affirmed through the appropriation of the sayings from Genesis 2:24 and in the use of the wedding and bridegroom motif to indicate the character of the divine reign of joy.

The place of these themes in the Jesus tradition makes abundantly clear that the abolition of marriage in the resurrection — or, as Luke has it, among those who already participate in the resurrection reality — by no means entails the abolition of the erotic or of sexuality. Sexuality is the crown of the divine creation: two becoming one flesh. But this union of desire and delight is not meant to entangle persons in the basic unit of production of the social, economic, and political values of the world that is characterized by division and domination.

But what is this union of desire and delight without its being appropriated into the mechanics and structures of the family? Clearly the Jesus tradition at every level regards the latter as an unacceptable compromise with the structures of the world, as an attempt to secure one's place in reality as presently constituted and so as a refusal of the in-breaking of the new reality, the reign of God.

The affirmation of sexuality is, of course, not a granting of permission to do violence to other persons, not permission to treat others unfairly, and not permission for willfulness or self-aggrandizing behavior. The sphere of sexuality, like all other spheres of life, is permeated by the values of love and justice, of generosity and joy, that embody the meaning of the arrival of the divine rule in the world created by God for precisely this goal.

That the institution of the family, and so marriage insofar as it is a perpetuation of this institution, is regarded as inherently contradicting these values is the clear sense of the Jesus tradition. This institution appears to belong to the sphere of possession and domination that is antithetical to the new reality announced and enacted by Jesus.

How does the affirmation of uninstitutionalized sexuality relate to our theme of same-sex eroticism and relationships? Clearly no ground exists here whatsoever for rejecting same-sex eroticism as such. On the contrary, the expression of delight and desire without undertaking to reproduce the systems of patriarchy and possession would seem to be at least as compatible with same-sex as with cross-sex relationships.

And indeed we have found confirmation of this concept in our consideration of the significance of the relationship between Jesus and the man he loved. This same-sex relationship is capable of serving as a model not only for same-sex relationships but also as a paradigm for the liberation of heterosexual relationships as well. Already Aelred of Rievaulx noticed this connection when he used this model of same-sex relationships to propose that cross-sex relationships should also be understood as aiming toward mutuality rather than subordination of the one to the other.

What both same-sex and cross-sex relationships at their best have in common is that they aim at freely chosen loyalty to one another grounded in the joyous recognition that "this at last" is the counterpart to desire and the fulfillment of delight. They may have in common an expression of sexual or erotic friendship. We may even suppose that these different forms of sexual relationship complement one another. Cross-sex relationships are seemingly more often characterized by lifelong attachment, while same-sex relationships are seemingly characterized by free mutuality of friendship. These are, however, only ideal types. Each individual relationship has its own character, its own challenges, its own defeats and victories as it struggles to adequately express the love that is its foundation and goal.

The Gospels clearly develop perspectives on marriage and family and wedding feasts that are quite consistent with a gay-affirmative perspective, further substantiating the reading I have proposed of homoerotic traditions in the biblical narratives concerning Jesus. If Jesus' primary affectional relationship was to another man, then that relationship could exhibit the values of desire and delight without becoming complicitous in the structures of possession and self-preservation characteristic of marriage and family values. Their relationship was one that the ancients would recognize as friendship, but distinguished from the relationship to the others Jesus called friends by its intimate and erotic character.

Chapter 12

Sexuality and Procreation

In the last chapter, I suggested that the celebration of wedding feasts and the suspicion of marriage in the Gospels combine to produce a positive view of sexuality that is not subordinated to the perpetuation of family structures. In order to clarify how such a view is possible on New Testament grounds, we need to attend to the view that sexuality should be governed by the goal of procreation.

One of the ways in which sexual relations between persons of the same sex has been regularly disqualified is by advancing the idea that legitimate uses of sexuality should be related to procreation. Insofar as the aim of sexuality is procreation, then nonprocreative sex is contrary to the aim of sexual activity and so is to be proscribed as "contrary to nature" or as illicit. This chapter approaches biblical literature from the standpoint of this question. The discussion obviously bears upon the plausibility of the interpretation of the Jesus tradition that has been advanced in parts 1 and 2, especially as regards the appropriateness of a sexual mediation of the relationships explored there.

I seek first to show that the idea of biological reproduction that appears in Genesis 1 is replaced in the New Testament by the idea of missional reproduction. Thus the call to "be fruitful and multiply" of Genesis 1 is transformed to "proclaim and make disciples."

I also draw attention to the way in which sexuality is separated from the question of procreation in most New Testament texts. In fact, in only one text — 1 Timothy — is procreation brought into discussions related to sexuality, and this connection happens in such a way as to contradict the general New Testament view.

The discussion of procreation that I advance here depends upon a discussion of the attitude taken in the Jesus tradition toward family relations generally. Thus I do not attempt here to replicate that discussion.

211

Background

The Christian view of sexuality and procreation that came to predominate in the emergence of the Catholic Church is one that may be regarded as a compromise between Jewish and Roman insistence on the importance of marriage and family and a hellenistic religious and philosophical suspicion directed against the body in general and sexuality in particular.

The view of rabbinic Judaism was rather like what today would be called "compulsory heterosexuality" (Adrienne Rich). On this view, it is incumbent upon people to propagate, if not the species then, at least, the people. Hence marriage and procreation were generally regarded as obligatory.

The modifications of normative Judaism in early Christianity challenge this view in important ways. The early church knew that at least Jesus and Paul failed to comply with the marital imperatives of Judaism and of Rome. Moreover certain sayings of both Jesus (on eunuchs) and Paul (on marrying) appear on principle to undermine this compulsory heterosexuality. That is, Jesus and Paul seem to recommend nonmarrying to their followers.

This policy would certainly seem scandalous from the point of view of Judaism and of many pagan cultures as well. On the other hand, this tradition could be viewed as liberating for those who had their own reasons for not desiring the married estate — for example, women could thereby find release from the controls of patriarchal institutions. The role of widows and virgins in the early community may have provided a real liberation for women. Indeed we can see in the attempt to rein in or limit admission to these roles a recognition on the part of some men of the dangers to male authority and control posed by the proliferation of women in the movement who either had not been married (called "virgins") or who were no longer married (called "widows"). The critical thing with respect to virgins and widows is not a question of their sexual experience or lack of it, but their freedom with respect to the institution of marriage.

The explicit and implicit critique of marriage contained within elements of the emerging Christian tradition brought it into contact with other traditions within the hellenistic world that took a decidedly negative attitude toward sexuality, procreation, the body, and marriage.[1] Certainly some

---

1. See Aline Rouselle, *Porneia: On Desire and the Body in Late Antiquity,* trans. Felicia Pheasant (Oxford: Blackwell, 1988), 129–93; and Peter Brown, *The Body and Society: Men, Women, and Sexual Renunciation in Early Christianity* (New York: Columbia University Press, 1988), 5–32.

Christians found themselves attracted to a widespread hellenistic revulsion toward the body and sexuality. In general, the view went: the body is corruptible, undergoes birth and death. Salvation consists in being rescued from this sphere of corruption in order to live in the sphere of the eternal, the unchanging, and so on. Hence the life that is on the way to salvation is one that refuses to participate, so far as possible, in the sphere of the physical, the bodily, the sexual.

The difficulty with assimilating this worldview was that it entailed unacceptable contradictions with other elements of the Christian tradition. In some versions (Marcion, some gnostics), this outlook meant separating the God of Jesus from the Creator. In still other versions, it meant denying the incarnation, or the passion, or the resurrection of the body. These doctrinal consequences were faced at various points and rejected by what came to be the dominant forms of Christianity.

Nevertheless the suspicion directed toward sexuality seemed to have some basis in the traditions of the community and to connect with very prestigious forms of hellenistic popular philosophy.

The result of this collision was a view that sought to regulate sexuality without simply repudiating it. By the end of the second century, we can see the basic elements of this compromise coming into focus, above all in the work of Clement of Alexandria. Clement's view is that through Christianity even the most ordinary and untrained common people come to live lives worthy of philosophers. An essential ingredient in his viewpoint is that the extremism of those who seek to abolish marriage and sexuality is avoided, but that sexuality between husbands and wives is ordered toward procreation, thus making sexuality "rational." We need to propagate the species; sex is the way to do this; we engage in sex to fulfill our philosophical or rational duty, and not therefore simply to indulge in whims or to satisfy our lusts or desires.[2]

This view obviously undergoes additional modifications. A strong and indeed growing institutionalization develops for the nonprocreation option (celibacy) and, within this framework, further suspicion is directed

---

2. Clement of Alexandria, *Miscellanies* Book III, in *Alexandrian Christianity*, ed. Henry Chadwick (Philadelphia: Westminster Press, 1954), 40–92. Interestingly, this Alexandrian compromise did not commend itself to Judaism, which remained less susceptible to the ascetic impulse to restrain the body. Although the importance of procreation was not forgotten, Judaism seems never to have accepted the view that nonprocreative sex was sinful. Procreation was desirable — a couple should endeavor to have at least two children — but sex itself had other legitimate expressions. For a discussion of attitudes toward sexuality in Judaism, see Daniel Boyarin, *Unheroic Conduct: The Rise of Heterosexuality and the Invention of the Jewish Man* (Berkeley: University of California Press, 1997).

against even procreative sex. This suspicion is found, for example, in Augustine's view of the act of procreation, or rather its attendant lust/desire as the agent that transmits original sin to the one conceived by the sexual act.[3] This suspicion of sexuality obviously goes further than Clement of Alexandria's. But Augustine is careful not to fall into the Manichean error of alleging that procreative sex is itself sinful.[4]

Ultimately this view is made systematic by Aquinas's appropriation of Aristotelian biology to produce the view that all nonprocreative sexual acts are sinful, in that they violate the natural aim of sex in creation. This view characterizes Catholic moral teaching at present.

Protestantism rejected the option of celibacy and so indicated an apparent return to the compulsory heterosexuality of Judaism. In Puritan and Anglican treatises of the seventeenth century, the view that sex has only the purpose of procreation also came under criticism. Ironically both the rejection of celibacy and the critique of procreation theories of sexuality are often forgotten as soon as the topic is changed from heterosexual marriage to homosexuality. Then we regularly find even conservative Protestants talking about celibacy as an option for some people (them) and stigmatizing homosexual activity as nonprocreative and therefore illicit.

The question we must ask therefore goes back behind the formulations of Clement of Alexandria to ask whether in fact sexuality is regarded in the New Testament as necessarily procreative and whether the noncelibate are obligated to procreate.

Multiplication

The call to be fruitful and multiply is often regarded as generally binding upon humanity. Thus, noting the ways in which the New Testament, especially the Gospels, deals with the fruitfulness of Christian disciples is of some interest.

The image of fruitfulness is introduced at the baptism of Jesus with the descent of the dove. Although it has become the international symbol of peace, in the ancient Near East the dove was the symbol of procreative fecundity. Its appearance as the concrete representation of spirit or life force marks the inauguration of Jesus' mission and ministry as the beginning of the birth of a new humanity. The dove represents the procreative fecundity of the new humanity that will be born of the water and the spirit.

---

3. Augustine, *City of God,* Book XIV, ch. 16–18
4. Ibid., chaps. 22–26.

This image is complemented in the Synoptic Gospels by the sending out of the disciples two-by-two. In Mark and Matthew, the twelve are sent in this way, while in Luke a group of seventy are sent two-by-two to engage in the work of mission. Going out "two-by-two" recalls the way in which animal life was saved in the flood (Gen. 6:20; 7:9). They enter the ark two-by-two so as to become the breeding stock for replenishing the planet (Gen. 8:17). The disciples are sent in pairs as well, not in order to engage in biological propagation of the species, but in order to engage in the missiological propagation of God's reign.

Upon reflection the reason that the task of "be fruitful and multiply" is removed from the sphere of biological reproduction and placed instead in the sphere of mission becomes obvious. The promise to Abraham had been one of descendants, and the promise came to be understood in terms of the multiplication of progeny to become a great nation or people. That the promise will be realized is clear from the prolific character of Jacob, who has twelve sons who become the ancestors of the tribes of Israel. But the new promise actualized in Jesus is not a new nation but a new movement that will be consummated in a new creation. In this context, one can understand how it is that Jesus has not twelve sons but twelve disciples. They in turn are called to create disciples from among all nations of the earth.

This contrast becomes the subject of explicit reflection in the Gospel of John. The theme is announced already in the prologue concerning the word who was made flesh, "but to all who received him, who believed in his name, he gave power to become the children of God, who were born not of blood, or the will of the flesh or the will of man, but of God" (John 1:12–13).

The being "born of God" is here explicitly contrasted with the means of human generation: blood (the woman), the desire of the flesh (sexual desire), the will of the man (the male). Thus the male, the female, and the sexual desire that unites them are here not the instrument of the promise of progeny. Rather faith is the instrument of conception.

This theme is subsequently picked up again in the discussion with Nicodemus concerning birth. Here we learn that the origin of life has nothing to do with procreation but with the operation of the Spirit: "very truly, I tell you, no one can enter the reign of God without being born of water and Spirit. What is born of the flesh is flesh, and what is born of the Spirit is spirit" (3:5–6).

Here again we have the contrast of the two means of generation, flesh and spirit. The new reality is not dependent upon (re)entering the mother's womb (3:4) but upon the action of the spirit. The significance of this contrast is brought out in the contrast between the predictability of those who are born of flesh and the unpredictability of those who are born of the spirit/wind. This contrast is often obscured by supposing that the emphasis falls here on the unpredictability of the wind whose whence and whither is invisible and uncontrollable. But what is said is that this unpredictability applies to those who are "born of the spirit" (3:8).

This contrast is crucially important. People whose origin is biological procreation are predictable indeed. Birth is destiny, locating one ineluctably in gender, family, tribe, nation, class, caste, and epoch. The very point of a fertility-based ethic, whether of the tribal sort or the class sort or the "marriage and family values" sort, is to secure the perpetuation of the status quo: to maintain social predictability and control. But where the origin is from above or "like the wind," then the various forms of social control and conformity lose their force. No binding of family, tribe, nation, class, caste, or gender is present. A new and dynamic situation arises that cannot be comprehended within the terms of the old order.

A similar contrast is exhibited in an episode recounted in the Gospel of Luke. Jesus has been explaining the significance of his work of exorcism. "While he was saying this, a woman in the crowd raised her voice and said to him, 'Blessed is the womb that bore you and the breasts that nursed you!' But he said, 'Blessed rather are those who hear the word of God and obey it!' " (11:27–28).

Here again is an explicit contrast between natural procreation and the spiritual procreation that occurs through the speaking and hearing (and heeding) of the word. This comment is by no means a devaluation of women as such. On the contrary, Luke's Gospel gives more emphasis to the ministry and mission of women than any other New Testament text. For Luke, as for John, biology is not destiny; nor is biology "origin" either.

The transfer of emphasis from procreation to proclamation as the means for the propagation of life permeates the New Testament. The contrast that we have discussed between those born of the flesh and those born of spirit helps to explain the radical critique that we encounter in the Synoptic Gospels of the institutions of marriage and family, institutions that may be understood as perpetuating the status quo. Fruitfulness and multiplication are transferred from the sphere of sexuality to the sphere of mission and evangelization.

This transfer is not initially accomplished through a suspicion of sexuality as such. The transfer is accompanied by a critique of the family institution but not of sexuality. But now sexuality can no longer be understood as the instrument of propagation or procreation. What then becomes of sexuality?

Paul on Sex

Paul gives in 1 Corinthians an extended discussion of sexuality. The first part of this discussion (chapters 5 and 6) deals with questions of sexual immorality in the Corinthian church. The two cases are, first, sex with one's (step)mother, and, second, the issue of the frequenting of prostitutes.

In chapter 7, Paul deals with the general issue of (heterosexual) marriage. Paul supposes in general that it is better not to marry but that marriage is permissible and in certain circumstances advisable. His view that it is better not to marry is, of course, at variance not only with the views of emerging forms of Judaism but also with the views of the majority of gentile or pagan traditions. Thus, from the standpoint of the upholders of traditional marriage and family values and institutions, Paul is already decidedly heterodox.

Paul does not give as a reason for remaining unmarried the view that sexuality is itself suspect or under suspicion. Rather his objections are entirely prudential. If you are married, you will be preoccupied with satisfying your partner and have correspondingly less time and energy to devote to the life of the community. If married, you take on responsibilities for a household, for the domestic arrangements of housing, eating, and so on. The analogy Paul uses is that of being engaged in commerce. If you are married, try to act as if you were not; if you are engaged in commerce or trade, try to behave as if you are not. That is, don't become preoccupied with this, keep your priorities straight; don't be consumed by the things of this world.

But to be married, while behaving as if you were not does not mean to be married and not have sex. Having sex is in some way what married people are supposed to do, but not in order to have children. What Paul says is as follows:

> The husband should give to his wife her conjugal rights, and likewise the wife to her husband. (7:3)

> Do not deprive one another except perhaps by agreement for a set time, to devote yourselves to prayer, and then come together again so that Satan may not tempt you because of your lack of self control. (7:5)

Paul seems to take for granted that each partner in the relationship has an obligation to give the other partner the sexual satisfaction that is the basis of the marriage relationship. In order to see this point even more clearly, we can look at the reasons that Paul gives for marriage being necessary in some cases. Two statements are relevant:

> To the unmarried and the widows I say that it is well for them to remain unmarried as I am. But if they are not practicing self-control, they should marry. For it is better to marry than to be aflame with passion. (7:8–9)

> If anyone thinks that he is not behaving properly toward his maiden, if his passions are strong, and so it has to be, let him marry as he wishes; it is no sin. Let them marry. (7:36)

The basic reason for marrying according to Paul is because of desire or passion. Marriage is the way to satisfy sexual passion.

Because of this fact, refusing sexual pleasure to a partner would be a form of fraud. Of course, what Paul says in this regard supposes a radically egalitarian relation between the partners in the relationship. Both partners place their bodies at the service of the other:

> The husband should give to the wife her conjugal rights, and likewise the wife to her husband. For the wife does not have authority over her own body, but the husband does; likewise the husband does not have authority over his own body, but the wife does. (7:3–4)

Nothing here smacks of the notion that the man's sexual satisfaction is more important than the woman's. Nor does Paul indicate suspicion of the sexual needs of either party to the relationship. This is not to say that Paul's comments are without problem. But if what Paul says here had been heeded in Christian tradition, we would have been spared a great many deformations in this tradition. Paul offers a full acceptance of the sexual needs of men and of women, a matter-of-fact view that people get together in order to have sex, and the refusal to place this sexuality under suspicion.

Perhaps even more surprising given the way the tradition ultimately developed, Paul does not suggest that the reason for getting married is to have children. The reason for marrying is to mutually satisfy one another's sexual needs, and the reason for sexuality is not related here or elsewhere in this text to procreation.

To be sure, children come in for a bit of attention in this passage. Children born to a Christian (whether the Christian parent is the male or the female) are presumed somehow to be sanctified. The reference here is obviously not to baptism since Paul has earlier in the letter made clear that baptism is of no great concern to him. Children born to any Christian are "holy" rather than "unclean." Still Paul does not use this condition as a reason for having children. Indeed from the perspective developed by Paul, the sexual practices that were less likely to produce progeny would be better for Christians to perform. Procreative sex not only involves one in attempting to care for your partner and the household that you form, but producing children also increases the cares of this world and the number of distractions from what Paul considers the true business of the Christian. Thus Paul's argument here would lead us to say that nonprocreative sex is "better" than procreative sex. Both may give sexual satisfaction to the partners, but nonprocreative sex has the further advantage of not increasing the distractions and cares that make it so difficult to attend to the work of salvation.

From Paul's point of view, tradition got it backwards. This passage ultimately persuaded the Puritans that marital sex was not directed only to procreation but to the comfort and consolation of one another in this vale of tears.

Now a part of what makes Paul's view possible is precisely that the question of procreation is set aside. To be sure this has partially to do with Paul's view that the end is near, but also with the way in which the Christian tradition has already made the spread of the gospel the means of being fruitful and multiplying. The awakening of faith in the other multiplies, gives birth, raises, and nurtures. Paul's notion is not a gnostic one that would cast suspicion on biological procreation. If it happens fine, if not fine. It's not a big deal. Once this approach is taken, then sex itself is freed to be viewed simply as the giving and receiving of what is due, the mutual satisfaction of need and desire.

Trouble

If Paul's view in 1 Corinthians had been the basis of subsequent reflection on sexuality, many problems might have been avoided. This view has not, however, been shared universally. The most blatant illustration of the point of view that was to gain ascendancy in the church is found in 1 Timothy. Here, for the first and only time in New Testament literature, sexuality appears to be linked with childbearing:

Let a woman learn in silence with full submission. I permit no woman ꞌ to teach or to have authority over a man; she is to keep silent. For Adam was formed first, then Eve; and Adam was not deceived, but the woman was deceived and became a transgressor. Yet she will be saved through child bearing, provided they continue in faith and love and holiness, with modesty. (2:12–15)

So I would have younger widows marry, bear children, and manage their households, so as to give the adversary no occasion to revile us. (5:14)

Although a couple of points of contact occur here with ideas put forward in 1 Corinthians (with respect to women being silent), a completely different attitude is present. In the first place, only here is Eve blamed for the fall. In 1 Corinthians and in Romans that blame belongs to Adam. Only here is women's place clearly "in the home," and indeed, pregnant.

To be sure, the situation grew worse. Nothing here yet expresses the suspicion of sexuality that will come to permeate much of the tradition, a suspicion that will limit licit sexual activity to that which is procreative. The text still opposes tendencies toward asceticism (4:1–5), and does not explicitly link sexuality to procreation. Indeed the text has a good deal to commend it. But the spirit of mutuality, of good sense, and of theological creativity and acuity is distinctly absent here. Unfortunately the worst aspects of this text would prove to be the most influential, and the best of it would soon be forgotten.

The point of citing this text is to show that the establishment of the connection between sexuality and procreation takes considerable time to develop. Even at the late stage represented by 1 Timothy, the connection is still far from definitive, but we can see some of its elements beginning to take shape before our eyes. Seeing this development may help to underscore the absence of that connection in the New Testament tradition that is antecedent to this text. At least another generation, perhaps two, would pass before the connection is explicitly made. Before the theory is fully developed, theory makers would emerge as a separate class of persons largely without sexual experience.

Conclusion

The review that we have made of the New Testament view of sexuality shows that sex is not connected even at the end of that tradition with procreation. By the time of 1 Timothy, we can see the beginnings of that view, and we can also see that it is linked to a negative view of women and their contribution to the life of the community.

Far more striking, however, is the refusal of the earlier tradition to make this connection between sex and procreation. This refusal flies in the face of much influential pagan popular philosophy. Why the refusal to make this connection?

The first reason concerns the way in which faith was understood as the true beginning of life. On this view, the fruitfulness of the new creation is expressed in the activity that either inaugurates new communities or that builds up communities in faith. This view represents the new, evangelical meaning of "be fruitful and multiply." Yet until this perspective is connected with the antisexual ethos of the hellenistic world, no extreme suspicion yet falls on sexuality as such. To be sure, sin may appear within this sphere, but sin is much less important in this respect than, for example, gossip or envy or enmity which all receive far more attention in the texts.

At this juncture, then, sexuality may be viewed fairly soberly as the sphere of desire and need and thus as the sphere of mutual and concrete service to one another. As long as this perspective is kept clearly in view, no need exists to "police" this sphere with all kinds of restrictions and regulations. Common sense and a due regard for one another's rights and needs are all that is essential.

I do not suppose that this position is adequate. Paul is not very aware of pleasure and play, of joy and celebration. He still has something to learn from the celebrative aspect of the Jesus tradition. But even taking Paul's view as it stands, especially in connection with what we have seen of the Jesus tradition, we could go a good ways toward undoing the worst aspects of a tradition that is anti-erotic and anti-body.

Now specifically with respect to the issue of a gay-affirmative rereading of the New Testament, we can say that the view of sexuality as oriented to the need and desire of the other means that no basis in principle exists for the disqualification of same-sex relationships, whether between women or men. These relations are just as capable as cross-sex relations of providing the concrete bodily service of the beloved with respect and mutuality. From this perspective, no objection can arise to the sexual mediation or expression of same-sex relationships on the grounds that such expression would be nonprocreative. This viewpoint applies, of course, to the relationship between Jesus and the man he loved, as well as to the centurion and his beloved youth.

The realignment of sexuality and procreation together with the extreme suspicion that tradition has directed against the sexual sphere has produced the monstrosity that is traditional Christian sexual ethics. This monstrosity seeks to stigmatize same-sex relations as nonprocreative and thus as sinful. An unmasking of the bad faith of this tradition is an important step not only in overcoming homophobia and heterosexism but also in overcoming the erotophobia to which generations of Christians, gay and straight, have been subjected.

In part 1 we uncovered the "dangerous memory" of Jesus' relationship with another man as represented in the Gospel of John. We saw that the least forced reading of the texts that deal with the man Jesus loved is one which understands this relationship as one of physical and emotional intimacy, and that nothing in the text in any way precludes the sexual mediation of this relationship which one might expect of similarly constructed relationships.

In part 2 we saw additional traces of this relationship in the Markan tradition as well. The Gospel of Matthew, while it does not attribute such a relationship to Jesus, does nonetheless represent Jesus as open to such relationships with others as part of Matthew's inclusion of the sexually marginalized in this Gospel. Luke obscures without eliminating this relationship in the interest of reducing some elements of scandal in the Jesus tradition for readers attracted to the traditions of Israel. However, all the Gospels retain elements of the gender role subversion that we have seen to be characteristic of the Jesus tradition.

One of the principal ways that this "dangerous memory" has been obscured for subsequent generations of readers of these texts is the presupposition that the New Testament generally (and therefore Jesus) is supportive of the marriage and family values that are alleged to legitimate a disapproval of same-sex eroticism.

Our study of the traditions concerning Jesus has shown that, far from supporting or legitimating those institutions and values, the Jesus tradition is relentlessly critical of them. Thus the opposition to the institution of the family and the suspicion directed against marriage as the reproduction of that institution attest to a radical vision of human relationships that is consistent with the acceptance of same-sex relationships. Moreover this critique of the familial structure is not couched in terms of asceticism and so cannot be attributed to the erotophobia that characterizes later Christian tradition. Rather the critique seems to be produced as an element within an overall assessment of structures of domination.

Finally we have seen that the New Testament does not accept the view, already current in some hellenistic circles, that sex is for procreation —

a view subsequently introduced into Christianity to buttress heterosexism and that later becomes an element in the prohibition of same-sex eroticism.

Thus any use of marriage and family values to disparage either same-sex eroticism or a gay-affirmative rereading of the Gospels requires a complete disregard for the unanimous witness of the traditions concerning Jesus. That normative Christianity has succeeded in closing its eyes to this manifest reality makes it less surprising that it has failed to detect the affirmation of same-sex erotic relationships in these same texts. Indeed one wonders whether this blindness to Jesus' critique of the institution of marriage and family has not been produced in order to obscure as far as possible the dangerous memory of Jesus' love for another man and his acceptance of such relationships in others. In any case, the price of heterosexism and homophobia is an inability to recognize or deal with consistent features of the traditions concerning Jesus.

Chapter 13

Marriage, Family, and Slavery

A study of the narrative traditions of the New Testament shows a vigorous critique of the institutions of marriage and family. But defenders of these same institutions often cite other New Testament documents that seem supportive of marriage and family. I do not seek to ignore these texts but to show how they are complicitous with another equally essential institution (at least as far as the hellenistic world is concerned): that of slavery.

To put it another way, the attitude taken toward the relation of husband and wife and father and child closely parallels the attitude taken toward the relationship of masters and slaves. We shall see that this holds true for several texts, indeed for all that seem to valorize the institution of marriage and family. The bulk of these texts are from the epistolary corpus that tradition has assigned to Paul, although most of these documents are attributed by modern scholars to a post-Pauline and, in some cases, anti-Pauline tradition of theologizing.

1 Corinthians

The earliest text that specifically deals with the question of marriage appears to be 1 Corinthians, chapter 7. We have already had occasion to note that this text understands sexuality apart from the question of procreation and that the relationship between man and woman insofar as it is sexual, is understood in terms of equality and mutuality.[1]

The bulk of this and the two previous chapters deal with assorted questions of sexuality, but we also notice that Paul connects his advice

---

1. We leave aside here the issues with which Paul deals in chapter 11, for example, that of head-covering (1 Cor. 11:2–16) as well as the possibility of the insertion of 1 Cor. 14:34–35 about women keeping silence in the churches. For a good discussion of these texts, see Neil Elliott, *Liberating Paul: The Justice of God and the Politics of the Apostle* (Maryknoll, N.Y.: Orbis Books, 1994), 52–54.

concerning marriage with his advice concerning the condition of slavery. These concepts in turn are connected to the issue of circumcision and uncircumcision.

> Let each of you lead the life the Lord has assigned, to which God has called you. This is my rule in all the churches. Was anyone at the time of his call already circumcised? Let him not seek to remove the marks of circumcision. Was anyone at the time of his call uncircumcised? Let him not seek circumcision. Circumcision is nothing, and uncircumcision is nothing; but obeying the commandments of God is everything. Let each of you remain in the condition in which you were called.
>
> Were you a slave when called? Do not be concerned about it. Even if you can gain your freedom. Make use of your present condition now more than ever. For whoever was called in the Lord as a slave is a freed person belonging to the Lord, just as whoever was free when called is a slave of Christ. You were bought with a price; do not become the slaves of human masters. In whatever condition you were called, brothers and sisters, there remain with God. (7:17–24)
>
> Are you bound to a wife? Do not seek to be free. Are you free from a wife? Do not seek a wife. (7:27)
>
> A wife is bound as long as her husband lives. But if the husband dies, she is free to marry anyone she wishes, only in the Lord. But in my judgment she is more blessed if she remains as she is. (7:39–40a)

Much in this passage rewards scrutiny and requires critical comment. But for our purposes what is most striking is the way in which Paul seeks to warrant his views concerning marriage by way of an appeal to the condition of slavery as a parallel case.

Clearly Paul seems to regard one situation in these pairings as intrinsically better than the other. In the case of Judaism, he appears to suggest a kind of equality. This suggestion is only illusory as we see easily from a comparison between trying to undo circumcision and trying to undo uncircumcision. The former is clearly difficult;[2] the second is possible but proscribed. (This proscription is the subject of intense argumentation in Galatians.) In the case of slavery Paul wants the reader not to seek to become free as though this were necessary in order to belong to Christ. But

---

2. But not impossible. See 1 Maccabees 1:15.

he is adamant in insisting that those who have been claimed by Christ cannot — must not — enslave themselves to another: "you were bought with a price; do not become the slaves of human masters." In the third case, Paul wants to maintain that marriage is to be avoided wherever possible, for men and women, although he recognizes that one may be impelled by desire and need to marry. Here again Paul does not counsel divorce to attain the desirable state of freedom, but he does want to warn his readers against the encumberments of marriage. Thus, concerning the widow he says, "in my judgment she is more blessed if she remains as she is."

In this argumentation, one's religion (Jew or gentile), one's class (free or slave), and one's marital status are regarded as in some way parallel. In subsequent texts, the question of religious status drops out of the picture. But the association of marriage and slavery and the application of the values of the one structure to those of the other remain constant.

Colossians

The next text that comes in for consideration is from Colossians. The authorship of this letter is disputed and no consensus seems likely.

> And whatever you do, in word and deed, do everything in the name of the Lord Jesus, giving thanks to God the Father through him.
>
> Wives, be subject to your husbands, as is fitting in the Lord. Husbands, love your wives and never treat them harshly.
>
> Children, obey your parents in everything, for this is your acceptable duty in the Lord. Fathers, do not provoke your children, or they may lose heart.
>
> Slaves, obey your earthly masters in everything, not only while being watched and in order to please them, but wholeheartedly, fearing the Lord. Whatever your task, put yourselves into it, as done for the Lord and not for your masters. Since you know that from the Lord you will receive the inheritance as your reward; you are slaves of the Lord Christ. For the wrongdoer will be paid back for whatever wrong has been done, and there is no partiality. Masters, treat your slaves justly and fairly, for you know that you also have a master in heaven. (Col. 3:17–4:1)

In general we may see that the admonitions have a similar structure, save for the expansion of the admonition to slaves. The pattern for wives and husbands is repeated for children and fathers, slaves and masters.

The first term of the pair is urged to obey (or submit), the second term is ordered to be kind.

The relationships here described are "economic" in that they are relations in which the second term not only has power or authority but also has ownership rights with respect to the first term (wives, children, slaves). This is made clear by the extended attention to the obligations of the slave.

The author certainly seeks to humanize or even "christianize" these institutions by pointing to a more fundamental relationship to Christ that relativizes the authority of the husband, father, master. The author is not concerned to invent new institutions or to abolish the old ones but rather, taking the world as he finds it, seeks to ameliorate conditions on the basis of the gospel.

We notice here a clear retreat from the more radical assertions of egalitarianism that may be found in Galatians and even in the letter to Philemon, where the old institutions of the household are undercut. This radicalism has not been entirely lost, since an attempt is still made to place the relationships under the heading of obedience to Christ. But this attempt later leads to an absolutizing of the inequalities that this text may be understood as relativizing.

Ephesians

A more extended treatment of "household duties" may be found in Ephesians, which even fewer scholars attribute to Paul. The "ethical section" of the argument begins with the admonition: "Therefore be imitators of God as beloved children, and live in love, as Christ loved us" (5:1–2). The section specifically concerned with the household begins with the admonition: "Be subject to one another out of reverence for Christ" (5:21). This discussion at least attempts to permeate the given relations of society with the new reality of the gospel, and the basic principle is the same for all. In this respect, the argument is even more egalitarian in emphasis than much of the actual argumentation of 1 Corinthians. Let us attend to the passage.

> Wives, be subject to your husbands as you are to the Lord. For the husband is head of the wife just as Christ is head of the church, the body of which he is the Savior. Just as the church is subject to Christ, so also wives ought to be, in everything, to their husbands.
>
> Husbands, love your wives, just as Christ loved the church and gave himself up for her, in order to make her holy by cleansing her with the washing of water by the word, so as to present the church

to himself in splendor, without a spot or wrinkle or anything of the kind — yes, so that she may be holy and without blemish. In the same way, husbands should love their wives as they do their own bodies. He who loves his wife loves himself. For no one ever hates his own body, but he nourishes and tenderly cares for it, just as Christ does for the church, because we are members of his body. "For this reason a man will leave his father and mother and be joined to his wife, and the two will become one flesh" [Gen. 2:24]. This is a great mystery, and I am applying it to Christ and the church. Each of you, however, should love his wife as himself, and a wife should respect her husband.

Children, obey your parents in the Lord, for this is right. "Honor your father and mother" — this is the first commandment with a promise: "so that it may be well with you and you may live long on the earth" [Exod. 20:12; Deut. 5:16].

And fathers, do not provoke your children to anger, but bring them up in the discipline and instruction of the Lord.

Slaves, obey your earthly masters with fear and trembling, in singleness of heart, as you obey Christ; not only while being watched, and in order to please them, but as slaves of Christ, doing the will of God from the heart. Render service with enthusiasm, as to the Lord and not to men and women, knowing that whatever good we do, we will receive the same again from the Lord, whether we are slaves or free.

And masters, do the same to them. Stop threatening them, for you know that both of you have the same Master in heaven, and with him there is no partiality. (Eph. 5:22–6:9)

This version of household duties is more clearly related to the gospel than is the version from Colossians and is even more potentially subversive of these institutions.

Nevertheless, most significant for our purposes is the no less clear correlation between the status of wives, children, and slaves on the one hand, and that of husbands, fathers, and masters on the other. This clear correlation retrospectively illumines the severe critique of such relationships of marriage and family in the Gospel.

1 Peter

Another illustration of this same structure is to be found in the document known as 1 Peter. Here no reference appears to the situation of children and fathers but the discussion of wives/slaves in relation to husbands/ masters has a familiar pattern. Here the series in fact begins with the admonition to "accept the authority of every human institution" (2:13). The meaning of these and other admonitions in this letter is to prevent the community from being denounced as subversive; the situation of persecution is clearly in mind. The author does not suppose that avoiding this persecution is possible, but he wants to insist that members of the community should not make things easy for the persecutors to claim that Christians are an unruly people. In this context appear admonitions to slaves and wives and a brief admonition to husbands (not to masters).

In the admonition to slaves (2:18–25), they are told to endure suffering at the hands of unjust masters as Christ endured unjust suffering.

In the admonition to wives, "in the same way" the wife's submission is to be a way of winning over by the wife's conduct (3:1–6).

The admonition to husbands concludes the series:

> Husbands, in the same way, show consideration for your wives in your life together, paying honor to the woman as the weaker sex, since they too are also heirs of the gracious gift of life — so that nothing may hinder your prayers. (3:7)

The community to which this letter is addressed seems to be made up largely of slaves and women who share the experience of brutish men.

Pastoral Epistles

The pastoral epistles (1 and 2 Timothy and Titus), which ascribe themselves to Paul, are regarded by most scholars to be from a later period of the churches' life. The letter that seems to be most personal and to be closest to Pauline authorship is 2 Timothy. Significantly this letter does not address itself to "household duties" at all.

The letter to Titus echoes the instruction of 1 Peter concerning submission to authorities generally: "remind them [the members of the congregations in Crete] to be subject to rulers and authorities, to be obedient" (3:1). In this context, we are told that a bishop or overseer of the life of the church must be "someone who is blameless, husband of one wife, whose children are believers, not accused of debauchery or rebellion" (1:6). Thus the leadership of the church is depicted as the model Roman paterfamilias. We are very far here from Paul's advice to male Christians to avoid marriage, let alone the views of Jesus as represented in the Gospels. The young women are to be encouraged to be "submissive to their husbands, so that the word of God may not be discredited" (2:5). Note here the lack of the justification of this concept within a situation of persecution (as in 1 Peter). Here the motive is that Christianity should conform to the norms of pagan respectability.

Within this same context then, we should not be surprised at the corresponding instruction for slaves. "Tell slaves to be submissive to their masters and to give satisfaction in every respect; they are not to talk back, not to pilfer, but to show complete and perfect fidelity, so that in every thing they may be an ornament to the doctrine of God our Savior" (2:9–10). No instruction is given here to masters to reciprocate in some way the good behavior of the slaves.

The Letter to Titus then embodies the ethic of submission that applies to wives and to slaves (and children) with the apparent aim of making Christianity seem to be not subversive of the basic institutions of Roman society.

This impression is all the stronger when we come to 1 Timothy, which not only develops this ethic of submission to an extraordinary degree but also, in the case of women/wives, does so by means of a novel and ultimately quite influential interpretation of the story of creation and fall.

With respect to these matters, 1 Timothy inaugurates the series with a phrase that will ultimately warm the cockles of Constantine's heart. "First of all then, I urge that supplications, prayers, intercessions, and thanksgivings be made for everyone, for kings and for all who are in high positions, so that we may lead a quiet and peaceable life" (2:1–2).

The bishop is then described in terms that makes him a beneficent king: "He must manage his own household well, keeping his children submissive and respectful in every way — for if someone does not know how to manage his own household, how can he take care of God's church?" (3:4–5). Again we are far removed from Paul's view that not to be married is better. Here marriage and attentiveness to the regulation of the household become a prerequisite for ecclesiastical responsibility.

Having adopted the view of the Roman paterfamilias, the view that women are to be placed in a situation of submission is not surprising, and is now outfitted with a kind of theological justification:

Let a woman learn in silence with full submission. I permit no woman to teach or have authority over a man; she is to keep silent. For Adam was formed first, then Eve; and Adam was not deceived, but the woman was deceived and became a transgressor. Yet she will be saved through childbearing, provided they continue in faith and love and holiness, with modesty. (2:11–15)

This passage marks the first and only appearance in Scripture of the interpretation of Genesis as a justification for male rule. The text is in marked contrast to the way in which Paul, for example, associates the fall with Adam rather than Eve (1 Cor. 15:45ff; Rom. 5:12ff).

We should not be surprised, then, at the way in which "family values" come to be absolutized. In the instruction concerning widows we read, "So I would have younger widows marry, bear children, and manage their households, so as to give the adversary no occasion to revile us" (5:14). This viewpoint is obviously the opposite of what Paul proposed in 1 Corinthians 7:8, 40.

We may also note the absolutizing of family values: "And whoever does not provide for relatives, and especially for family members, has denied the faith and is worse than an unbeliever" (5:8). This is obviously as far as possible from the recollection of the Jesus tradition as inscribed in the roughly contemporaneous Gospel according to Luke: "Whoever does not hate mother and father... "

The ethic of total submission to authority is carried out, as we should expect, also in relation to the duties of slaves:

Let all who are under the yoke of slavery regard their masters as worthy of all honor, so the name of God and the teaching may not be blasphemed. Those who have believing masters must not be disrespectful to them on the ground that they are members of the church; rather they must serve them all the more, since those who benefit from their services are believers and beloved. (1 Tim. 6:1–2)

No longer does an exhortation to the masters to be kind appear. We are in the sphere of total acquiescence in the status quo of Roman despotic household values that are designed to mirror and reinforce the structures of the social order. These words were obviously of great comfort to the slave-holding Christians of the New World.

Conclusion

The texts we have examined (with the exception of 1 Peter) claim to derive from the hand of Paul, although this ascription is in dispute save for (virtually all of) 1 Corinthians. The tradition deriving from Paul is separated by a widening chasm from the simultaneous development of narrative texts that seek to recall the words and deeds of Jesus. Without positing a contradiction between Paul and Jesus, we may certainly see how the traditions that appear to derive from these figures do diverge, until a chasm separates them. Indeed this same chasm appears to divide the Paul of 1 Corinthians and Galatians from the pseudo-Paul of the later epistles.

The suspicion directed against the whole sphere of "marriage and family values" in the various versions of the Jesus tradition inscribed in the narrative texts of the Gospels is completely overturned in the pseudo-Pauline literature. If we recall that the development of the literature that we call Gospels was roughly parallel to the development of epistolary literature, then we may say that we confront here two contemporary but radically opposed versions of Christianity. In the Gospels, the "dangerous memory" of the Jesus tradition continues to undermine structures of domination. In the letters, the authority of Paul (or Peter) is used to sanctify structures of domination. The result of the latter tradition is that Christianity comes increasingly to present itself as the bulwark of stabilizing values of all kinds, so that the one who was crucified by the system can become its principal defender and legitimation. The writer of 1 Timothy claims to be concerned that the name of God not be "blasphemed" by the masters of the system of domination. The result has been that women, children, and slaves have been provoked to blaspheme against the God who protects the perpetrators of violence and violation. Yet the Gospels have been there to remind us that Jesus was in this sense the one who was executed by the system for blasphemy against the god of the system.

This rapid review of texts that stand outside the Jesus tradition may help to suggest some of the reasons for the suspicions directed against marriage and family values in the Gospels. The ease with which the family was assimilated to the institution of slavery in the ancient world gives added cogency to the repudiation of family structures by those traditions most closely connected to the memory of Jesus.

Chapter 14

Was Jesus Gay?

Was Jesus gay? I have already explained why the question as thus framed admits of no simple answer. Modern categories of gay and straight or of heterosexual or homosexual (or bisexual) do not readily capture the experience and behavior of the people of antiquity. Moreover, any conclusions about the sexual experience or practices of particular individuals in antiquity must in the nature of the case be inferential and tentative since the available sources almost never tend to be explicit. This statement is to a significant degree true also of our contemporaries, but the sources for the reconstruction of lives of persons widely separated from us in time and culture pose additional difficulties — all the more true of a figure like Jesus. While we have a number of sources for his life, they are all heavily determined by the theological interests of the writers and of the communities that transmitted these writings. Hence a great many things about Jesus' mission, ministry, words, and deeds are open to serious scholarly debate.

Despite these important and weighty caveats, however, we have seen that considerable evidence supports the view that Jesus' primary affectional relationship was with another man, one who is called in the Gospel of John "the disciple Jesus loved." Moreover we have seen that the reading of the references to this relationship that makes the most sense is one which infers a relationship of physical and emotional intimacy, a relationship that we might otherwise suppose would be the potential subject of erotic mediation, of sexual expression. The worldview of the Gospel of John, like that of the other Gospels, is one that seems to oppose the ascetic views that would preclude this sexual expression. Therefore we should most likely think of this relationship as sexual in character.

Moreover this Gospel does not stand alone. We have found confirmation of something quite similar in the Gospel of Mark, especially when read in connection with the fragment known as the Secret Gospel of Mark.

233

Indeed this fragment helps us to see in a new light episodes in the canonical Gospel (the look of love, the nude youth in the garden) that are otherwise quite puzzling. The evidence therefore mounts that Jesus was remembered as one who had an erotic relationship with a (young) man who also was or became one of his followers.

Even in the Gospels (Matthew and Luke) that seem not to give evidence of this "dangerous memory," we find indications that Jesus was remembered as being open to and affirmative of a relationship (between the centurion and his youth) that appears to conform to models of hellenistic pederastic love.

We have also seen that the Jesus tradition carries the marks of a strong subversion of gender roles, roles that were sometimes used to discredit same-sex relationships in the Roman hellenistic world and which have continued to be used in that way in our own century. The Jesus tradition affirms the very sort of gender subversion that was then sometimes associated with same-sex love. This affirmation occurs in these documents despite the fact that contemporaneous developments in the Christian tradition (Pauline and post-Pauline letters) seek to reinstate traditional gender role expectations in the Christian community.

The reading that I have proposed of the Jesus tradition has often been precluded by using the New Testament to affirm what today are called marriage and family values. Part 3 made clear that the Jesus tradition is heavily critical of these same values. One of the benefits of a gay-affirmative reading of the Gospels is that it permits us to see and make sense of this dimension of the Jesus tradition so long obscured by heterosexism.

At the beginning of this study, I referred to the work of counterhomophobic exegesis that has greatly reduced the number of biblical texts that may plausibly be used to license homophobia. The result of that labor is that the biblical foundation for opposition to same-sex love has been reduced to two verses in the Hebrew Bible of decidedly late provenance, two verses of the Pauline corpus of disputed meaning, and two words whose relevance is generally disputed appearing in two further verses attributed to Paul. At most then, six verses of the Bible are adduced to oppose what we now call homosexuality.

In contrast, the material that seems hospitable to same-sex relations includes, as we have seen, all four Gospels of the New Testament. Not just six verses, but entire books of the New Testament offer a positive view of same-sex erotic attachment. Nor are they narratives tucked away in a corner somewhere but they are obviously central to the biblical story, at least insofar as Christians are concerned.

Yet the tiny and dubious scraps have come to overwhelm the powerful and central narratives. While academics and churches argue about the six verses, the homoerotic traditions of biblical narrative have been largely ignored. For that reason I have chosen in this study to largely ignore the scraps on the floor over which the dogs of contention growl so noisily and to focus instead upon the feast set upon the table of New Testament narrative.

In considering these narratives, I have not sought to develop arbitrary or fanciful interpretations — airy confections that may be sweet to the palate but that provide no solid nourishment. Instead, I have attempted to show that these narratives give solid support to a homoerotic interpretation of the relationship between Jesus and the man he loved, as well as offer to the reader a narrative world that is hospitable to the development and expression of same-sex relationships.

I have not sought in this study to be exhaustive in the examination of biblical narratives that may be understood in a gay-affirmative light. I have chosen instead to focus on those narratives that have an especially important place in the canon of Christendom as the bearers of the traditions concerning Jesus.

I do not imagine that my readings of these texts will simply be accepted without further ado. The subject matter is too much in dispute for that. But I do hope the discussion will be one about the texts and their context. I am persuaded that we have been too often blinded to the texts by cultural or religious presuppositions that tell us that they cannot possibly mean what they seem to mean.

In contrast, the gay-affirmative reading I have proposed does not require us to do violence to any passage of Scripture. This approach does not need to ignore the evidence nor to invent evidence. It needs only attend to the text, and follow where it leads. What is at stake here, then, is not only the question of our attitude toward gay and lesbian relationships, but our attitude toward the Bible. I do not mean here that the question is about whether the Bible is the Word of God. I simply mean whether we can treat it with the sort of decent respect and openness that we should accord any document whatever, but especially one to which we owe a debt of gratitude for insight into how to live as human beings encountered by the transcendent claim of justice and love.

Homophobia is a key element in the long history of the expropriation of the Bible to legitimate injustice: the injustice of rapacious economic systems, violent political systems, institutions of racism and slavery, of patriarchy and heterosexism. All of these "interpretations" may lay claim to a long and hallowed tradition, but that does not make them true.

I hope that the fact that the interpretations offered here run counter to similarly long-established traditions will not prevent readers from taking them seriously enough to attend to the biblical texts to which they refer.

Index of Biblical and Ancient Literature

Index of Names